dBASE III® Handbook

dBASE III®

Handbook

George Tsu-der Chou

Que™ Corporation
Indianapolis, Indiana

Library of Congress Catalog No.: 85-60691
ISBN 0-88022-159-3

Editorial Director
David F. Noble, Ph.D.

Editors
Jeannine Freudenberger, M.A.
Katherine Murray

Technical Editor
Ron Holmes

89 88 87 86   8 7 6 5 4 3

Interpretation of the printing code: the rightmost double-digit number is the year of the book's printing; the rightmost single-digit number, the number of the book's printing. For example, a printing code of 84-3 shows that the third printing of the book occurred in 1984.

Dedicated to

my wife, Jane-Wen
and our children
Doris, Tina, and Tom

About the Author

George Tsu-der Chou of Vancouver, Washington, is a consultant in the field of database design and development. He has developed numerous database management systems for a large number of clients, such as Gregory Government Securities, Morley Capital Management, Hi-Tech Electronics, West Coast Lumber Inspection Bureau, NERCO, Inc., and others. These systems include analytical managerial database systems and administrative database management programs that deal with inventory and accounting functions.

Dr. Chou earned his Ph.D. in the area of Quantitative Methods, with supporting areas in Computer Science, Economics, and Econometrics, from the University of Washington. He is currently a full professor at the University of Portland in Oregon, where he teaches courses in business data processing and data management, quantitative methods, operations research, business forecasting, and others. He has taught computer programming in FORTRAN, COBOL, BASIC, and IBM Assembler.

Dr. Chou is the author of *Microcomputer Programming in BASIC* and *Computer Programming in BASIC,* both published by Harper & Row. The former has been translated into Spanish and published in Mexico; reprints of this book have also been distributed in the Philippines. Dr. Chou has also written a financial analytical modeling software program, COMPASS, *Computer Assisted Portfolio Planning Management System.* Combining database and analytical tools, this software represents the first major effort in the computerization of portfolio management. COMPASS, marketed by Morley & Associates, has now been adopted by many major banks and financial institutions in the United States and Canada.

Contents

361 Appendix E: Built-In Functions

Trademark
Acknowledgments

Screens printed courtesy of
DOMUS Software, Ltd.
Ottawa, Ontario, Canada

Composed in Wiedeman
by Que Corporation

Cover designed by
Listenberger Design Associates

Book designed by
Positive Identification, Inc.
Indianapolis, Indiana

Introduction

Welcome to the wonderful world of dBASE III. Just a few years ago, the power of database management could be enjoyed only by users of large, expensive computer systems. However, the introduction of dBASE II changed the way data is organized and manipulated on small cost-effective but powerful microcomputers. As a result, small businesses and individuals can now benefit from these types of database management programs.

Although many different database management programs are now available and new products are being added to the market almost weekly, dBASE II has maintained its leading share of the market. Because dBASE II was designed for the early generations of microcomputers and has limited memory capacity and computational power, the size of the database and the processing speed of the program have been compromised. In addition, because the program emphasizes programming features, dBASE II is not considered user friendly. However, the introduction of dBASE III has effectively addressed these problems.

Even though dBASE III evolved from dBASE II, dBASE III is a drastically different computer program designed to take advantage of current microcomputers. The program's data storage capacity and computational speed have been greatly increased; and without sacrificing dBASE II's programming capability, dBASE III is very easy to use. Some other database management programs may be more user friendly than dBASE III, and these programs are adequate for many small-scale, simple database applications. But larger databases need the strong, flexible programming features offered by dBASE III, features that have not been matched by any other program.

How Do You Use dBASE III?

As a database management tool, dBASE III has two processing modes. In an interactive mode, you can create and manipulate data files by typing the commands directly from the keyboard. Because the computer responds instantly, you can monitor the input and output processes with easy-to-use, English-like commands.

The other processing mode is batch processing, which represents one of the most important utilities provided by dBASE III. Batch processing offers all the power and flexibility necessary for designing an integrated menu-driven database management system.

A primary objective of the *dBASE III Handbook* is to demonstrate how the dBASE III commands can be used for effective database management. To maintain clarity of principle, the examples in this book have been kept simple and concise. To maintain continuity of the examples, the same database is used to illustrate as many different commands as possible. Because of all the features incorporated, simple examples give you a better understanding of the underlying principles. Once you fully understand the principles of database management and the correct uses of the dBASE III commands, you can easily design a more sophisticated database system of your own.

The *dBASE III Handbook* is not intended as a substitute for the dBASE III manual but as a user's guide that goes beyond the basics of the manual. The book shows you how the commands can be integrated to perform useful tasks. In addition, because the dBASE III commands are grouped by functions, the *dBASE III Handbook* may be used as a comprehensive reference manual.

Who Should Use This Book?

If you own dBASE III, you should own this book. While the dBASE III manual serves as a dictionary that lists and describes the commands and vocabulary, the *dBASE III Handbook* shows you how to compose with these commands and vocabulary. The dBASE III manual introduces the basic musical notes, but the *dBASE III*

Handbook teaches you how to make music. From the easy-to-follow examples, you can learn how to design and create a database for your own data management needs. By duplicating the examples, you can learn firsthand how those commands are used for various functions. When it comes to mastering the dBASE III commands, no approach is better than "doing it yourself."

If you do not own dBASE III but are considering purchasing the program, this book is also for you. Chapter 1 introduces the concept of a database and gives you a general understanding of how a database can be used to manage your data needs. "Introduction to dBASE III," Chapter 2, provides an overview of dBASE III and ways you can use this program to perform the functions of database management. Examples in the subsequent chapters demonstrate the powerful utilities offered by the dBASE III program.

If you are a dBASE II user, the *dBASE III Handbook* is also for you. In addition to the comprehensive comparison of dBASE II and dBASE III in Appendix B of this book, the *dBASE III Handbook* provides in-depth discussions of the new commands and programming features offered by dBASE III. From this information you may see how you can significantly increase your programming productivity by switching from dBASE II to dBASE III.

What Is in This Book?

Chapter 1, "An Introduction to the Database Concept," discusses the basic concept of database management. The text introduces some commonly used models for data organization and explains the differences between hierarchical databases and relational databases. In this chapter, you will see the simplicity of a relational database, which is the model chosen by dBASE III.

Chapter 2, "Introduction to dBASE III," covers the specific features of dBASE III and the development of the program from dBASE II. In addition, this chapter explains the design philosophy that makes dBASE III a more powerful computer program than other programs currently on the market.

Chapter 3, "Getting Started," introduces the basic steps involved in preparing the computer for processing the dBASE III program. The chapter begins with a brief discussion of the basic components of an IBM Personal Computer and then explains how to initialize the disk operating system (DOS). The text explains how you can configure the system disk to specify the number of files and data buffers needed for dBASE III.

Chapter 4, "Creating, Editing, and Displaying Data," begins the discussion of the dBASE III commands that can be used in the interactive mode to perform some basic database management functions. The chapter explains the initial steps for defining a data structure and creating a database file. You learn how to use simple commands to edit the contents of the database file. The chapter also discusses the commands for displaying data records.

Chapter 5, "Sorting, Indexing, and Manipulating Data," covers the commands used to rearrange the data records of a database file: the methods of data record sorting and file indexing. The text describes how these two methods work and explains why one is better than the other. Examples are used to illustrate these operations in detail. In addition, this chapter introduces dBASE III commands you can use to generate summary statistics, such as calculating the sum, total, or average.

Chapter 6, "Memory Variables, Expressions, and Functions," discusses storing data in temporary memory locations called variables. The chapter introduces the usefulness of expressions in data manipulation and shows how you can take advantage of built-in functions to perform sophisticated mathematical operations and to convert data from one type to another.

Chapter 7, "Generating Reports," introduces the ways to generate custom reports. In addition to explaining the dBASE III commands used to design and produce reports, this chapter discusses the powerful built-in label and report generators of dBASE III. With these label and report generators, you can design custom labels and reports without tedious, laborious steps.

Chapter 8, "Fundamentals of Command File Programming," introduces the mode of batch processing. The text explains how a set of dBASE III commands can be assembled as a program file, which is then processed as a batch of instructions to be carried out by the computer. Through the use of numerous examples, this chapter shows the power and flexibility of batch mode. Most important, this chapter shows how easily you can use this mode to accomplish rather complicated data management applications.

Chapter 9, "Input and Output Commands," discusses the ways in which input and output operations can be performed by commands in a program file. The chapter covers the program segments you can use to edit or append the data records in a database file and shows how you can produce custom reports on a monitor or a printer by command file programming.

Chapter 10, "Conditional Branching and Program Loops," covers using the DO WHILE procedure for performing database management functions that require repetitious operations. This procedure is one of the vital links between interactive command processing and command file programming. The power of command file programming lies in the DO WHILE procedure.

Chapter 11, "Program Demodulation," discusses the concept of structure programming. In this chapter, you learn how to divide a database management system into several smaller easy-to-manage subsystems and then link them through a multilevel menu. You also learn how to design a database management program that uses several different database files.

Chapter 12, "Integrated Database System," presents a model that illustrates a complete database management system for a small business. In this chapter, you see how to design and integrate various data management functions such as billing, inventory, and account maintenance in a menu-driven dBASE program.

The Appendixes

The dBASE III Handbook contains five useful appendixes. Appendix A presents the standard ASCII character codes. The differences between dBASE II and dBASE III are summarized in Appendix B. Appendix C is a summary of the function and control keys in dBASE III, and Appendix D is a summary of dBASE III commands with many examples. The program's built-in functions are listed in Appendix E. These handy reference sections should prove to be valuable to both beginning and experienced users of dBASE.

Introduction to the Database Concept

An Overview

Database management systems have long been used to organize and manipulate large collections of business data. These systems are powerful computer programs that can effectively manage a huge number of data elements. However, the systems are expensive and run only on large, sophisticated computers.

These restrictions were removed by the introduction of dBASE II, the first database management program for microcomputers. With dBASE II, users of smaller computers could begin to enjoy computerized data management at an affordable price. Because of the advent of dBASE III and a new generation of microcomputers, new programs have capabilities approaching those of earlier programs that were designed only for large computer systems and cost tens of thousands of dollars.

dBASE III performs most database management functions. The program is actually a set of tools with which you can organize and manipulate data in a simple yet effective manner. However, the effectiveness of these tools can be fully realized only by the user who has a clear understanding of the underlying concept of database management. This chapter introduces those database management concepts that are necessary for the effective use of the dBASE III commands discussed in the following chapters.

The basic topics covered in this chapter are the following:

Database management system (DBMS)
Organization of data in a database
Types of commonly used databases
Fundamentals of a relational database
Basic components of a relational database
Functions of a database
A computerized relational database program, dBASE III

The following special terms are introduced in the chapter:

Database
Hierarchical database
Relational database
Alphanumeric data
Numeric data
Relational database file
Database structure
Data record
Data field

Definition of a Database

The term *database management system* (DBMS) has long been used to define a systematic approach to organizing and managing a large collection of information in a large computer system. Although used by data processing personnel for some time, the term has become more generally known since the introduction of programs like dBASE II for microcomputers. In the past, only computers with a large memory capacity and fast processing speed could effectively handle the task of a practical database management system. Because of the introduction of powerful microcomputers such as the IBM Personal Computers (IBM PC, PC XT, and PC AT) and the availability of low-cost, high-capacity memory devices, a reasonably large database management system can be implemented with only a limited investment. As a result, more database management systems are being developed for personal and business applications.

A *database* is a collection of useful information organized in a specific manner. For instance, you can view a personal telephone directory as a database:

James C. Smith	(206) 123-4567
Albert K. Zeller	(212) 457-9801
Doris A. Gregory	(503) 204-8567
Harry M. Nelson	(315) 576-0235
Tina B. Baker	(415) 787-3154
Kirk D. Chapman	(618) 625-7843
Barry W. Thompson	(213) 432-6782
Charles N. Duff	(206) 456-9873
Winston E. Lee	(503) 365-8512
Thomas T. Hanson	(206) 573-5085

This telephone directory is a listing of names and telephone numbers arranged randomly as they were entered. However, you can organize these telephone numbers in a specific order or form according to your preference. For example, you can group the entries by area codes and then alphabetically by the last names:

Charles N. Duff	(206) 456-9873
Thomas T. Hanson	(206) 573-5085
James C. Smith	(206) 123-4567
Albert K. Zeller	(212) 457-9801
Barry W. Thompson	(213) 432-6782
Harry M. Nelson	(315) 476-0235
Tina B. Baker	(415) 787-3154
Doris A. Gregory	(503) 204-8567
Winston E. Lee	(503) 365-8512
Kirk D. Chapman	(618) 625-7845

Data

Depending on the nature of the information and how it will be used, data may be classified into two main categories: alphanumeric and numeric.

Alphanumeric Data

Alphanumeric data consists of alphabetic characters (letters A through Z), numerals (0 through 9), and some special symbols (such as # and $). For instance, the model number for a television set, RCA-XA100, is alphanumeric data. Account numbers and employee identification numbers are also examples of alphanumeric data.

Numeric Data

Numeric data can be quantified and represented by a set of numeric digits. In a payroll database, the number of hours worked by an employee (for example, 38.5 hours) is an example of numeric data. The number of students in a class, the credit limit for a customer, and the level of inventory for a given item are other examples of numeric data.

Although both alphanumeric and numeric data are information stored in a database, the two types play different roles in their applications. Numeric data in a database is used as numbers in computational applications. Alphanumeric data, on the other hand, can be used only as text for identification or labeling purposes. Alphanumeric data cannot be used in a formula. For instance, if you use the set of digits 83024 as an alphanumeric string that represents the identification number of an employee, the string is treated only as a label. Even though the string may resemble a numeric value, you cannot use the string in a formula.

Types of Databases

Information stored in a database can be organized, or viewed, in a number of ways. As a result, you can define many different kinds of databases according to how the information is organized. The two most popular kinds of databases for database management are the hierarchical database and the relational database.

Hierarchical Databases

A *hierarchical database* organizes its contents in a hierarchical tree model. Besides identifying the data elements in the database, the hierarchical tree defines the relationships among these data elements. Several types of hierarchical models are available. The simplest one is the model that organizes all the data elements in the database in one-to-one relationships. Other hierarchical database models view the relationships among the data elements as one-to-many or many-to-many. The tree model of the organization of a classroom database illustrates the concept of a hierarchical database (see fig. 1.1).

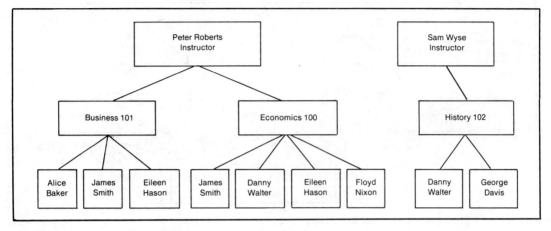

Fig. 1.1. Hierarchical tree model.

The data elements in this database include names of instructors, classes, and students in these classes. When the tree is viewed from bottom to top, the link between a student and a class is defined as a one-to-one relationship; that is, any one student in the tree model belongs to only one class. When James Smith takes more than one class, his name appears twice in the hierarchical database as two separate data elements. (One belongs to Business 101; the other to Economics 100.) A one-to-one relationship between two data elements is shown by a single line. You can also use a similar one-to-one relationship to describe the link between the name of a class and the instructor.

However, when the hierarchical database shown in figure 1.1 is viewed in a top-to-bottom fashion, one-to-many relationships are used to describe the links between an instructor and the classes taught or between the class and the students in that class. For instance, instructor Peter Roberts "owns" two classes: Business 101 and Economics 100. Each class, in turn, has several students.

The classroom database can also be organized as another version of a hierarchical model. For instance, the network tree model shown in figure 1.2 gives a different view of the relationships among the same data elements.

When you organize the data elements of the classroom database as illustrated in figure 1.2, for some students the links with classes taken are defined as many-to-many relationships. For example, student James Smith belongs to more than one class, and each class has more than one student. Multiple lines link James Smith and the

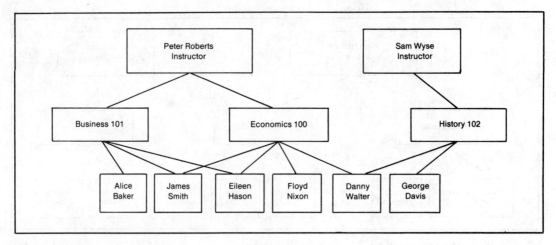

Fig. 1.2. Network tree model.

classes he takes: Business 101 and Economics 100. In such a network model, each data element is unique. The name of a student, even though he or she belongs to several classes, appears as only one data element in the model. For this reason, the number of data elements in the network model are fewer than in the previous model; however, the links among the data elements in a network model are more complex. Therefore, in choosing a database model, you should consider the trade-offs between the number of data elements and the complexity of the links in a database model.

Relational Databases

You can also organize a database as a relational model. The *relational database* structure was originally developed for use on large computer systems. With this structure, nonprogrammers can set up and manipulate interactively a large amount of information. Relational databases have recently become popular applications for microcomputers because of the simple structure that defines the relationships among the data elements in the database.

A relational model organizes a database as a two-dimensional table consisting of rows and columns. Each row contains information that belongs to a given entry in the database. Data within a row is subdivided into several items that are held in the columns in the table. For example, the classroom database can also be viewed in a relational model (see fig. 1.3).

Row #	Column #1 Instructor	Column #2 Class	Column #3 Student
1	Peter Roberts	Business 101	Alice Baker
2	Peter Roberts	Business 101	James Smith
3	Peter Roberts	Business 101	Eileen Hason
4	Peter Roberts	Economics 100	James Smith
5	Peter Roberts	Economics 100	Danny Walter
6	Peter Roberts	Economics 100	Eileen Hason
7	Peter Roberts	Economics 100	Floyd Nixon
8	Sam Wyse	History 101	Danny Walter
9	San Wyse	History 101	George Davis

Fig. 1.3. Relational model.

Organization of a Relational Database

As seen in figure 1.3, elements in the classroom database are organized in a table of nine rows and three columns. Each row is a data record, and each column is a data field. A data field can be assigned a field name, which may be an alphanumeric string or a label (INSTRUCTOR, CLASS, STUDENT, etc.). As each data record is entered, it is given a number (similar to a row number in a table). This number represents the order in which the data item is stored in the database. The different parts of the record fall into different columns, or fields. As a result, any data element in the database can be identified by its record number and field name.

The telephone directory used earlier in this chapter may also be organized as a relational database with the data fields defined as the following:

Field Number	Field Name
1	FIRST NAME
2	INITIAL
3	LAST NAME
4	AREA CODE
5	PHONE

With these defined fields, you can view the data elements in the relational database as the table shown in figure 1.4, which has ten

RECORD NO.	FIRST NAME	INITIAL	LAST NAME	AREA CODE	PHONE
		Data Field			
1	James	C	Smith	206	123-4567
2	Albert	K	Zeller	212	457-9801
3	Doris	A	Gregory	503	204-9801
4	Harry	M	Nelson	315	576-0235
5	Tina	B	Baker	415	787-3154
6	Kirk	D	Chapman	618	625-7843
7	Barry	W	Thompson	213	432-6782
8	Charles	N	Duff	206	456-9873
9	Winston	E	Lee	503	365-8512
10	Thomas	T	Hanson	206	573-5085

Fig. 1.4. Telephone directory as a relational database.

rows and five columns. Each column, or data field, contains an item of the directory listing for one person. Each row represents a data record that contains a person's name and telephone number.

Basic Components of a Relational Database File

A *relational database file* consists of two main parts. One part defines the structure of the data records, and the other contains the actual data.

Data Record

As seen in previous examples, the contents of a relational database are organized into data records and fields. A *data record* holds the data items for a single entry. In the telephone directory database, for example, the full name and telephone number of a specific person make up a data record.

Data records in a database are usually arranged in the order in which they are entered. Each data record is assigned a sequential record number when the record is added to the database. Users can subsequently identify these data records by their record numbers.

Data Field

A *data field* is a storage unit for holding a single data item within a data record. Each data field is given a name by which it is identified in the database. A field name contains a fixed number of characters, which may be a combination of letters, numbers, and certain symbols.

The contents of a data field may be an alphanumeric string or a numeric value. An alphanumeric string may be as short as a single letter or as long as a paragraph. A numeric value is an integer or a number with a decimal point. The length of an alphanumeric string and the number of digits reserved for a value in a data field must be clearly defined in the data structure before the data field is used.

In some database management systems, including dBASE III, other data fields can also be defined; these fields are date, memo, and logical fields. Some of these fields are special cases of alphanumeric fields, and others are data fields reserved for holding data in a special format.

Database Structure

A database structure consists of detailed descriptions of each field in a data record. These details include the following:

Field name—name or identification of the data field

Field type—kind of data field

Field width—dimension of the data field

Defining the structure serves several purposes. During data manipulation, you can use the field name specified in the structure to recall and refer to data stored in that field. For instance, you can use the field name LAST NAME throughout a database application to locate all the information associated with a particular last name.

Specification of the data type dictates how the information is to be used. If you define an item in a data field as a numeric value, the item can be recalled and included in a formula; but data specified as an alphanumeric string can be used only as a label or as the object in a searching operation. An alphanumeric string can never be included in a formula.

Because most database management systems assume a fixed length for the size of a data field, the dimension of a data field is defined as the maximum number of characters to be used by the data item. If the number of letters for the longest last name in your database is ten, you must declare the dimension of the field LAST NAME to be ten even though some last names require fewer than ten letters. By declaring the dimension of a data field, you reserve the necessary storage space for the anticipated data items.

Applications of a Relational Database

As illustrated in the examples, a relational database provides an effective means for maintaining and manipulating a large amount of information. Some useful functions you can perform on a relational database include the following:

Maintaining and updating the contents of the database

Locating and retrieving data that meets a given set of specifications

Sorting or rearranging a set of data items into a predetermined sequence or order

Linking data items in different database files to have indirect indexing on the data items

Data maintenance involves adding data to the database, changing part or all of the contents of the database, and deleting items from the database. New data records can be inserted in a relational database, and any part of an item can be modified or deleted. In the telephone database, for example, a new telephone number can be added to the database by appending the record to the end of the file. Any item in the database, such as an area code or a local number, can be modified or replaced. This data maintenance capability is also a useful tool for inventory management.

Another important function in database management is the ability to locate and retrieve data in the database by referring to the item's record number and field name. In a relational database, finding a record that contains a specific item in one field is a relatively simple task.

The ability to sort, or rearrange, the data records in a database is another valuable feature in a relational database management system. For instance, in a mailing label application, having all the names and addresses in descending or ascending order by ZIP code is often desirable; and telephone numbers are usually sorted alphabetically by the person's name.

Linking data elements in different database files is also a powerful feature in a data management system. For instance, by using the account number as a data field in several files, you can link all the files through a given account number by means of indirect indexing.

These functions are discussed more fully in later chapters in this book.

A Relational Database Computer Program: dBASE III

dBASE III is a relational database management system. The program is designed to be used on IBM Personal Computers for maintaining and manipulating data stored in relational databases. Data is stored in the database as a relational data table. Information in the relational database can be processed in two ways. One way to handle the information in a database file is the method of interactive command processing. Information in the database may be manipulated interactively by commands entered from the keyboard. After each command is entered, results are displayed on an output device, such as a monitor or a printer.

Another method for processing information in dBASE III is batch command processing. Processing tasks are defined in a set of command procedures. These commands are then executed as a batch. The collection of commands is stored in a command file, which is considered to be a computer program. With a batch command file, a processing menu can be designed so that users can select specific tasks during execution.

The main objective of this book is to introduce the dBASE III tools for these two processing methods. You need these tools to handle effectively the information stored in a relational database.

Chapter Summary

A database is a collection of useful information organized in a specific manner. The type of information stored in a database may be alphanumeric text or numerical values. Alphanumeric text consists of information in the form of letters, numbers, and special symbols.

Information stored in a database can be organized in several ways. A database can be defined as a hierarchical database or a relational database. Data in a hierarchical database is organized as a tree structure that assumes one-to-one, one-to-many, or many-to-many relationships. A relational database organizes the data in the form of a table that has rows and columns. Each column of a relational database is called a data field, and each row is called a data record.

A database consists of a set of data records, each of which contains the data elements that belong to a single entry. Each data record is divided into data fields. Each data record within a database file is given a record number. Data fields are identified by a name, or label. Names of data fields and type of data to be stored in each field are specified in the data structure of the database.

A relational database provides an effective means for maintaining and manipulating a large amount of information. Important functions of a database system include the ability to locate and access any item in the database, to sort a data set into a desired order, and to link database files with indirect indexing. These procedures are essential tools for managing business databases.

The term *database management system* (DBMS) has long been used to define a systematic way to organize and manage databases in a large computer system. Because of the introduction of powerful microcomputers and computer programs like dBASE III, database management on microcomputers is now possible. The main objective of this book is to introduce the dBASE III tools that can be used effectively to manage a database.

2

Introduction to dBASE III

An Overview

The preceding chapter introduced the basic concepts of a database management system with organizational models. The material in this chapter concentrates on a specific computer program with which you can easily perform versatile functions of database management. This computer program is dBASE III.

dBASE III is a relational database management system that organizes data elements in a logical, easy-to-read data table. After reading this book and learning the simple and English-like dBASE III commands, you should be able to create a useful database without any other special knowledge of computer programming.

dBASE III can be used in two processing modes. By using the interactive mode and entering your commands directly from the keyboard, you can monitor all the input and output steps involved. Once you understand the dBASE III commands, you will be ready to enjoy the powerful features offered by batch command file programming.

To provide a better understanding of the strengths and limitations of dBASE III, this chapter presents historical perspectives of the program's design philosophy. You will also be introduced to the basic structure and technical specifications of a dBASE III database file. The following special terms discussed in this chapter are related to a dBASE III database file:

> File name
> Character fields
> Date fields
> Numeric fields
> Logical fields
> Memo fields
> Memory variables

A Brief History

dBASE III is designed to be used on an IBM Personal Computer (including the IBM PC, Portable, PC XT, and PC AT) or an IBM-compatible microcomputer. As the developer claims, dBASE III is the new database management standard for today's 16-bit microcomputers.

dBASE III evolved from an earlier database management program. The original version, dBASE II, which was developed several years ago, ran on 8-bit microcomputers that used the CP/M-80 disk operating system. The program was used on several microcomputers, such as the TRS-80, the Osborne, the Kaypro portable, and the Apple // (with a CP/M card installed). Version 2.4 was released in September, 1983, for IBM Personal Computers running under PC DOS V1.1, 2.0, or 2.1.

Before the introduction of dBASE II, database management systems were used mainly on large computers because these systems required a powerful processor and a huge amount of computer memory. The processing language for these database management systems was foreign to most nonprogrammers, and professionally trained programmers were required to write codes or programs to process data with these systems. Because of the high costs of purchasing and operating these systems, the power of database management could be enjoyed only by users of larger computer systems. The release of dBASE II represented a bold and admirable attempt to tap the power of recently developed microcomputers for database management applications. Since its release, the program has been the best-known software for database management on microcomputers. However, the limited processing strength and memory capacity of the early microcomputers often compromised the power of dBASE II. Nevertheless, dBASE II revolutionized the way information was handled on a microcomputer.

Early criticism of dBASE II pointed out the slow processing speed and the small size of the databases supported. Nonprogrammers often complained that the programming language was difficult and time-consuming to master. The problem of slow processing speed and the size limit of a database was due partly to the restricted processing power of microcomputers. Because the design philosophy of dBASE II was largely adapted from that of large computers for professional programmers, dBASE II was not user friendly. In addition, the computer language in which dBASE II was developed was not designed for performing the type of processing tasks required by a large database management system. As a result, the computational power of dBASE II was not satisfactory for some database management applications.

Since the introduction of dBASE II, computer technology has advanced rapidly. A more powerful 16-bit microprocessor has become commonly used in microcomputers. The 16-bit microprocessors process much faster than the 8-bit processors. Inexpensive, large memory capacity also is now readily available. New and more powerful computer languages, such as the C language, have been developed and perfected. In response to the technical advances in hardware and software, dBASE III was introduced in 1984.

Although evolved from dBASE II, dBASE III is drastically different from its predecessor; therefore, dBASE III cannot be considered simply an upgraded version of dBASE II. dBASE III is designed for the 16-bit microprocessor; and because the program is written in the efficient C language, the processing speed of dBASE III has been greatly increased. dBASE III also has a much larger memory capacity than dBASE II. The major differences between dBASE II and dBASE III are summarized in Appendix B at the end of this book.

The strength of dBASE II lies in its programming features. The programming commands provide powerful tools for designing programs to handle database management applications, but the program is not designed to support menu-driven processing, which is easy for nonprogrammers to use for managing databases. dBASE III has corrected most of the deficiencies of dBASE II. With the help screens (detailed helpful hints accessed by a single keystroke) and the ASSIST command, microcomputer users can start manipulating data in a relatively short time. However, because of the program's tremendous power and flexibility, considerable time and effort are required to master the operational rules before serious business applications can be run.

Design Philosophy

As mentioned earlier, the creators of dBASE III adopted most of their design philosophy from database management systems used on large computers. A predominant mode of processing on large computers is batch processing. In this mode, tasks of data processing and computation for a given application are first laid out in a series of detailed steps. Each step is coded into a command, or an instruction, that follows a set of clearly defined rules. The collection of these commands constitutes a computer program, which is fed into the computer as a batch of commands. Without any further human intervention, the computer processes, or executes, the batch of commands. As a result, a complex application can be handled by a large set of commands that were coded and assembled before processing.

Batch processing is an effective way to handle data management, and both dBASE II and dBASE III support batch processing. In this respect, dBASE III can be considered a computer programming language for processing database management applications. This outstanding feature in dBASE III is not shared by many other user-friendly database software programs designed for microcomputers.

Another method of data handling in dBASE III is the interactive mode. This mode of processing differs from batch processing in the way the commands are executed. In the batch processing mode, the whole set of instructions is fed to the computer in one file. Interactive command processing requires that each command be individually entered from the keyboard. Consequently, in the interactive mode, the tasks of data processing and computations can be carried out and monitored step by step.

This immediate feedback from the computer for each command is one advantage of the interactive mode. The feedback helps nonprogrammers understand what is going on during the processing stage. The immediate interaction between the user and the computer also permits instant correction of mistakes in the command. This advantage is one of the chief reasons that many recent developers of database management programs have chosen the interactive mode as the primary method for handling the data in a database. The interactive mode makes database management software more user-friendly for nonprogrammers. Because of the nature of interactive processing, however, a complex application cannot be carried out with an easy-to-use menu design, and an untrained user cannot operate complex programs effectively.

However, dBASE III can be operated in both modes; a database can be easily set up in the interactive mode, and complex tasks can be done by a command program in batch processing mode. The provision of two processing modes makes dBASE III an easy-to-use, flexible, and powerful database management system.

Organization of Data

As a relational database management system, dBASE III operates on the premise that all the information to be stored in a database is defined in a relational structure. The items are arranged in rows and columns of a data table, where each row is a data record and each field is a column. Information in a data table is stored in memory as a data file.

Depending on the nature of the information, many different types of data files are available; each is reserved for storing a specific kind of data. A database may consist of several data files of different types. Because information in a database is usually stored on an external memory device, such as a floppy disk, a data file is often called a disk file.

Types of Disk Files

A data or disk file represents the memory space reserved for holding the information in memory. Because different types of information are used in a database application, different kinds of data structures are defined in disk files. The types of disk files that can be set up in dBASE III are the following:

    Database files
    Database memo files
    Index files

Command files
Format files
Label files
Memory files
Report form files
Text output files

Database Files

A *database file* is equivalent to the relational data table (described in Chapter 1) in that the data elements are in records and fields. The contents of a database file consist of information in one of the following forms:

A string of alphanumeric characters, such as James C. Smith or (206) 456-9873

A date in the form of mm/dd/yy, such as 03/25/85, where mm, dd, and yy denote the numeric codes for month, day, and year, respectively

A numeric value, such as 135.78 or -25.89

A logical character of T for true or F for false, or Y for yes or N for no

Database Memo Files

A *database memo file*, similar to a database file, is used to store large blocks of text that are called memos. A database memo file provides supplementary memory space for a database file. The memo text may be defined as a data field in a database file, but the contents of the data field are stored in a memo file that is separate from the database file itself. Details of database memo files are discussed in later chapters.

Index Files

Sorting data into a desirable order is an important function in database management; dBASE III indexes the contents of a database file in a specific manner and achieves the effect of a sorting operation. An *index file* provides the necessary working spaces for an indexing operation. With an index file, a set of data can be used in a logical order rather than the order in which the records were entered in the database.

Command Files

A *command file* stores the collection of commands that are to be processed in batch processing mode. Because the set of instructions is often called a program, a command file is also referred to as a command program file. The commands can be entered in the command file through the text editing program, which is a part of dBASE III; or the command file can be created by a word-processing program in nondocument mode.

Format Files

A *format file* stores information that specifies the format of output. The format defined in a format file is used with the data items in a database to generate custom reports. The contents of a format file are created by the command language in dBASE III and by the auxiliary program dFORMAT.

Label Files

Label files contain information for printing labels with the LABEL command in dBASE III. A label file, which is similar to a format file, stores the specifications for printed labels. The specifications may include the width and the height of the label, spacing between labels, and so forth. The contents of a label file can be created with the MODIFY LABEL command.

Memory Files

A *memory file* stores the contents of the active *memory variables*. Memory variables represent temporary memory locations that can hold computational results which may be used again for later processing. The contents of a memory variable may be an alphanumeric string or a numeric value. These values are entered in a memory file by the SAVE and RESTORE commands. The use of a memory variable to keep track of the last invoice number issued, for example, plays an important role in data manipulation.

Report Form Files

Report form files contain information for generating reports with the REPORT command. Information in a report form file specifies the contents of reports and their format, such as information in the heading of the report and the data items to be used in the reports. Report form files are created with the MODIFY REPORT command.

Text Output Files

A *text output file* stores text that can be shared with other computer programs. For instance, a table of data created in dBASE III may be written to a text output file. Then after you have exited from dBASE III, the contents of the file can be read by other software, such as a word-processing program or other database management programs. A text output file provides the necessary links for information exchange among different computer programs.

Disk File Names

For reference, each disk file must be assigned a file identification. The identification of a disk file consists of two parts: a file name and a file identifier. A unique file name is assigned by the user. A file identifier designates the type of file. The file identifier consists of a period (.) and any of the following letter combinations:

.dbf or .DBF	Database file
.dbt or .DBT	Database memo file
.ndx or .NDX	Index file
.prg or .PRG	Command (or program) file
.fmt or .FMT	Format file
.lbl or .LBL	Label file
.mem or .MEM	Memory file
.frm or .FRM	Report form file
.txt or .TXT	Text output file

A *file name* consists of a string of no more than eight characters. Except for the first character, which must be a letter of the alphabet, these characters can be letters, numbers, or the underscore (_). No blank spaces are allowed as part of a file name. The following strings of characters are acceptable file names:

PHONES.DBF
Accounts.dbf
PAYCHECK.FMT
ID_NO.DBF
LETTERS.DBT
mailing.lbl
ATABLE.TXT
Billing.prg

A file name, together with its file extension (for example, .DBF, .PRG, etc.), represents a symbolic name for the disk file. The file name provides a unique reference for the disk file.

Types of Data Fields

A *data field* is a division of a data record. Five different types of data fields can be used in dBASE III:

Character (or text) fields
Memo fields
Numeric fields
Logical fields
Date fields

Each type of data field is used to store one kind of data. The type of data field dictates the form in which the data must be entered and the way the data can be used in a certain kind of application. Character fields and memo fields store text, which may include letters, numbers, special symbols, and blank spaces. Any characters defined by the American Standard Code for Information Interchange (ASCII) can be a text character. A list of the ASCII characters is given in Appendix A at the end of this book. However, character fields and memo fields are different. A *character field* can store a short text, but only a *memo field* can store a large block of text. In addition, the text stored in these two fields is used differently. Details of these differences are the subjects of later chapters.

Any values or numbers in a database can be saved in a numeric field. *Numeric fields* are of two types: integer and decimal. The sign (positive or negative) associated with a number or value is considered a part of the field contents. Contents of a numeric field are used for computational applications.

A *date field* is used to store dates, which may be represented in various forms. A common format for a date is mm/dd/yy, where mm, dd, and yy represent the numeric codes for the month, day, and year, respectively. A date in dBASE III is treated differently from text or a number. The date must be used only as a date in data manipulation. Dates cannot be treated as a normal alphanumeric string. The numeric codes in a date cannot be used in a formula without conversion.

Logical fields are designed to accommodate a single character that represents a true (T) or false (F) state in a logical comparison. A logical field can therefore divide the contents of a database file into two groups: one with a true state and the other with a false state. For example, a database consisting of a set of students' records may include a logical field to identify the sex of a student. A T entered in the logical field MALE indicates that the student is a male, whereas the records of all the female students will have F stored in that field.

System Requirements

dBASE III is designed to be run on the IBM PC, IBM Portable, IBM PC XT, IBM PC AT, COMPAQ, and other IBM-compatible microcomputers. The minimum computer memory required is 256K, which can hold about 256,000 characters. During data manipulation, the computer memory is used as a working space, so more memory usually increases processing speed.

dBASE III also requires MS-DOS or PC DOS Version 2.0 or greater. The computer should have two 360K double-sided floppy disk drives or one 360K floppy drive with a hard disk drive. The computer program usually resides on one of the floppy disks, and all the database files are saved on the other floppy disk (or the hard disk). The maximum data storage on a floppy disk is about 360,000 characters. A two-disk drive may be sufficient for handling small-to-medium-size databases. However, for faster accessing and large databases, a hard disk is highly recommended. Other hardware includes a printer with at least an 80-column capacity.

System Limitations

The type of processor used in the microcomputer and the amount of computer memory available impose certain size limits. Furthermore, the available storage space on the floppy disk determines the number of files that can be stored. Ten database (.DBF) files can be active at one time, and seven index (.NDX) files may be created from a database file. However, for each database file, only one format file can be specified. Still, a total of fifteen different files of any type may be activated at any one time during processing. Note that a database file containing a memo field is counted as two files.

A database (.DBF) file may contain up to two billion characters of information or a maximum of one billion data records. Each data record may hold as many as 4,000 characters and be divided into as many as 128 data fields. However, each data record in a database memo (.DBT) file can store up to 512,000 characters of text.

A character field can store up to 254,000 characters of information, whereas a memo field can hold up to only 4,096 characters of text. A numeric field may store up to 19 characters, which may include digits, decimal points, and the sign of a value, but no commas. Smaller yet, a date field holds a string of eight characters (mm/dd/yy), and a logical field may contain only one character (T or F, Y or N).

Chapter Summary

In 1984, dBASE III, a relational database management program with a 16-bit microprocessor structure, was released for the IBM PC. Although dBASE III evolved from dBASE II, the two programs have significant differences in their design philosophy and processing power.

Because of the type of processor used in the microcomputer and the amount of computer memory available, certain size limits are imposed. Inasmuch as dBASE II was designed for 8-bit microprocessors, its processing speed is much slower than that of dBASE III, and a dBASE II database is much smaller than a database in dBASE III. The power of dBASE III lies in its built-in programming language, which provides an effective batch processing mode. Because of the added features of help screens and ASSIST commands, dBASE III can be used efficiently in both batch processing mode and interactive mode.

dBASE III uses a relational database model in organizing its data elements. Data in a database is stored in disk files. Various types of data files can be used for holding different kinds of information in the database. A database file, equivalent to the data table in a relational database, contains the data structure and all the data records. The data structure defines the detailed attributes of the data fields within a data record. A memo file is used to hold large blocks of text in the database. Format files, label files, and report files are used to store the details needed for generating custom reports. All the batch processing commands in the form of a computer program are held in a command file. Index files and memory files contain information that may assist the operations of data manipulation. A text file can be used to save text that can be shared by other computer programs.

In dBASE III, five different types of data fields are available to accommodate different kinds of data elements. A character/text field and a memo field are reserved for holding alphanumeric data. Numbers or values are stored in a numeric field. Dates are saved in a

date field in the form of dd/mm/yy. A logical field is used to
contain a character that represents a true or false (T or F, Y or N)
state in a logical comparison.

3

Getting Started

An Overview

Because dBASE III is specifically designed to run on an IBM PC, a thorough understanding of that computer system is vital for effective use of the program. Therefore, this chapter is written for the reader who has little prior knowledge of microcomputers. The text begins by discussing the basic components of an IBM PC system. Next, the steps necessary to start the disk operating system (DOS) are explained, followed by the procedures for formatting a data disk and for activating the dBASE III program itself.

However, before use, the dBASE III system disk, which is supplied by the manufacturer, must be configured to accommodate the maximum number of database files and data buffers you will need. In another configuration step, you should designate the default disk drive, where the data disk is to be found before the dBASE III program starts. These configuration steps are explained in the latter part of this chapter, and you may want to verify them before you proceed further.

The special terms introduced in this chapter include the following:

    System unit
    Microprocessor
    Internal memory
    Auxiliary memory
    Read-only memory (ROM)
    Random-access memory (RAM)
    Data backup system
    Disk operating system (DOS)
    Booting a computer system
    Cold boot procedure
    Warm boot procedure
    Configuring the DOS system disk
    Configuring the dBASE III system disk

The following disk operating system (DOS) commands are explained in this chapter:

    FORMAT
    dBASE
    COPY CON: CONFIG.SYS
    COPY CON: CONFIG.DB
    TYPE

The Microcomputer System

Electronic computers, originally developed as computational tools to help perform tedious, time-consuming, and often complex calculations, are now widely used as microcomputers to assist business managers in problem solving and database management functions. Over the years, various types of computers have been developed; but until recently, business computers were large and expensive and required specially trained operators. Computers were used mostly for handling the data processing needs of professional programmers. The procedures for using these types of computers were usually complicated and difficult for nonprogrammers to understand. Most business applications also required specially tailored computer programs. As a result, electronic computers were not used for decision-making and problem-solving tools by management until the recent development of microcomputers.

The introduction of the IBM Personal Computer (IBM PC) represented a significant milestone in computer development. Because of the machine's immense computational power and ease of use, IBM PCs have become an increasingly important tool for business applications, including word processing, accounting operations, financial analyses, and database management.

Basic Components of the IBM PC

The basic components of a microcomputer system usually include the following four parts: the input unit, the processing unit, the auxiliary memory, and the output unit. The basic components of an IBM PC and their functional relationships are summarized in figure 3.1.

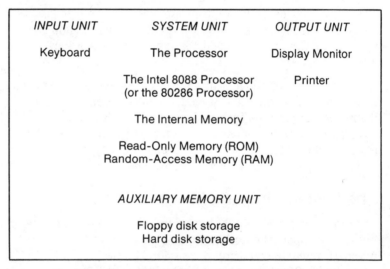

INPUT UNIT	SYSTEM UNIT	OUTPUT UNIT
Keyboard	The Processor	Display Monitor
	The Intel 8088 Processor (or the 80286 Processor)	Printer
	The Internal Memory	
	Read-Only Memory (ROM) Random-Access Memory (RAM)	
	AUXILIARY MEMORY UNIT	
	Floppy disk storage Hard disk storage	

Fig. 3.1. Basic components of a microcomputer system.

The Input Unit—the IBM PC Keyboard

Although you have different ways to enter information into a computer, the keyboard is the most important input device. A diagram of the IBM PC keyboard is shown in figure 3.2.

Like an electric typewriter, the keyboard has a set of alphanumeric keys on which information can be typed and transmitted into the computer. However, the PC also has a set of ten special keys that are not found on a typewriter keyboard. These keys, labeled F1 through F10, are located on the left side of the keyboard and are called *function keys*. Each function key can be programmed to perform a predefined function. Several other keys, such as the Esc,

Fig. 3.2. The IBM PC keyboard.

Ctrl, and cursor (or arrow) keys are also unique to the IBM PC keyboard. The functions of these keys in dBASE III are summarized in Appendix C, and the uses of the keys are explained as they are introduced.

One important point about using an IBM keyboard is that when you enter information from the keyboard, the information appears on the monitor but goes no farther. The information is received, or "understood," by the computer only after the RETURN key (which is labeled ↵) has been pressed. Therefore, you must press the RETURN key at the end of every command line.

The System Unit and Microprocessors

The *system unit* of an IBM PC houses the "brain" of the computer. The main component of the system unit is the processing circuits, which use Intel's 8088 microprocessor for the IBM PC and IBM PC XT or the 80286 microprocessor for the IBM PC AT. Another part of the system unit includes the control unit, which acts as a traffic controller that regulates data flow within the computer system. Internal memory in the form of ROM (read-only memory) and RAM (random-access memory) is also part of the system unit. Auxiliary memory devices—floppy disk drives and a hard disk drive—are the other components of a system unit.

All the computations are carried out by the arithmetic circuits in the *microprocessor*. The logic unit within the processor performs the decision-branching operations, such as comparing two values and determining whether one is greater than, less than, or equal to the other.

Most computer users do not need to understand the engineering aspects of these microprocessors. The two microprocessors perform similar functions, except that one may perform faster computations and provide more accuracy in numeric manipulation than the another.

The Read-Only Memory (ROM)

Two types of *internal memory* devices are built in the system unit. The first is the *read-only memory*, or ROM. It is the internal storage facility that you use for all the programs or instructions necessary for controlling the computer operations and for interpreting the programming instructions typed from the keyboard. Because the information stored in ROM can only be read, or retrieved, you cannot modify the contents of ROM. They are normally preset by the computer manufacturer and usually do not concern most programmers or users.

The Random-Access Memory, RAM

The second internal memory of the system unit is the *random-access memory*, or RAM. The user can view or read the contents of RAM and deposit, or write, information to the memory at random. Therefore, RAM is used to store application programs and data. For instance, the set of processing commands and the contents of a database file in dBASE III are stored in RAM during processing. You have full control of the contents of the random-access memory: you can create, modify, or delete any information in RAM.

The size of the memory is usually measured by bytes. A byte consists of 8 binary bits, each of which can be represented by a digit, 0 or 1. Although the practice is not universal, many computers use 8 bits to represent a character; so a byte is the memory capacity needed for storing a character. The size of RAM in the IBM PC is determined by the RAM circuit chips available on the system circuit board. You can add RAM chips to the system by using a plug-in memory board and thus increase the size of the RAM. The RAM chips usually come in increments of 64K (about 65,536 bytes), where one K(ilobyte) is equivalent to 1,024 bytes. The maximum RAM on a microcomputer is also dictated by the disk operating system. To learn the maximum size of RAM for your system, check the reference manual for your disk operating system.

Auxiliary Memory Devices

You may need *auxiliary memory* devices to supplement the internal memory for storing large amounts of information, such as a large database. Common external memory devices include floppy disks and hard disk drives. Cassette recorders may be used as auxiliary memory devices, but recorders are so slow in transferring data that they are not recommended for most database applications.

Floppy disks are one of the most commonly used storage media for the IBM PC. It uses 5 1/4-inch disks. Floppy disks are an economic means for storing large amounts of information as programs and data files.

The amount of information that can be stored on a floppy disk is determined by the type of disk drive and the *disk operating system*. The IBM PC uses a single-sided or a double-sided disk drive. The disk operating system can be PC DOS V1.1, V2.0, or any later versions. With very minor differences, PC DOS is equivalent to MS-DOS. When used with a double-sided drive and under PC DOS V2.0 or 2.1, a floppy disk holds 320K of information. A double-sided drive on the IBM PC AT under PC DOS V3.0 may store 1.2 million bytes (1.2 megabytes) of information on a high-density floppy disk.

The popularity of hard disks as auxiliary memory devices has recently increased dramatically because of the disk's improved efficiency and reliability. The storage capacity of a hard disk drive is much greater than that of a floppy disk. The amount of information that you can store on a hard disk may range from 5 megabytes to about 250 megabytes. The amount of time for a hard disk to transfer information from the disk to the processor is much faster than that for a floppy disk drive. Because of these advantages, hard disks are widely used on business computer systems.

The Output Unit

The output unit in a computer system displays the results of computations or data processing. Output can be displayed temporarily on a monitor similar to a television screen or printed on a printer.

Display Monitors

The most common output device is a display monitor. Two types of display monitors can be used with the IBM PC. With the proper circuit boards in the system unit, results can be displayed on a green monochrome monitor or on a color graphics monitor. An IBM monochrome monitor displays on a green screen textual information in lines up to 80 characters long. The color graphics monitor is used for displaying text on 40- or 80-character lines and graphs (line graphs, bar graphs, etc.) with colors. For displaying results in dBASE III, either an IBM monochrome monitor or a color monitor can be used.

Printers

Printers are important output devices because printers provide the means to generate a permanent copy (hard copy) of the output. In general, two types of printers are available. The types are differentiated by the way characters, or symbols, are generated. One type is a dot-matrix printer, which forms each character by a combination of dots (usually in a pattern of 7 by 9, or 63, dots). Dot-matrix printers are fast and versatile and can print different type fonts. However, because each character is formed by a pattern of discrete dots, the characters do not look as sharp as those produced by an electric typewriter.

Another type of printer is the letter-quality, or type-quality, printer. The printing mechanism of a letter-quality printer may be a daisywheel, which is a thimble-shaped printing cap. Letter-quality printers can generate output that looks as good as output from an electric typewriter. However, a letter-quality printer is slow and has a limited number of type fronts.

With recent developments in printer technology, some printers use a high-density matrix pattern. As a result, a better print quality, called correspondence-quality, can be achieved without sacrificing printing speed. In addition to text, many printers can produce graphics documents that have continuous lines and figures. Many more expensive printers are also capable of producing color charts and graphics and color texts.

Data Backup System

Although a hard disk is an effective means of data storage for a microcomputer, hard disks are also vulnerable to hardware failures. Malfunctions of a hard disk often result in locking the disk-retrieval mechanism. Consequently, none of the data on the disabled disk can be accessed, and repairs on the hard disk unit usually erase the contents of the disk. Therefore, regular systematic *data backup* is essential to ensure that all data is maintained. Data backup means making an extra copy of the data and storing the backup copy in a safe place. Then, if the hard disk should fail, the data on the backup disk can be used.

You can choose from a number of storage devices for backup. The most common is a streamer-tape unit that uses magnetic tape. Some units copy the contents of the whole hard disk to a tape cartridge; others provide the flexibility of copying the data file by file. The tape backup system is convenient and cost-effective for data backup.

The Procedure for Starting the Microcomputer

The procedure of starting a microcomputer is usually referred to as *booting the computer*. Before a computer can perform any tasks, instructions must be fed to the processor. Some instructions are stored in ROM and can be carried out by the processor as soon as the computer is activated. Instructions that govern how the information on the disk drives is to be retrieved and processed must also be furnished by a program called the disk operating system (DOS).

Starting DOS

The *disk operating system*, or DOS, is stored on a floppy disk supplied by the manufacturer. The disk operating system, such as IBM's PC DOS V2.0, comes as a part of the contents of the disk labeled DOS System Disk. The system disk must be in the disk drive (usually in drive A) before the DOS program is retrieved.

The Cold Boot

DOS can be started two different ways. The first way to start the computer is called a *cold boot*. You perform a cold boot by doing the following:

1. Put the disk operating system disk in drive A.

2. Turn on the computer's power switch.

As soon as the power is turned on, the processor is activated. By executing the instructions stored in ROM, the computer begins to perform various functions, such as checking the random-access memory (RAM) and activating the input and output devices (the keyboard, monitor, and printer). The computer then attempts to access DOS by turning on the default disk drive, usually drive A. If found, DOS is loaded into the computer memory, and you see the following prompt on the screen (after responding to **Enter current date** and **Enter current time**):

A>

This DOS prompt indicates that drive A is the active disk drive. At this point, the computer is ready to receive further instructions. If you are using a hard disk (for instance, on an IBM PC XT or PC AT), you can copy the disk operating system to the hard disk, which may be designated as drive C or D, and initiate the booting procedure from there.

The Warm Boot

The second way to start the disk operating system is the *warm boot*. This procedure restarts the disk operating system by interrupting the current processing task. For a warm boot, hold down both the control key (Ctrl) and the Alt key and press also the delete key (Del). The current processing job is halted, and DOS is reinitiated and displays the A>. A warm boot takes less time because it does not direct the processor to perform checks on the RAM as in a cold boot.

Preparing a Data Disk

Before dBASE III is activated, you must prepare data disks for storing the database files you will create. A blank floppy disk cannot be used for data storage without being formatted. Formatting a disk involves writing on it various record markings that tell the disk unit where and how information is to be saved on the disk.

Formatting a Floppy Disk

If you are using a system with two floppy disks, you can format a disk by following these steps:

1. Put the disk operating system disk (such as DOS V2.0 or 2.1) in drive A.

2. Start the system with a cold boot or a warm boot.

3. Enter the date and time as requested by the computer.

4. When the A> appears, type the phrase

    FORMAT B:

This command tells the computer to format a disk in drive B. Be sure to press the RETURN key after each line you type.

5. Put a blank disk is drive B and follow the instructions given by the computer.

6. When formatting is done, put the formatted disk away for later use.

Formatting a Hard Disk

Storage space on a hard disk is usually divided into volumes, each of which can be viewed as a disk drive like drive B in a floppy system. However, volumes of a hard disk are usually designated as drives C, D, E, and so on. The procedure to format a volume in a hard disk is like formatting a floppy disk. In a system with one floppy disk and one hard disk, a disk volume of the hard disk (designated, for example, drive C) is formatted by following the steps given for the floppy disk but typing *C:* instead of *B:* in step 4 and eliminating steps 5 and 6. You may also format only a portion of a disk volume in a hard disk. Check your reference manual for the hard disk for details.

Preparations for Starting dBASE III

dBASE III is a computer program that instructs an IBM PC to perform the tasks required for managing a database. The computer program consists of a set of commands that are coded and stored on the dBASE III system disk. Before dBASE III is loaded into memory, the computer must be informed about the environment in which the program is to be operated. For example, the number of files to be used in the program and the amount of memory to be reserved for data storage must be specified before the program is processed. The default disk drive for data storage must also be designated so that the disk operating system can locate the data files when they are needed. You specify this information by the procedure called system configuration.

System configuration involves specification to DOS of the necessary parameters, such as the number of files and the size of reserved memory, and the designation of the default disk drive on the dBASE III system disk.

Configuring the DOS System Disk

Booting the computer begins the execution of the instructions stored in ROM. The computer is instructed to set up the necessary input and output devices and to allot memory space for normal processing. The number of files is normally set to 8 by the computer; however, 5 files are used by DOS, leaving only 3 for the user. Because dBASE III can accommodate a total of 15 files by the user, you must set the number of files to 20 during system configuration.

The processor sets aside a certain amount of computer memory as temporary working space for data manipulation. This temporary working space is reserved in blocks of RAM that are called memory buffers. The more buffers you reserve, the faster processing is achieved. The total number of buffers is restricted by the amount of RAM available on the computer system. Because the dBASE III program itself and the active data files used in the program compete with buffers for memory space, the number of buffers should not be set too high. Otherwise, you will not have enough memory for storing your database files during processing. With a minimum of 256K RAM on the computer, you should be safe to designate 24 memory buffers, as recommended by the dBASE III developers.

Unless the default setting is chosen, information about the number of files and the number of memory buffers is communicated to the computer through a file named CONFIG.SYS. This file must be on the DOS system disk when the computer is booted. Whenever the computer is booted, the system tries to locate the CONFIG.SYS file on the DOS system disk in drive A. If the file is found, the information in the file is retrieved, and the numbers of files and buffers are set accordingly. Otherwise, the default values are used.

You can create the CONFIG.SYS file and save it on the DOS system disk with the following steps. Do not forget to press the RETURN key after each line you type.

1. Put the DOS system disk in drive A.

2. Boot the system.

3. When the A> appears, type

   COPY CON: CONFIG.SYS

4. Then type

   FILES=20

5. Next type

   BUFFERS=24

6. Press the F6 function key and then the RETURN key.

Step 3 instructs the computer to create a COPY of the file named CONFIG.SYS on the console (CON:), or monitor. Steps 4 and 5 supply the contents to the file in line-by-line sequence. The final F6 keystroke (equivalent to holding down the Ctrl key and pressing Z) signals the end of the file contents. As soon as the RETURN key is pressed, the file CONFIG.SYS is created and saved on the DOS system disk.

After the CONFIG.SYS file is created and saved on the DOS system disk, the A> is again displayed. If you want to verify the configuration procedure and to examine the contents of the CONFIG.SYS file, enter the following command after the A>:

TYPE CONFIG.SYS

The screen displays the contents of the CONFIG.SYS file for your verification (see fig. 3.3). If you find a mistake, re-create the file.

```
A>COPY CON: CONFIG.SYS
FILES=20
BUFFERS=24^Z
        1 File(s) copied

A>TYPE CONFIG.SYS
FILES=20
BUFFERS=24
A>
```

Fig. 3.3. The CONFIG.SYS file.

Once the CONFIG.SYS is correct and has been saved on the DOS system disk, the file does not have to be created again. CONFIG.SYS remains valid for use with dBASE III. If, however, you need to change the contents of CONFIG.SYS, just re-create the file.

Configuring the dBASE III System Disk

dBASE III is designed to be used on a system with two floppy disks or one floppy disk and one hard disk. The dBASE III system disk is normally assumed to be in drive A, and the files created by the program are stored on the second floppy disk (drive B) or on a hard disk designated as drive C, drive D, etc. The disk drive that is to hold the database files must be specified before data manipulation takes place.

Specification of a default data disk drive can be done in two ways. One way is to provide the drive identification (drive B, drive C, etc.) through a CONFIG.DB file on the dBASE III system disk. Another way is to enter the drive identification after dBASE III is activated. The first method is preferred. When the dBASE III system disk is configured with information about the default disk drive, data manipulation can begin as soon as the program is activated.

Configuration of the dBASE III system disk involves the creation of the CONFIG.DB file, a process similar to setting up the CONFIG.SYS file. CONFIG.SYS, however, is saved on the DOS system disk, whereas CONFIG.DB is saved on the dBASE III system disk. To create on the dBASE III system disk a CONFIG.DB file designating drive B (B:) as the default disk drive, follow these steps:

1. Put the DOS system disk in drive A.

2. Boot the system.

3. When the A> appears, place the dBASE III system disk in drive A.

4. Type

    COPY CON: CONFIG.DB

5. Type

    DEFAULT=B:

6. Press the F6 function key (or Ctrl-Z) and then the RETURN key.

You can display the contents of the CONFIG.DB file by entering the following command after the A> appears on the screen:

TYPE CONFIG.DB

The screen display in figure 3.4 shows the command lines and their results for creating and displaying the CONFIG.DB file on the dBASE III system disk.

Starting the dBASE III Program

After you have configured the DOS system disk and the dBASE III
disks, you are ready to start the actual dBASE III program.

```
A>COPY CON: CONFIG.DB
DEFAULT=B:^Z
          1 File(s) copied

A>TYPE CONFIG.DB
DEFAULT=B:
A>
```

Fig. 3.4. The CONFIG.DB file.

To start the dBASE III program, use the following procedure:

1. Boot the system with the DOS system disk in drive A (if you
    have not done so).

2. Insert a formatted blank data disk in drive B (if a two-disk
    system is used).

3. When the A> appears, place the dBASE III system disk in
    drive A and type

    dBASE

You are greeted by dBASE III with the message shown in figure 3.5.

As you can see in figure 3.5, at the end of the message in the lower
left corner of the screen is a dot (.), called a *dot prompt*. The
presence of the dot prompt tells you that the computer is under
dBASE III control. You can now enter a dBASE III command from
the keyboard. You must press the RETURN key after every
command line; and the command lines may be written in capital
letters, lowercase letters, or a combination.

One command that is useful even before you begin processing any
data is the HELP command. To activate the HELP command, type
the word *help* or *HELP* after the dot prompt:

    . HELP

The HELP command brings up information about dBASE III
commands and their operational rules. These help messages are self-

```
dBASE III  version 1.00 IBM/MSDOS ***

COPYRIGHT (c) ASHTON-TATE 1984
AS AN UNPUBLISHED LICENSED PROPRIETARY WORK.
ALL RIGHTS RESERVED.

Use of this software and the other materials contained in the software package
(the "Materials") has been provided under a Software License Agreement (please
read in full).  In summary, Ashton-Tate grants you a paid-up, non-transferrable,
personal license to use the Materials only on a single or subsequent (but not
additional) computer terminal for fifty years from the time the sealed disk
has been opened.  You receive the right to use the Materials, but you do not
become the owner of them.  You may not alter, decompile, or reverse-assemble the
software, and YOU MAY NOT COPY the Materials.  The Materials are protected by
copyright, trade secrets, and trademark law, the violation of which can result
in civil damages and criminal prosecution.

dBASE, dBASE III and ASHTON-TATE are trademarks of Ashton-Tate.


Press the F1 key for help
Type a command (or ASSIST) and press the return key (◄┘).

.
```

Fig. 3.5. The dBASE III opening message and dot prompt.

explanatory. At any time, you can interrupt the help message and return to the dot prompt by pressing the escape (Esc) key. At the dot prompt, you can exit from dBASE III and return to the DOS prompt (A>) by typing *QUIT* or *quit*.

Chapter Summary

An IBM PC consists of four major components: the input unit, which is the keyboard; the system unit, which consists of the microprocessor and internal memory as ROM and RAM; the auxiliary memory, such as a floppy disk drive or a hard disk unit; and the output unit, which can be a monitor or a printer. An IBM keyboard has a set of alphanumeric keys by which information can be given to the computer plus a set of unique keys that are used to perform predefined operations.

ROM and RAM are memory units that hold information in a computer system. Systems programs, such as those governing the operations of the input/output devices, are stored in ROM, or read-only memory. RAM, or random-access memory, holds user programs and data files. Auxiliary memory units in the form of floppy disk drives or hard disk units are devices for storing user programs and data files as permanent records. A streamer-tape unit is a memory device that can backup a large amount of information, such as that stored on a hard disk.

The procedure for starting a computer system is called booting. You use a cold boot when you turn on the computer. You can restart the computer system by a warm boot, which interrupts the current processing task.

Before starting dBASE III, you must prepare the computer for handling the computer program. In addition, data disks must be prepared and formatted before data can be saved on the disks. The computer must also be informed of the anticipated memory usage— that is, the number of files and the size of the memory buffer to be used. You must also specify the default data disk. You can accomplish these tasks by setting up the CONFIG.SYS file on the DOS system disk and the CONFIG.DB file on the dBASE III system disk. Once these tasks have been completed, you can activate the dBASE III program. When dBASE III is successfully activated, a dot prompt (.) is displayed. You now are in the world of dBASE III and can enter the commands for performing the database management functions.

4

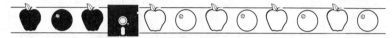

Creating, Editing, and Displaying Data

An Overview

This chapter explains how to design and create a database file. You can use a database file to store data elements as simple as employee information or as complicated as an accounting system.

The chapter also highlights the simplicity of database management with easy-to-use dBASE III commands. When you master these simple commands, you can perform many sophisticated data management functions. The chapter explains how to do the following:

Edit information on screen
Create a new database file
Define the structure of a database file
Enter data in a database file
Display the database file directory

Display the structure and contents of a database file
Edit or modify contents of a database file
Copy a database file to another file
Rename a database file
Delete a database file

This chapter introduces the following dBASE III commands:

Commands	Functions
CREATE	Creates a database file
USE	Activates a database file
DISPLAY, LIST, BROWSE	Display data
APPEND, INSERT	Add data records
LOCATE, CONTINUE, SKIP, GOTO, GO TOP, GO BOTTOM	Locate a data record
MODIFY, EDIT, BROWSE, CHANGE, REPLACE	Modify data records
DELETE, PACK, RECALL, ZAP, ERASE	Delete data records
DIR, COPY FILE, RENAME, ERASE	File manipulation

Creating a Database File

When the dot prompt is displayed, you can create a new database file. To create a new database file, type CREATE after the dot prompt. An active database file is stored in the computer's random-access memory (RAM). A nonactive database file is usually saved in auxiliary memory such as on a floppy disk or a hard disk. When you create a database file, you assign a unique name to the file for later identification. The format of a CREATE command is

. CREATE <database file name>

To enter a command line, you must press the RETURN key. The less than (<) and greater than (>) symbols signify the name of the database file to be created. These symbols are not a part of the command and should not be entered.

Naming a Database File

The name of a database file can include up to eight characters, the first of which must be a letter of the alphabet. The remaining characters can be letters, numeric digits, or underscores. Following are a few acceptable database file names:

EMPLOYEE
Directry
PHONES
INVENTRY
Accounts
ADDRESS
COURSES
ITEMSOLD

Because dBASE III automatically converts all letters to uppercase, you can enter a file name in upper- or lowercase letters. To access a file, you can enter the name in upper- or lowercase. For example, the database file EMPLOYEE can be recalled as *Employee* or *employee*. When the directory is displayed, however, all file names appear uppercase.

A database file name cannot contain spaces or symbols other than the underscore (_). Because dBASE III recognizes a space as a separator between two data items, a file name with a space is not accepted by the program. The period (.), the slash (/), the colon (:), and the semicolon (;) are reserved for special functions in dBASE III and should be excluded from file names. Some examples of illegal file names are

PHONE NO
PART1;35
BUS/101
MODEL:A

When you enter an illegal file name, you will see one of the following error messages:

Syntax error or **File is not accessible**

The message **Syntax error** means that the item was entered incorrectly and violates the syntax rules for a processing command. If you enter the phrase PHONE NO, dBASE III reads the name as two separate file names, and an error message is returned. Two database files cannot be created with one CREATE command.

The error message **File is not accessible** appears when you use a symbol in a file name. When a database file name is assigned with more than eight characters, no warning message is displayed, but only the first eight characters are saved. For example, when the following CREATE commands are entered, no error message is displayed:

. CREATE PARTS_RCA100
. CREATE PARTS_RCA200

Because only the first eight characters are recognized, the commands will create the same database file name (PARTS_RC).

Defining the Data Structure of a Database File

After you enter an acceptable file name, the field definition form for the data structure appears. Figure 4.1 shows the definition form after the CREATE EMPLOYEE command is accepted.

The name of the database file appears in the upper left corner of the field definition form. dBASE III adds the file identifier *.DBF* to the

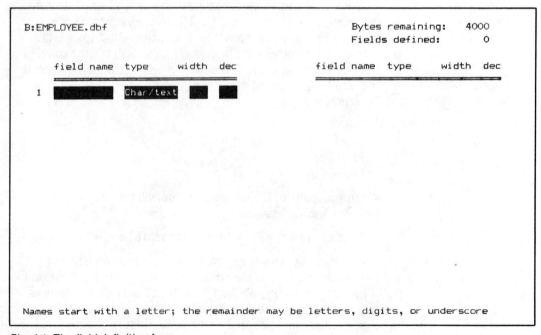

Fig. 4.1. The field definition form.

file name to indicate the type of data file involved. The upper right corner shows the amount of available memory (in bytes or characters) and the number of fields that have been defined. The information is updated as new fields are defined and added to the data structure. The main body of the form provides space to define the specifications of each data field, such as

name of data field
type of data field
width of data field

Entering the Data Field Name

After you enter the CREATE command, the cursor is shown at the beginning of a data field on the field definition form. Now the data field name can be entered. The name of a data field can contain up to ten characters, and the first character must be a letter. The remaining characters may be in the form of letters, numeric digits, or underscores. Similar to database file names, no blank spaces are allowed. Underscores are often used for separating words in a field name. Some examples of acceptable data field names are the following:

FIRST_NAME
LAST_NAME
MIDDLE_INT
AREA_CODE
PHONE_NO
ACCOUNT_NO
GROSS_WAGE
BIRTH_DATE
ANNUAL_PAY

The definition form provides space for ten characters in a field name. When the space is filled, the cursor automatically moves to the next data field on the form, and a beep sounds. You can enter a field name with less than ten characters by pressing RETURN after the last character of the name. The RETURN keystroke moves the cursor to the next item on the form, and no beep is heard.

Entering the Data Field Type

Five types of data fields can be defined in dBASE III to store different kinds of information. The five field types are the following:

C	Character/text fields
N	Numeric fields
D	Date fields
L	Logical fields
M	Memo fields

To enter the field type to the structure, type one of the five letters (C, N, D, L, or M) when the cursor is in the field type. The default field type is the character/text field and can be selected by pressing the RETURN key. You can choose a field type other than the one displayed by pressing the space bar. To select a new field type, press the space bar and then the RETURN key.

Entering the Data Field Width

The width of a data field is the maximum number of characters allowed in the field. In character/text or memo fields, the field width determines the possible length of the text. All letters, numeric digits, symbols, and spaces are considered part of the text.

A date field is always eight characters wide and stores the numeric codes for the month, the day, the year, and the slashes that separate the codes. The standard date format is mm/dd/yy.

A logical field accepts only one character in a true/false value, so the width of the field is always one character.

The width of a numeric field is defined two ways. First, you define the maximum number of digits allowed in the value, including the sign and the decimal point if one is used. Then you determine the number of spaces after the decimal point. For example, to store a number up to 9999.99, set the width of the field to seven and define two decimal places. An integer does not require decimal places defined in the field width. Commas or dollar signs (such as $9,999.99) cannot be used as part of the value.

A Sample Data Structure

To illustrate the process of defining the data structure, we have created a database file to store the information of a firm's employees. Employee information is stored in each data record in the file. Each item shown in figure 4.2 can be defined as a data field.

The data fields FIRST_NAME, LAST_NAME, AREA_CODE, and PHONE_NO are defined as character/text fields to store the

```
 B:EMPLOYEE.DBF                                 Bytes remaining:   3950
                                                Fields defined:       7

      field name  type      width  dec      field name  type    width  dec
      ════════════════════════════════      ════════════════════════════════
   1  FIRST_NAME  Char/text    12
   2  LAST_NAME   Char/text    10
   3  AREA_CODE   Char/text     3
   4  PHONE_NO    Char/text     8
   5  MALE        Logical       1
   6  BIRTH_DATE  Date          8
   7  ANNUAL_PAY  Numeric       8     2




 Names start with a letter; the remainder may be letters, digits, or underscore
```

Fig. 4.2. A sample database file.

employee's name and phone number. The width of these fields is set to accommodate the number of alphanumeric characters in the fields.

The logical field MALE identifies the sex of the employee, and accepts only a single character for a true (T) or false (F) reply.

As an alternative, you could define a character/text field named SEX to store a variable for male or female. However, a logical field can be searched more efficiently than a character/text field.

An employee's birth date is defined as the date field BIRTH_DATE in the form of dd/mm/yy. Remember that a date field is not a character/text field, although the date field may contain a string of alphanumeric characters. Only the contents of a date field can later be manipulated with date operators.

The numeric field ANNUAL_PAY is used to store the employee's annual salary. The maximum length of the numeric field is set to eight characters, so you can enter up to 99999.99 in value.

When all the fields are defined, you can terminate the process by pressing the RETURN key or the Ctrl-End keystroke combination. To use Ctrl-End, simply press and hold down the Ctrl key while you also press the End key. After you press either of the alternatives, you will see the following message:

Hit RETURN to confirm--any other way to resume

If you press RETURN again, the data structure will be saved, and the following message will appear on screen:

    Input data records now? (Y/N)

Entering Data in a Database File

If you answer Y to the question, the program displays the data entry form on screen. For example, after you have defined the EMPLOYEE database file structure, the computer will display the first data entry form (see fig. 4.3).

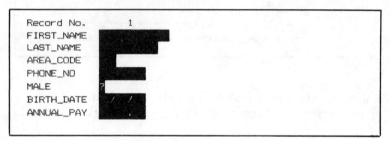

Fig. 4.3. The data entry form.

Each data record is given a record number that appears at the top of the screen. Below the record number, the data entry form shows the names of the data fields defined in the data structure.

By positioning the cursor in the desired field, you can enter the contents of the data fields in the space provided on the entry form. When the field is full, the cursor moves to the next field. You can move the cursor by pressing RETURN after you type a data item. When the last data field is filled, a new data entry form is displayed. You can return to the last record by pressing the PgUp key. Figure 4.4 shows four data records that have been entered in the database file.

Terminating the Data Entry Process

Data entered in a database file is saved record by record. As soon as the last field of a data record has been completed, the record is

```
Record No.        1            Record No.        3
FIRST_NAME   James C.          FIRST_NAME   Doris A.
LAST_NAME    Smith             LAST_NAME    Gregory
AREA_CODE    206               AREA_CODE    503
PHONE_NO     123-4567          PHONE_NO     204-8567
MALE         T                 MALE         F
BIRTH_DATE   07/04/60          BIRTH_DATE   07/04/62
ANNUAL_PAY   22000.00          ANNUAL_PAY   16900.00

Record No.        2            Record No.        4
FIRST_NAME   Albert K.         FIRST_NAME   Harry M.
LAST_NAME    Zeller            LAST_NAME    Nelson
AREA_CODE    212               AREA_CODE    315
PHONE_NO     457-9801          PHONE_NO     576-0235
MALE         T                 MALE         T
BIRTH_DATE   09/20/59          BIRTH_DATE   02/15/58
ANNUAL_PAY   27950.00          ANNUAL_PAY   29000.00
```

Fig. 4.4. Sample data records.

added to the database file. Then you can terminate the data entry process.

To terminate data entry, you can press RETURN when the cursor is at the first field of a new data entry form. For example, when you have entered data in the last field of data record 3, the form for record 4 is displayed. At this point, the data from record 3 has already been added to the database file. Pressing RETURN now will terminate the data entry procedure and return the program to the dot prompt. The last data record added to the database file would be record 3.

You can also use Ctrl-W to end the data entry process. Ctrl-W saves the displayed data record and returns the program to the dot prompt. The Ctrl-W operation can be activated anytime, regardless of the cursor position on the entry form. If Ctrl-W is pressed before all data fields are filled, the remaining data fields are filled with blank spaces.

The Esc (Escape) key can be used to stop any function in progress and return to the dot prompt in dBASE III. However, such a method should be used with care. Improper use of the Escape function can cause data to be lost.

When you press the Esc key, the computer "forgets" the most recent operation and returns to the dot prompt. What constitutes the most recent operation may vary from one type of procedure to another. For example, if you press the Esc key from the data entry mode, any data entered to the current record is disregarded. Data entered to the last record would not be affected, however, because that data was saved before the current record was displayed.

Appending Data to the Database File

New data records can be added to the database file in one of two ways. One way is to *append* a new data record to the end of the file, and the other way is to *insert* a data record within the database file.

APPEND

The APPEND command can be used to add data records to the end of a database file. The format of this command is

   . APPEND

APPEND tells the computer to display an entry form for the new record following the last record in the database file. For example, if three data records are stored in a database file, the APPEND command displays the data entry form for the fourth record. The APPEND command adds data, one record at a time, to the active database file. Before entering the APPEND command, you must know which database file is currently in use.

The EMPLOYEE.DBF file was the last database file to be activated, so the file remains active. If you apply the APPEND command now, EMPLOYEE.DBF will be the object of the data-appending operation. If another file, such as PAYROLL.DBF, had been created after EMPLOYEE.DBF, PAYROLL.DBF would be the active file. In that case, the APPEND command would add data to the PAYROLL.DBF database file.

If you want to enter new data to the EMPLOYEE file when PAYROLL is the active file, EMPLOYEE must be reactivated before APPEND is entered. To activate a database file, enter the USE command at the dot prompt.

USE

Database files are usually saved in auxiliary memory, such as on a floppy disk or a hard disk. To conserve memory, only the active database files are stored in random-access memory (RAM) for quick access. The USE command tells the computer to retrieve the contents of a file from the auxiliary memory and store the contents in RAM. Although several database files may remain active, only one active file can be used at a time. The format of the USE command is

. USE <database file name>

The following USE command will activate the database file EMPLOYEE.DBF:

. USE EMPLOYEE

Because only database files can be accessed with USE, you do not need to enter the file identifier .*DBF*. After you enter USE, the contents of the database file are copied from the disk to RAM, and a dot prompt appears on the screen. Then you can enter other dBASE III commands, such as APPEND. Figure 4.5 shows an example.

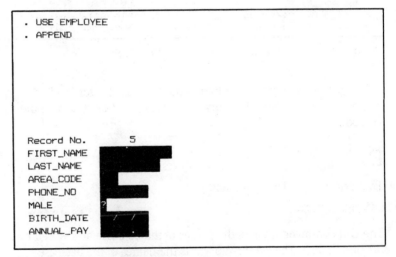

Fig. 4.5. The USE and APPEND commands.

The APPEND command adds a new data record at the end of the file by displaying the entry form for record 5. Figure 4.6 shows the next six data records appended to the database file EMPLOYEE.DBF.

Displaying a Database File

After the database has been created, you can display the contents of the file. A database file contains the name of the database file, the

```
Record No.        5          Record No.        8
FIRST_NAME   Tina B.         FIRST_NAME   Charles N.
LAST_NAME    Baker           LAST_NAME    Duff
AREA_CODE    415             AREA_CODE    206
PHONE_NO     787-3154        PHONE_NO     456-9873
MALE         F               MALE         T
BIRTH_DATE   10/12/56        BIRTH_DATE   07/22/64
ANNUAL_PAY   25900.00        ANNUAL_PAY   13500.00

Record No.        6          Record  No.       9
FIRST_NAME   Kirk D.         FIRST_NAME   Winston E.
LAST_NAME    Chapman         LAST_NAME    Lee
AREA_CODE    618             AREA_CODE    503
PHONE_NO     625-7845        PHONE_NO     365-8512
MALE         T               MALE         T
BIRTH_DATE   08/04/61        BIRTH_DATE   05/14/39
ANNUAL_PAY   19750.00        ANNUAL_PAY   34900.00

Record No.        7          Record No.       10
FIRST_NAME   Mary W.         FIRST_NAME   Thomas T.
LAST_NAME    Thompson        LAST_NAME    Hanson
AREA_CODE    213             AREA_CODE    206
PHONE_NO     432-6782        PHONE_NO     573-5085
MALE         F               MALE         T
BIRTH_DATE   06/18/55        BIRTH_DATE   12/24/45
ANNUAL_PAY   24500.00        ANNUAL_PAY   28950.00
```

Fig. 4.6. Data records appended to EMPLOYEE.DBF.

data structure, and the data stored in the records. To verify a file
name, you can display a directory of the files saved on disk with the
DIR command.

DIR

The format of the DIR command is

. DIR

The DIR command displays the names of the database files stored on
the default disk. The file directory lists the names of the database
files, the total number of records, the amount of memory used by
the records, and the date when the records were last updated. A
sample file directory is shown in figure 4.7.

```
. DIR
Database files    # records    last update    size
EMPLOYEE.DBF            10      03/14/85       1024


     1024 bytes in      1 files.
  136192 bytes remaining on drive.
.
```

Fig. 4.7. The DIR command.

DISPLAY STRUCTURE

To verify the data structure of the active file, you can use the DISPLAY STRUCTURE command. DISPLAY STRUCTURE shows the data field specifications defined when you created the structure. The format of the command is

. DISPLAY STRUCTURE

DISPLAY STRUCTURE displays the structure of the current database file. If the file you desire is not currently active, you can display the structure of the file by activating the database file with a USE command. The screen display of figure 4.8 shows an example.

```
. USE EMPLOYEE
. DISPLAY STRUCTURE
Structure for database : B:EMPLOYEE.dbf
Number of data records :        10
Date of last update    : 03/14/85
Field  Field name  Type       Width    Dec
    1  FIRST_NAME  Character     12
    2  LAST_NAME   Character     10
    3  AREA_CODE   Character      3
    4  PHONE_NO    Character      8
    5  MALE        Logical        1
    6  BIRTH_DATE  Date           8
    7  ANNUAL_PAY  Numeric        8       2
** Total **                     51

.
```

Fig. 4.8. The DISPLAY STRUCTURE command.

Other database file structures created to illustrate database management operations can be found in Appendix D.

DISPLAY ALL

You can use DISPLAY commands to show all or part of the records in an active database file. The unconditional DISPLAY ALL command is used to display all the records in a file. You can display selected records with the conditional DISPLAY FOR command. The format of the DISPLAY ALL command is

. DISPLAY ALL

When DISPLAY ALL is applied to the EMPLOYEE database file, you see the results shown in figure 4.9.

```
. USE EMPLOYEE
. DISPLAY ALL
Record#   FIRST_NAME   LAST_NAME   AREA_CODE  PHONE_NO  MALE  BIRTH_DATE  ANNUAL_PAY
      1   James C.     Smith       206        123-4567  .T.   07/04/60      22000.00
      2   Albert K.    Zeller      212        457-9801  .T.   10/10/59      27950.00
      3   Doris A.     Gregory     503        204-8567  .F.   07/04/62      16900.00
      4   Harry M.     Nelson      315        576-0235  .T.   02/15/58      29000.00
      5   Tina B.      Baker       415        567-8967  .F.   10/12/56      25900.00
      6   Kirk D.      Chapman     618        625-7845  .T.   08/04/61      19750.00
      7   Mary W.      Thompson    213        432-6782  .F.   06/18/55      24500.00
      8   Charles N.   Duff        206        456-9873  .T.   07/22/64      13500.00
      9   Winston E.   Lee         503        365-8512  .T.   05/14/39      34900.00
     10   Thomas T.    Hanson      206        573-5085  .T.   12/24/45      28950.00
.
```

Fig. 4.9. The DISPLAY ALL command.

The DISPLAY ALL command shows all the records in the EMPLOYEE database file. Because monitors are limited to a screen width of 80 characters, records with more than 80 characters are printed to the screen in a wrap-around fashion. To fit the screen width, you can display only certain fields of the data records. Selected data fields can be specified in a DISPLAY ALL command, such as

. DISPLAY ALL <field name#1, field name#2, . . . >

Figure 4.10 shows an example.

```
. DISPLAY ALL FIRST_NAME, LAST_NAME
Record#   FIRST_NAME   LAST_NAME
      1   James C.     Smith
      2   Albert K.    Zeller
      3   Doris A.     Gregory
      4   Harry M.     Nelson
      5   Tina B.      Baker
      6   Kirk D.      Chapman
      7   Mary W.      Thompson
      8   Charles N.   Duff
      9   Winston E.   Lee
     10   Thomas T.    Hanson
.
```

Fig. 4.10. The conditional DISPLAY ALL command.

DISPLAY FOR

You can use a conditional DISPLAY command to display selected records when you add a logical relation or qualifier. To display only the records in EMPLOYEE with an area code of 206, you can enter

. DISPLAY FOR AREA_CODE="206"

The format of the DISPLAY command is

. DISPLAY <a qualifier>

The qualifier can be defined as

FOR <the search key><relationship><the search object>

Character/text or numeric fields can be used as search keys in a qualifier. The type of the search object must match the type of the search key. For instance, only an alphanumeric string can be used as a search object for a character/text search key. A numeric field can be searched with only a number or value. A memo field cannot be used as a search key in the qualifier. A logical field may be used in a conditional display command, but this field does not need a search object in the qualifier.

A date field must be converted to an alphanumeric string before you define the field as a search key. After conversion, the field can be compared to an alphanumeric string. The conversion operation involves a built-in dBASE III function that is covered in a later chapter.

Here are two examples of conditional display commands. The first uses a character/text search key, and the second involves a numeric search key:

. DISPLAY FOR AREA_CODE="206"
. DISPLAY FOR ANNUAL_PAY>=28000

The first command tells the computer to search and display records with 206 stored in the field AREA_CODE. AREA_CODE is the search key, and the search object is the string 206. The qualifier (AREA_CODE ="206") defines the condition that must be met before the DISPLAY action takes place. The equal sign (=) is called a relational operator and defines the relationship between the search key and the search object. The search object (206) is enclosed in quotation marks because AREA_CODE was defined as a character/text field when the structure was created. For this reason, the area code 206 cannot be treated as a numeric value.

The second example uses the number *28000.00* as a search object for the numeric key field ANNUAL_PAY. Because the field type of the search key is numeric, the search object must be also a numeric value and be entered without quotation marks. The symbol >= is another relational operator.

You can show different relationships between the search key and the search object with relational operators. Acceptable relational operators are listed in table 4.1.

Table 4.1
Description of Acceptable Relational Operators

Relational Operator	The Relation
=	Equal to
<> or #	Not equal to
>	Greater than
>=	Greater than or equal to
<	Less than
<=	Less than or equal to

Using qualifiers with different relational operators, you can display records many different ways. Here are some examples of DISPLAY commands with various conditions as qualifiers:

. DISPLAY FOR LAST_NAME="Smith"
. DISPLAY FOR PHONE_NO="123-4567"
. DISPLAY FOR AREA_CODE>="415"
. DISPLAY FOR AREA_CODE<>"206"
. DISPLAY FOR LAST_NAME<="Smith"
. DISPLAY FOR ANNUAL_PAY>=28000

When you use the relation of equal to (=), the condition will be satisfied only when the contents of the search key and the search object are identical. For instance, if the search object is Smith, as in

. DISPLAY FOR LAST_NAME="Smith"

the condition will be met only if the contents of LAST_NAME is *Smith*; not *smith* or *SMITH*. Capital and lowercase letters are treated as unique characters in a data record, so the string of *Smith* is not equal to *smith*.

When you use the relational operators greater than (>) or less than (<), the strings are compared character by character to determine which string meets the condition. The order of alphanumeric characters defined by the American Standard Code for Information Interchanges (ASCII) is listed in table 4.2. A character with a higher

Table 4.2
The Order of Alphanumeric Characters

Lowest Order							
	blank space	0	@	P	]	p	
	!	1	A	Q	a	q	
	"	2	B	R	b	r	
	#	3	C	S	c	s	
	$	4	D	T	d	t	
	%	5	E	U	e	u	
	&	6	F	V	f	v	
	'	7	G	W	g	w	
	(	8	H	X	h	x	
	)	9	I	Y	i	y	
	*	:	J	Z	j	z	*Highest*
	+	;	K	X	k		*Order*
	, (comma)	<	L	Y	l		
	-	=	M	Z	m		
	. (period)	>	N	[	n		
	/	?	O	\	o		

order designation is greater than a character with a lower order designation.

In keeping with the order defined in table 4.2, each of the following relations is considered to be true:

"smith" > "Smith"
"Samson" > "Sam"
"JOHN" < "john"
"ABC123" < "ABC12"
"(206)" < "206"
"Smith, James" <> "Smith,James"

Note that the string *smith* is greater than *Smith*. The reason is that the first character of *smith* (s) has a higher order designation than the first character of *Smith* (S). Figure 4.11 shows the records in the EMPLOYEE database file with last names greater than or equal to *S*.

```
. DISPLAY FOR LAST_NAME >= "S"
Record#  FIRST_NAME    LAST_NAME    AREA_CODE  PHONE_NO  MALE  BIRTH_DATE  ANNUAL_PAY
      1  James C.      Smith        206        123-4567  .T.   07/04/60    22000.00
      2  Albert K.     Zeller       212        457-9801  .T.   10/10/59    27950.00
      7  Mary W.       Thompson     213        432-6782  .F.   06/18/55    24500.00
```

Fig. 4.11. The conditional DISPLAY FOR command.

To use a logical field in the qualifier, you only need to enter the name of the logical field in the conditional DISPLAY command. Figure 4.12 shows such an example.

```
. DISPLAY FOR MALE
Record#   FIRST_NAME    LAST_NAME    AREA_CODE  PHONE_NO  MALE  BIRTH_DATE  ANNUAL_PAY
       1  James C.      Smith        206        123-4567  .T.   07/04/60    22000.00
       2  Albert K.     Zeller       212        457-9801  .T.   10/10/59    27950.00
       4  Harry M.      Nelson       315        576-0235  .T.   02/15/58    29000.00
       6  Kirk D.       Chapman      618        625-7845  .T.   08/04/61    19750.00
       8  Charles N.    Duff         206        456-9873  .T.   07/22/64    13500.00
       9  Winston E.    Lee          503        365-8512  .T.   05/14/39    34900.00
      10  Thomas T.     Hanson       206        573-5085  .T.   12/24/45    28950.00
.
```

Fig. 4.12. The DISPLAY command with a logical field.

The conditional command retrieves only the data records with T in the logical field MALE. To display the records with F contained in the logical field, use the relational operator .NOT. (see fig. 4.13).

```
. DISPLAY FOR .NOT. MALE
Record#   FIRST_NAME    LAST_NAME    AREA_CODE  PHONE_NO  MALE  BIRTH_DATE  ANNUAL_PAY
       3  Doris A.      Gregory      503        204-8567  .F.   07/04/62    16900.00
       5  Tina B.       Baker        415        567-8967  .F.   10/12/56    25900.00
       7  Mary W.       Thompson     213        432-6782  .F.   06/18/55    24500.00
.
```

Fig. 4.13. Using a relational operator with DISPLAY.

When you use .NOT., you tell the computer to display all records where MALE does NOT contain a true state. You can also define multiple relations by using a logical operator as a qualifier with DISPLAY. Figure 4.14 shows an example of multiple relations.

```
. DISPLAY FOR AREA_CODE="206" .OR. AREA_CODE="503"
Record#   FIRST_NAME    LAST_NAME    AREA_CODE  PHONE_NO  MALE  BIRTH_DATE  ANNUAL_PAY
       1  James C.      Smith        206        123-4567  .T.   07/04/60    22000.00
       3  Doris A.      Gregory      503        204-8567  .F.   07/04/62    16900.00
       8  Charles N.    Duff         206        456-9873  .T.   07/22/64    13500.00
       9  Winston E.    Lee          503        365-8512  .T.   05/14/39    34900.00
      10  Thomas T.     Hanson       206        573-5085  .T.   12/24/45    28950.00
.
```

Fig. 4.14. Multiple relations.

The command instructs the computer to search and display all records with area codes equal to 206 or 503. You can also use the logical operator .AND. to specify multiple relations in a qualifier. The operator .AND. requires that all relations are true before the command is carried out. Figure 4.15 shows an example of .AND.

```
. DISPLAY FOR MALE .AND. ANNUAL_PAY>=28000
Record#   FIRST_NAME   LAST_NAME   AREA_CODE  PHONE_NO  MALE  BIRTH_DATE  ANNUAL_PAY
      4   Harry M.     Nelson         315      576-0235  .T.   02/15/58     29000.00
      9   Winston E.   Lee            503      365-8512  .T.   05/14/39     34900.00
     10   Thomas T.    Hanson         206      573-5085  .T.   12/24/45     28950.00
.
```

Fig. 4.15. The .AND. operator.

The logical operator .NOT. is similar to the relational operator of <> when used for searching character/text and numeric fields. For instance, the following two commands produce the same results:

. DISPLAY FOR AREA_CODE<>"206"
. DISPLAY FOR .NOT. AREA_CODE="206"

The first command tells the computer to display all the records with an area code not equal to 206. This is the same as the second command, which instructs the computer to display all the records where the condition (AREA_CODE="206") is NOT true.

When you use DISPLAY in an unconditional DISPLAY ALL command or a conditional DISPLAY FOR command, all the records in the file are searched. The condition specified in the qualifier (such as FOR AREA_CODE="206") is checked against each of the data records in the database file. This is one reason why the USE command must be entered before the DISPLAY functions can be performed.

The USE command retrieves the contents of a database file from disk and loads the data in RAM. The loading operation makes a copy of the file and stores the copy in RAM for further use. The contents of the file still remain on the disk. If there is enough memory in RAM, all the data records will be loaded at one time. Otherwise, the file will be loaded in sections. That is why a computer with more memory space may work faster when very large database files are involved.

Displaying a Data Record in the Database File

You can also display an individual record by identifying the record in the command line.

DISPLAY RECORD

When you create a data record, you assign an identifying number to that record. The command to display a specific record is

. DISPLAY RECORD <the data record number>

Figure 4.16 shows an example.

```
. USE EMPLOYEE
. DISPLAY RECORD 3
Record#  FIRST_NAME   LAST_NAME   AREA_CODE PHONE_NO MALE BIRTH_DATE ANNUAL_PAY
       3  Doris A.     Gregory     503        204-8567 .F.  07/04/62    16900.00
.
```

Fig. 4.16. The DISPLAY RECORD command.

The record number (RECORD 3) is used as an index for the logical location of the data record and should not be confused with the physical location, which is where the actual data is saved in RAM or on disk. For example, you may think record 3 and record 4 are stored next to each other, but the actual location of record 3 may be quite different from where record 4 is saved on disk. In dBASE III, you need to know only the logical location of the data record.

You can access only the active data record while data is being manipulated. A record pointer is used to keep track of the active data record by storing the active record number in memory. So without specifying the record number, you can display the active data record with the command

. DISPLAY

GOTO

A GOTO command can be used to point out any data record in the database file. Simply specify the destination of the GOTO instruction in the command, such as

. GOTO <data record number>

The example in figure 4.17 shows how data record 5 can be located and displayed.

```
. GOTO 5
. DISPLAY
Record#  FIRST_NAME    LAST_NAME   AREA_CODE  PHONE_NO  MALE  BIRTH_DATE  ANNUAL_PAY
     5   Tina B.       Baker       415        567-8967  .F.   10/12/56      25900.00
  .
```

Fig. 4.17. The GOTO command.

GO TOP, GO BOTTOM

The record pointer can be positioned at the first or the last data record in a file, using one of the following commands:

. GO TOP
. GO BOTTOM

To go to the very first record in a database, you can use the GO TOP command. The GO TOP command positions the record pointer to the first data record of the current database file. The first data record then becomes the active record.

Similarly, a GO BOTTOM command can be used to move to the last record of the current database file. Figure 4.18 illustrates the functions of the GO TOP and GO BOTTOM commands.

```
. GO BOTTOM
. DISPLAY
Record#  FIRST_NAME    LAST_NAME   AREA_CODE  PHONE_NO  MALE  BIRTH_DATE  ANNUAL_PAY
    10   Thomas T.     Hanson      206        573-5085  .T.   12/24/45      28950.00
. GO TOP
. DISPLAY
Record#  FIRST_NAME    LAST_NAME   AREA_CODE  PHONE_NO  MALE  BIRTH_DATE  ANNUAL_PAY
     1   James C.      Smith       206        123-4567  .T.   07/04/60      22000.00
  .
```

Fig. 4.18. The GO BOTTOM command.

Once a data record is selected with a GOTO, GO TOP, or GO BOTTOM command, the record remains active until another data record is selected. The active record number is saved in the record pointer. Other data records can be identified in relation to the record number of the current record. For example, if the record pointer currently points to record 5, a SKIP command can be used to point to the next data record (record 6).

SKIP

Any data record that is logically located before or after the current record can be selected by using the SKIP command. The formats of a SKIP command are

. SKIP <number of records to skip>
. SKIP

To move the pointer forward, you can enter a positive integer as the number of records to skip. You can move the pointer backward by assigning a negative integer to the variable. When the number of records is not specified, one data record will be skipped. Functions of the SKIP command are illustrated in figure 4.19.

```
. GOTO 2
. DISPLAY
Record#  FIRST_NAME   LAST_NAME  AREA_CODE PHONE_NO MALE BIRTH_DATE ANNUAL_PAY
      2  Albert K.    Zeller     212       457-9801 .T.  10/10/59     27950.00
. SKIP 5
Record no.       7
. DISPLAY
Record#  FIRST_NAME   LAST_NAME  AREA_CODE PHONE_NO MALE BIRTH_DATE ANNUAL_PAY
      7  Mary W.      Thompson   213       432-6782 .F.  06/18/55     24500.00
. SKIP -3
Record no.       4
. DISPLAY
Record#  FIRST_NAME   LAST_NAME  AREA_CODE PHONE_NO MALE BIRTH_DATE ANNUAL_PAY
      4  Harry M.     Nelson     315       576-0235 .T.  02/15/58     29000.00
. SKIP
Record no.       5
. DISPLAY
Record#  FIRST_NAME   LAST_NAME  AREA_CODE PHONE_NO MALE BIRTH_DATE ANNUAL_PAY
      5  Tina B.      Baker      415       567-8967 .F.  10/12/56     25900.00
.
```

Fig. 4.19. The SKIP command.

LOCATE FOR

In some applications, you may need to find a specific record without knowing the record number. A telephone operator, for example, may want to find the phone number of a person in the EMPLOYEE database file, without knowing the record number of the person's data record. For this application, you can use a LOCATE command with a qualifier, such as

. LOCATE <a qualifier>

For instance, to find the employee with the first name James, you can use a LOCATE FOR command, as shown in figure 4.20.

```
. LOCATE FOR FIRST_NAME="James C."
Record =        1
. DISPLAY
Record#   FIRST_NAME    LAST_NAME    AREA_CODE  PHONE_NO  MALE  BIRTH_DATE  ANNUAL_PAY
       1   James C.      Smith        206        123-4567  .T.   07/04/60      22000.00
   .
```

Fig. 4.20. The LOCATE FOR command.

The command searches all the data records and finds the first record containing the alphanumeric string *James C.* in FIRST_NAME field. The record pointer is set to that record number. The contents of the FIRST_NAME field may contain more than the alphanumeric string *James*. If the first five characters of FIRST_NAME matches *James*, the record is selected. The characters after the string are not considered. If there is more than one employee in the company who has the first name *James* (with different middle initials), the first *James* in the data records will be selected. The following LOCATE command finds the record of James C. Smith, because the data file has only one employee with a first name beginning with *J*:

. LOCATE FOR FIRST_NAME="J"

You can also specify multiple relations in a LOCATE command, using logical operators in the qualifier. The command finds the first data record that satisfies all the relations in the LOCATE command. The set of commands shown in figure 4.21 finds and displays the annual salary of James C. Smith.

```
. LOCATE FOR LAST_NAME="Smith" .AND. FIRST_NAME="James C."
Record =        1
. DISPLAY ANNUAL_PAY
Record#   ANNUAL_PAY
       1     22000.00
   .
```

Fig. 4.21. Multiple relations with the LOCATE command.

Using a conditional DISPLAY command, you can produce the same results by specifying the multiple relations as a qualifier:

. DISPLAY ANNUAL_PAY FOR LAST_NAME="Smith" .AND. FIRST_NAME="James C."

The LOCATE command moves the record pointer to the record containing the items desired (Smith and James). The last data record displayed becomes the current default record. Other data items in the record can be accessed without another search. When you use the DISPLAY command with a qualifier, however, the number of the displayed record is not retained. If you want to display a data field other than ANNUAL_PAY, the contents of the file must be searched again. Figure 4.22 shows the status of the record pointer after using the conditional DISPLAY FOR command.

```
. GO BOTTOM
. DISPLAY
Record#  FIRST_NAME    LAST_NAME   AREA_CODE PHONE_NO MALE BIRTH_DATE ANNUAL_PAY
     10  Thomas T.     Hanson         206       573-5085 .T.  12/24/45    28950.00
. DISPLAY ANNUAL_PAY FOR LAST_NAME="Smith" .AND. FIRST_NAME="James C."
Record#   ANNUAL_PAY
      1        22000.00
. DISPLAY
Record#  FIRST_NAME    LAST_NAME   AREA_CODE PHONE_NO MALE BIRTH_DATE ANNUAL_PAY
. SKIP
End of file encountered
      ?
SKIP
Do you want some help? (Y/N) No
.
```

Fig. 4.22. The record points after DISPLAY FOR.

As you can see, the record pointer was "confused" after the conditional DISPLAY FOR was executed. The contents of record 1 (found by the conditional DISPLAY FOR) are not displayed with the unconditional DISPLAY command. When you entered the SKIP command, the message **End of file encountered** indicated that the record pointer was at the last record in the file before the SKIP command was invoked.

CONTINUE

When the record pointer is on the active record, you can use the CONTINUE command to move the pointer to the next record. The format of the command is

. CONTINUE

For example, suppose that record 6 was found by a LOCATE command. When you enter the CONTINUE command, the record pointer moves to record 7.

LIST

Data records can be displayed with the LIST command. The LIST command is identical to DISPLAY, except that DISPLAY lists the records with periodic pauses, whereas LIST displays the records continuously. When the number of records to be displayed is small enough to be shown on one screen, both LIST and DISPLAY will produce identical results. For a long list of data records, however, the DISPLAY command is more appropriate because data records will be displayed with pauses. If the LIST command is used to display a long database file, part of the listing will be scrolled off the screen. The formats of the LIST command are

    . LIST STRUCTURE
    . LIST ALL
    . LIST <field name #1, field name #2, . . . >
    . LIST FOR <a qualifier>

Following are some examples of the LIST command:

    . LIST STRUCTURE
    . LIST ALL
    . LIST LAST_NAME, FIRST_NAME
    . LIST LAST_NAME, ANNUAL_PAY FOR
    ANNUAL_PAY>25000
    . LIST PHONE_NO FOR AREA_CODE="206"
    . LIST FIRST_NAME, LAST_NAME FOR .NOT. MALE
    . LIST FOR LAST_NAME="Smith" .AND. AREA_CODE="503"
    . LIST FOR .NOT. AREA_CODE="206"
    . LIST FOR LAST_NAME<>"Smith"

Displaying Data on a Printer

DISPLAY and LIST can be used to display the contents of a database file on screen. You can also display the output on the printer by adding the phrase TO PRINT at the end of the DISPLAY or LIST command. Before the command is executed, however, be sure that the printer is connected correctly and turned on. Otherwise, the program will be suspended. When this situation occurs, you can abort the printing process by pressing the Esc key. Following are some examples of DISPLAY and LIST commands with the TO PRINT clause:

. DISPLAY ALL TO PRINT

. LIST AREA_CODE,PHONE_NO FOR LAST_NAME="Baker" TO PRINT

. DISPLAY FOR .NOT. MALE .AND. ANNUAL_PAY>=20000 TO PRINT

. LIST ALL FIRST_NAME,LAST_NAME,BIRTH_DATE TO PRINT

Editing a Database File

After a database file is created, you can change the contents of the file at any time. Contents of a database file are divided in two parts: the data structure that defines the data fields in the file, and the actual contents of the data records in the database file.

MODIFY STRUCTURE

Data fields can be redefined, changed, and deleted with the MODIFY STRUCTURE command. The format of the command is

. MODIFY STRUCTURE

The MODIFY STRUCTURE command will display the structure of the active database for modification. The structure is displayed on a form identical to the one used when the structure was created. Figure 4.23 displays the data structure of the database file EMPLOYEE.DBF to be modified.

When the structure is displayed on screen, you can edit the structure by positioning the cursor (using the arrow or cursor keys) at the beginning of a field definition area. New items such as field name, field type, and field width can be entered at the cursor position. If the fields use more than one display screen, you can use the PgUp and PgDn keys to scroll the screen through the field definition areas.

You can insert a new field by positioning the cursor at the desired location and pressing Ctrl-N. A blank field will be displayed, and field definitions can then be entered as usual.

To delete a field, place the cursor at the beginning of the field and press Ctrl-U. Structure modification can be ended by pressing

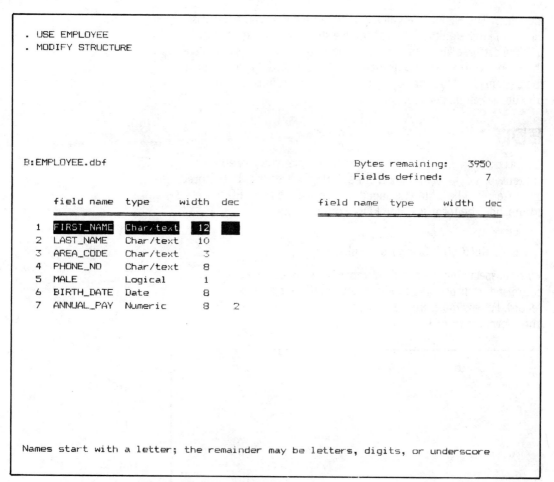

```
.  USE EMPLOYEE
.  MODIFY STRUCTURE




   B:EMPLOYEE.dbf                               Bytes remaining:    3950
                                                Fields defined:        7


        field name   type     width  dec       field name   type     width  dec
        ════════════════════════════════       ════════════════════════════════
    1  FIRST_NAME   Char/text   12           field name   type     width  dec
    2  LAST_NAME    Char/text   10
    3  AREA_CODE    Char/text    3
    4  PHONE_NO     Char/text    8
    5  MALE         Logical      1
    6  BIRTH_DATE   Date         8
    7  ANNUAL_PAY   Numeric      8     2







   Names start with a letter; the remainder may be letters, digits, or underscore
```

Fig. 4.23. The MODIFY STRUCTURE command.

Ctrl-End. After editing the structure, MODIFY STRUCTURE appends the database file to match the new structure. The contents of a character/text field will remain in the same field regardless of name modification. If the width of a numeric field is changed, the contents of the field are automatically adjusted to the new width. When a new field is added to the structure, blank spaces are written in the new field in all data records. When an existing data field is deleted from the structure, the contents will be erased automatically from the database file.

A working backup file is used to append existing data to a modified structure. A backup file is designated by the extension *.BAK* in the file name. The backup file will have the same name as the database file (.DBF) to be edited. The backup file stores the contents of the original database file. When the modification procedure is complete, the modified structure is automatically appended to the contents of the backup file. After the structure modification is finished, the backup file can be deleted.

EDIT

As was true for the structure of the database file, you can edit the contents of a data record at any time during processing. Data stored in a record can be edited, changed, or replaced with an EDIT command. The formats of the EDIT command are

    . EDIT
    . EDIT RECORD <a record number>

Without specifying the record number, you can use the EDIT command to display and modify the contents of a current data record. For example, the commands in figure 4.24 display the data entry form for record 5.

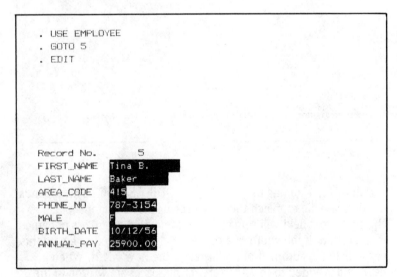

Fig. 4.24. The EDIT command.

You can edit the contents of data record 5 with the following command:

    . EDIT RECORD 5

When the record is displayed, you can use the arrow keys to position the cursor at the data field to be edited. As long as you move the cursor within the data fields shown, the current record remains on screen. However, if you move the cursor outside the current record, the previous record or the next record is displayed. For instance, if the cursor is positioned in the last field of data record 5 and the down-arrow key is pressed, the next data record (record 6) is displayed. Similarly, when the cursor is positioned at the first field of data record 5, an up-arrow keystroke moves the cursor to the previous data record (record 4).

When modification is complete (for example, the field PHONE_NO of record 5 has been changed from 787-3154 to 567-8967), you can exit from the editing mode or move to the previous or the next data record. At any point during the editing process, you can view either the previous data record by pressing the PgUp key or the next data record by pressing the PgDn key.

You can leave the editing mode two ways. You can press Ctrl-End, causing the edited data record to be saved and the program to return to the dot prompt. Or you can press the Esc key. However, this alternative aborts the editing process and causes your modifications on the current record to be lost.

BROWSE

Data in multiple records can be displayed and modified with the BROWSE command. The format of the BROWSE command is

. BROWSE

The BROWSE command displays the first seventeen records of the current database file on screen for reviewing or editing. In figure 4.25, a BROWSE command is applied to the EMPLOYEE database file.

Because of screen limitations, if a data record contains more than 80 characters, only the first 80 characters are displayed. However, you can display the fields within the screen size limit. You can display selective data fields by specifying the field names on the BROWSE FIELDS command, such as

. BROWSE FIELDS <field name #1>,<field name #2>, . . .

A BROWSE FIELDS command can be used to display only the names and telephone numbers of the EMPLOYEE database file (see fig. 4.26).

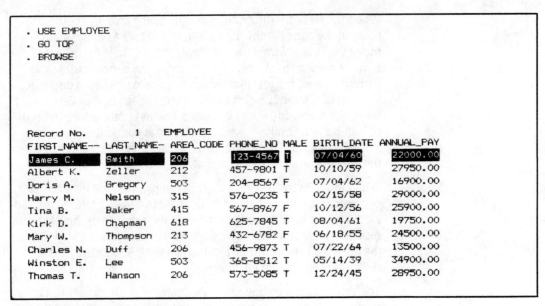

```
. USE EMPLOYEE
. GO TOP
. BROWSE




Record No.         1    EMPLOYEE
FIRST_NAME-- LAST_NAME- AREA_CODE PHONE_NO MALE BIRTH_DATE ANNUAL_PAY
James C.     Smith      206       123-4567 T    07/04/60   22000.00
Albert K.    Zeller     212       457-9801 T    10/10/59   27950.00
Doris A.     Gregory    503       204-8567 F    07/04/62   16900.00
Harry M.     Nelson     315       576-0235 T    02/15/58   29000.00
Tina B.      Baker      415       567-8967 F    10/12/56   25900.00
Kirk D.      Chapman    618       625-7845 T    08/04/61   19750.00
Mary W.      Thompson   213       432-6782 F    06/18/55   24500.00
Charles N.   Duff       206       456-9873 T    07/22/64   13500.00
Winston E.   Lee        503       365-8512 T    05/14/39   34900.00
Thomas T.    Hanson     206       573-5085 T    12/24/45   28950.00
```

Fig. 4.25. The BROWSE command.

```
. GO TOP
. BROWSE FIELDS FIRST_NAME,LAST_NAME,AREA_CODE,PHONE_NO




Record No.         1    EMPLOYEE
FIRST_NAME-- LAST_NAME- AREA_CODE PHONE_NO
James C.     Smith      206       123-4567
Albert K.    Zeller     212       457-9801
Doris A.     Gregory    503       204-8567
Harry M.     Nelson     315       576-0235
Tina B.      Baker      415       567-8967
Kirk D.      Chapman    618       625-7845
Mary W.      Thompson   213       432-6782
Charles N.   Duff       206       456-9873
Winston E.   Lee        503       365-8512
Thomas T.    Hanson     206       573-5085
```

Fig. 4.26. The BROWSE FIELDS command.

When the records have been displayed with BROWSE, you can use
several keystrokes to control cursor movement and edit the text.

You can see a summary of these keystrokes by pressing the F1
function key (see fig. 4.27).

```
Record No.         1     EMPLOYEEm

 CURSOR    <-- -->          UP   DOWN        DELETE        Insert Mode:   Ins
   Char:      ←   →   Record:  ↑    ↓      Char:  Del      Exit:         ^End
   Field: Home End    Page:  PgUp  PgDn     Field:  ^Y      Abort:         Esc
   Pan:      ^← ^→                           Record: ^U      Set Options: ^Home

FIRST_NAME-- LAST_NAME- AREA_CODE PHONE_NO MALE BIRTH_DATE ANNUAL_PAY
James C.     Smith      206       123-4567 T    07/04/60   22000.00
Albert K.    Zeller     212       457-9801 T    10/10/59   27950.00
Doris A.     Gregory    503       204-8567 F    07/04/62   16900.00
Harry M.     Nelson     315       576-0235 T    02/15/58   29000.00
Tina B.      Baker      415       567-8967 F    10/12/56   25900.00
Kirk D.      Chapman    618       625-7845 T    08/04/61   19750.00
Mary W.      Thompson   213       432-6782 F    06/18/55   24500.00
Charles N.   Duff       206       456-9873 T    07/22/64   13500.00
Winston E.   Lee        503       365-8512 T    05/14/39   34900.00
Thomas T.    Hanson     206       573-5085 T    12/24/45   28950.00
```

Fig. 4.27. Cursor movement screen with the BROWSE command.

The current data record is displayed in reverse video. The up-arrow
or down-arrow keys can be used to move through the data records
one at a time. You can also use the down-arrow key to scroll the
data records beyond the first 17 records by pressing the key until the
last record is displayed.

Left- and right-arrow keys can be used to pan the data fields of a
current data record. By positioning the cursor at the desired field of
a data record, you can enter new data to replace the existing
contents of the field. To move to the next data field, press RETURN.
You can press the PgDn key to skip to the last data record, or PgUp
to move to the first data record.

You can add a new data record to the file, using BROWSE. When
you use the down-arrow key to move the cursor beyond the last
data record, the message **Add new record? (Y/N)** appears at the
top of the screen. If you press Y, a row of blank spaces is displayed at
the bottom of the screen, and a new data record can be entered in
the corresponding fields. You can use this process to append as many
data records as necessary. Although data can be added to the end of
the file, a new data record cannot be inserted into the file during the
BROWSE procedure.

You can also delete records, using BROWSE. Two steps are required to delete a data record from the current database file. The first step involves marking the data record to be deleted. The second step actually removes the record from the database file, using a PACK command, which is discussed in the following section.

To mark a data record for deletion, position the cursor at the data record and press Ctrl-U. The short message *DEL* will appear at the top of the screen. The message indicates that the current data record is marked for deletion. To erase the deletion mark, press Ctrl-U once more. The *DEL* message will disappear, and the data record will be recovered.

REPLACE WITH

You can restore the contents of a specific field with a REPLACE command. A REPLACE command may be used with or without a qualifier. An unconditional REPLACE command specifies both the field to be replaced and the contents to replace the existing data. The format of the REPLACE command is

. REPLACE <Name of the field> WITH <new contents for the field>

The REPLACE WITH command replaces the contents of the specified field with the new contents given in the command. The data type of the new contents must be identical to that of the field to be replaced. Only an alphanumeric string can replace the contents of a character/text field, and the string must be enclosed in quotation marks. For instance, the REPLACE command in figure 4.28 replaces the contents of the field PHONE_NO with 567-7777.

```
. GOTO 5
. DISPLAY
Record#  FIRST_NAME    LAST_NAME    AREA_CODE PHONE_NO MALE BIRTH_DATE ANNUAL_PAY
      5  Tina B.       Baker        415       567-8967 .F.  10/12/56      25900.00
. REPLACE PHONE_NO WITH "567-7777"
      1  record replaced
. DISPLAY
Record#  FIRST_NAME    LAST_NAME    AREA_CODE PHONE_NO MALE BIRTH_DATE ANNUAL_PAY
      5  Tina B.       Baker        415       567-7777 .F.  10/12/56      25900.00
.
```

Fig. 4.28. The REPLACE WITH command.

The unconditional REPLACE command replaces only the contents of the data field in the active record. You can use a conditional

REPLACE command to replace the records that satisfy a specific condition. The format of a conditional REPLACE command is

. REPLACE <name of field> WITH <new contents> FOR <a qualifier>

Suppose that the area code 206 has been changed to 216. To change all the 206 area codes in the EMPLOYEE database file, you can use a conditional REPLACE command, such as

. REPLACE AREA_CODE WITH "216" FOR AREA_CODE="206"

Figure 4.29 shows the effect of this REPLACE command.

```
. USE EMPLOYEE
. LIST AREA_CODE,PHONE_NO FOR AREA_CODE<="300"
Record#   AREA_CODE PHONE_NO
       1  206         123-4567
       2  212         457-9801
       7  213         432-6782
       8  206         456-9873
      10  206         573-5085
. REPLACE AREA_CODE WITH "216" FOR AREA_CODE="206"
      3 records replaced
. LIST AREA_CODE,PHONE_NO FOR AREA_CODE<="300"
Record#   AREA_CODE PHONE_NO
       1  216         123-4567
       2  212         457-9801
       7  213         432-6782
       8  216         456-9873
      10  216         573-5085
.
```

Fig. 4.29. The REPLACE command.

INSERT

You can insert a record in a file with the INSERT command. The format of the command is

. INSERT

The INSERT command adds a new data record after the current record and places the program in the EDIT mode. To add a data record before the current record, you can enter the following command:

. INSERT BEFORE

If you want to add a new record between the third and the fourth record of the active file, you can use one of the following sets of commands:

    . GOTO 3
    . INSERT
    . GOTO 4
    . INSERT BEFORE

Both of these sets display the entry form for data record 4 and place dBASE III in an editing mode. New data can then be entered in the data entry form.

DELETE

The process of deleting a data record involves two steps that may or may not be carried out consecutively. First, you need to mark the data records to be deleted. Marking a data record for deletion with BROWSE was discussed earlier in this chapter. You can also use the DELETE command to mark a data record. The formats of this command are

    . DELETE RECORD <record number>
    . DELETE ALL
    . DELETE <a qualifier>

Some examples of DELETE include

    . DELETE RECORD 5
    . DELETE ALL
    . DELETE FOR AREA_CODE="503"
    . DELETE FOR MALE
    . DELETE FOR LAST_NAME="Smith" .AND.
    ANNUAL_PAY>20000

The first command sets the record pointer and places a deletion mark (*) in front of record 5. The DELETE ALL command marks every data record in the file without changing the current status of the record pointer. The last three commands mark only those data records where the conditions specified in the qualifiers have been met. Once you execute a DELETE command, the contents of the record pointer may be lost.

PACK

After the data records are marked for deletion, you can use a PACK command to remove the records. The PACK command can be carried out at any time during data manipulation. The format of the PACK command is

. PACK

PACK removes all data records marked for deletion. After removing the data records, the remaining data records will be repacked. A word of caution: Always be sure to backup your database files before using the PACK command. Once PACK is executed, the files are removed permanently.

RECALL

Data records marked for deletion are removed only when a PACK command is entered. You can erase deletion marks from data records, using the RECALL command. The formats of RECALL are

. RECALL RECORD <record number>
. RECALL ALL
. RECALL <a qualifier>

Following are the RECALL commands that can be used to reverse the DELETE commands shown previously:

. RECALL RECORD 5
. RECALL ALL
. RECALL FOR AREA_CODE="503"
. RECALL FOR MALE
. RECALL FOR LAST_NAME="Smith" .AND.
ANNUAL_PAY>20000

ZAP

All the data records in a database file can be erased with the ZAP command. The format for this command is

. ZAP

This command deletes the data records without erasing the data structure. The ZAP command achieves the same effect as a combination of the following two commands:

. DELETE ALL
. PACK

When the ZAP command is entered, dBASE III requests confirmation. The following message is displayed:

ZAP B:EMPLOYEE.DBF? (Y/N)

If you answer N, the ZAP command is aborted. Remember that once the data records are zapped, the records are erased from the file and cannot be recovered.

File Operations

Database files created in dBASE III can be renamed, duplicated, copied to files with different names, or erased altogether.

RENAME

An existing file can be assigned a different name without disturbing the contents of the file. The command to rename a file is

. RENAME <current file ID.> TO <new file ID.>

Both the current and new file identifications must include the file name and the file identifier. For example, the following command assigns the new name PERSONEL to the current database file named EMPLOYEE:

. RENAME EMPLOYEE.DBF TO PERSONEL.DBF

In most cases, the file identifier of the current file (.DBF) must be the same as that of the new file.

COPY FILE

The contents of a file can be copied to another file. The contents of a database file include the data structure and the data records. The format of the COPY FILE command is

. COPY FILE <source file ID.> TO <destination file ID>

An example of COPY FILE is

. COPY FILE ABC.DBF TO XYZ.DBF

The command copies the contents of the source file to a destination file. If the destination file has not been created, a new file will be made. If the destination file already exists and you attempt to copy another file to the destination file, you will see the warning

<destination file ID.> already exists, overwrite it? (Y/N)

If you answer Y, the contents of the existing file are replaced with the contents of the source file. Currently active files cannot be used in a COPY FILE command. If you try to copy an active file, you will see the message

File is already open

A similar error message will be displayed if you try to copy a file to an active file. As you can see, a file must be closed before it is used as a source file or a destination file in a COPY FILE command. To close a database file, you can use the following command:

. CLOSE DATABASES

You can also close other types of files. These are discussed in later chapters.

ERASE

A file in dBASE III can be permanently deleted with the ERASE command. The format of the ERASE command is

. ERASE <file ID>

The file identification should include the file name and the file identifier, such as

. ERASE EMPLOYEE.DBF

An ERASE command deletes a nonactive file's contents, which include the data structure and all the records in the file. Active files must be closed before being removed. Once the contents have been erased, the data cannot be recovered. For this reason, the ERASE command must be used with extreme care.

Chapter Summary

Database files are created with the CREATE command. To create a database file, you must first specify the data structure. It defines the attributes of the fields included in a data record. These attributes are field name, field type, and field width.

Once the structure is specified, you can enter data records in a number of ways. Data records can be added to the end of a file with an APPEND command, within a file with an INSERT command, or after the last record with the BROWSE command.

Contents of a data record can be modified with the EDIT command or the MODIFY command. A BROWSE command allows several data records to be viewed and modified on the same screen. The contents of an active record field can be modified with a REPLACE command.

A record pointer is used by dBASE III to keep track of the active data record. You can use commands such as GOTO, GO TOP, GO BOTTOM, SKIP, LOCATE, and CONTINUE to position the record pointer at the data record desired.

The contents of a database file can be displayed on the screen and printed. A DIR command gives a directory of all the database files on the default disk drive. You can display the structure and data records of a database file with the DISPLAY, LIST, and BROWSE commands. Conditional DISPLAY and LIST commands can be used to display data records that meet the conditions of a qualifier (FOR . . .). By adding the clause TO PRINT at the end of a DISPLAY or a LIST command, you can print data records.

Part or all of the contents in a database file can be marked for removal with the DELETE command. The PACK command deletes the marked data records from the database file. You can recover marked data records with the RECALL command.

An ERASE command deletes the whole database file, including the structure and all the data records in the file. To erase the data records without disturbing the data structure, you can use the ZAP command. Both ERASE and ZAP permanently delete the contents of a file.

All commands that involve editing, modifying, and displaying the contents of a database file affect only the active file. The command USE must be entered to activate the database file if the desired file is not currently active. The contents of a database file can be copied to a file with another name, using the COPY FILE command. You can rename a database file with RENAME. Before you can copy or rename a file, however, the file must be closed with the CLOSE DATABASES command.

5

Sorting, Indexing, and Summarizing Data

An Overview

This chapter explains how to arrange data to perform data management functions and introduces the two most important data arranging operations: sorting and indexing. The commands for generating summary statistics, such as totals and averages, are also introduced. The major topics discussed in this chapter are the following:

Sorting data records in a database file
Indexing a database file on data fields
Organizing data records with an indexed database file
File sorting versus file indexing
Organization of a sorted file
Structure of an indexed file
Applications of sorted files

Applications of indexed files
Counting data records
Summing numeric fields

The dBASE III commands used to perform the sorting, indexing, and related operations are the following:

Commands	Functions
SORT TO ON SORT TO ON FOR	Sort data records
INDEX ON TO TO USE INDEX SET INDEX TO REINDEX	Index a database file
FIND SEEK	Locate a data record
COUNT COUNT FOR COUNT FOR TO	Count data records
SUM SUM FOR	Accumulate values
AVERAGE AVERAGE FOR	Compute averages
CLOSE INDEX DIR *.NDX	Perform file operations

Organizing Data in a Database File

The contents of a database file are organized by data fields and data records. The definitions of the data fields in a data record are specified when the file is created. Data records are stored in a file in the order in which they are entered, and each record is assigned a record number for later reference. The ten data records created and stored in the EMPLOYEE database file are arranged in the order in which they were entered (see fig. 5.1).

Data records organized this way may not be suitable for your needs. Because the files are not arranged alphabetically, a listing of the records in the EMPLOYEE database file would not produce a

```
. USE EMPLOYEE
. LIST ALL
Record#   FIRST_NAME   LAST_NAME   AREA_CODE  PHONE_NO  MALE  BIRTH_DATE  ANNUAL_PAY
      1   James C.     Smith       216        123-4567  .T.   07/04/60    22000.00
      2   Albert K.    Zeller      212        457-9801  .T.   10/10/59    27950.00
      3   Doris A.     Gregory     503        204-8567  .F.   07/04/62    16900.00
      4   Harry M.     Nelson      315        576-0235  .T.   02/15/58    29000.00
      5   Tina B.      Baker       415        567-7777  .F.   10/12/56    25900.00
      6   Kirk D.      Chapman     618        625-7845  .T.   08/04/61    19750.00
      7   Mary W.      Thompson    213        432-6782  .F.   06/18/55    24500.00
      8   Charles N.   Duff        216        456-9873  .T.   07/22/64    13500.00
      9   Winston E.   Lee         503        365-8512  .T.   05/14/39    34900.00
     10   Thomas T.    Hanson      216        573-5085  .T.   12/24/45    28950.00
.
```

Fig. 5.1. EMPLOYEE database files are stored as entered.

satisfactory roster. As you can see, data records often need to be rearranged.

Sorting Data Records on a Single Key Field

You can use a sorting operation to arrange data records in ascending or descending order. Before the sorting process begins, a target file is created to serve as a working file. The records to be sorted are copied to the target file so that the original files remain intact while the sort is performed on the target file records. After the sorting operation is complete, the data records in the target file are arranged as specified in the key field(s).

SORT TO ON

To sort a database file, you need to specify the name of the target file and the key field on which the data records are to be arranged. The format of a basic SORT is

. SORT TO <name of sorted file> ON <name of key field>

This command rearranges the data records of the active file in ascending order based on the contents of the key field. With the SORT command, you can arrange data records alphabetically, chronologically, or numerically, by the key field specified in the command. The sorting order is ascending by default, which is the same as the ASCII order (see table 4.2).

When you are sorting an alphanumeric string, ascending order means that the strings are arranged from A to Z. If you use a date as the key field in a SORT command, the record with an earlier date will be placed before a record with a later date. When numeric values are sorted in ascending order, data records with smaller values are placed in front of those with larger values.

For example, to list an alphabetical roster from the EMPLOYEE database file, you can enter the following commands:

. USE EMPLOYEE
. SORT TO ROSTER ON LAST_NAME

ROSTER is the name of the target file for storing the sorted data records. The target file is treated as a database file and is assigned a file identifier of .DBF when the sorting operation is complete. The key field used to rearrange the data records is the LAST_NAME data field.

After you enter the commands, the sorting operation begins. The program continually monitors the sorting progress by displaying the percentage of the data records sorted. At the end of the sorting process, the message **100% Sorted . . . 10 Records sorted** is displayed (see fig. 5.2).

```
. USE EMPLOYEE
. SORT TO ROSTER ON LAST_NAME
  100% Sorted          10 Records sorted
.
```

Fig. 5.2. Message displayed during the sorting process.

When you see the message, the sorted data records have been saved in the target file ROSTER. Now you can display the sorted roster, using the DISPLAY ALL or the LIST ALL command after the sorted file has been activated with USE ROSTER (see fig. 5.3).

```
. USE ROSTER
. LIST ALL
Record#  FIRST_NAME   LAST_NAME   AREA_CODE  PHONE_NO  MALE  BIRTH_DATE  ANNUAL_PAY
     1   Tina B.      Baker       415        567-8967  .F.   10/12/56     25900.00
     2   Kirk D.      Chapman     618        625-7845  .T.   08/04/61     19750.00
     3   Charles N.   Duff        206        456-9873  .T.   07/22/64     13500.00
     4   Doris A.     Gregory     503        204-8567  .F.   07/04/62     16900.00
     5   Thomas T.    Hanson      206        573-5085  .T.   12/24/45     28950.00
     6   Winston E.   Lee         503        365-8512  .T.   05/14/39     34900.00
     7   Harry M.     Nelson      315        576-0235  .T.   02/15/58     29000.00
     8   James C.     Smith       206        123-4567  .T.   07/04/60     22000.00
     9   Mary W.      Thompson    213        432-6782  .F.   06/18/55     24500.00
    10   Albert K.    Zeller      212        457-9801  .T.   09/20/59     27950.00
.
```

Fig. 5.3. The USE ROSTER command.

You can also arrange the data records in EMPLOYEE.DBF
chronologically, using the BIRTH_DATE field as the sorting key.
Figure 5.4 shows the list of employees whose birth dates are
ordered chronologically.

```
. USE EMPLOYEE
. SORT TO BDATE ON BIRTH_DATE
  100% Sorted            10 Records sorted
. USE BDATE
. DISPLAY ALL FIRST_NAME,LAST_NAME,BIRTH_DATE
Record#  FIRST_NAME    LAST_NAME   BIRTH_DATE
      1  Winston E.    Lee         05/14/39
      2  Thomas T.     Hanson      12/24/45
      3  Mary W.       Thompson    06/18/55
      4  Tina B.       Baker       10/12/56
      5  Harry M.      Nelson      02/15/58
      6  Albert K.     Zeller      09/20/59
      7  James C.      Smith       07/04/60
      8  Kirk D.       Chapman     08/04/61
      9  Doris A.      Gregory     07/04/62
     10  Charles N.    Duff        07/22/64
  .
```

Fig. 5.4. File arranged chronologically.

To display a roster ranked by salaries, you can use the
ANNUAL_PAY field as a sorting key (see fig. 5.5).

```
. USE EMPLOYEE
. SORT TO PAYRANK ON ANNUAL_PAY
  100% Sorted            10 Records sorted
. USE PAYRANK
. LIST ALL FIRST_NAME,LAST_NAME,ANNUAL_PAY
Record#  FIRST_NAME    LAST_NAME   ANNUAL_PAY
      1  Charles N.    Duff         13500.00
      2  Doris A.      Gregory      16900.00
      3  Kirk D.       Chapman      19750.00
      4  James C.      Smith        22000.00
      5  Mary W.       Thompson     24500.00
      6  Tina B.       Baker        25900.00
      7  Albert K.     Zeller       27950.00
      8  Thomas T.     Hanson       28950.00
      9  Harry M.      Nelson       29000.00
     10  Winston E.    Lee          34900.00
  .
```

Fig. 5.5. File arranged by salary.

The data records of the EMPLOYEE.DBF file are arranged in
ascending order. You can sort the data records in descending order,
however, by adding /D at the end of a key field:

. SORT TO <name of sorted file> ON <name of key field>/D

The SORT command arranges the data records in descending order by the values stored in the key field ANNUAL_PAY (see fig. 5.6).

```
. USE EMPLOYEE
. SORT TO PAYRANK ON ANNUAL_PAY/D
  100% Sorted           10 Records sorted
. USE PAYRANK
. LIST ALL FIRST_NAME,LAST_NAME,ANNUAL_PAY
Record#   FIRST_NAME    LAST_NAME    ANNUAL_PAY
       1  Winston E.    Lee           34900.00
       2  Harry M.      Nelson        29000.00
       3  Thomas T.     Hanson        28950.00
       4  Albert K.     Zeller        27950.00
       5  Tina B.       Baker         25900.00
       6  Mary W.       Thompson      24500.00
       7  James C.      Smith         22000.00
       8  Kirk D.       Chapman       19750.00
       9  Doris A.      Gregory       16900.00
      10  Charles N.    Duff          13500.00
.
```

Fig. 5.6. File sorted by salary in descending order.

The name PAYRANK is used to store the target file of the sorting operation. To conserve disk memory space, a target file can be used over and over to store the contents of a sorted file. When an existing name such as PAYRANK.DBF is used for a sorted file, however, a warning message is displayed:

PAYRANK. DBF already exists, overwrite it? (Y/N)

If you answer Y, the contents of the existing file PAYRANK.DBF will be erased, and the file will be ready to become the target file of another SORT command.

SORT TO ON FOR

You can also sort portions of the data in a database file, using a conditional SORT command. A subset of the database file can be defined with a qualifier (FOR . . .). When you execute the command, only the data records that meet the condition(s) in the qualifier are sorted. The format of a conditional SORT command is

. SORT TO <sorted file> ON <key field> FOR <a qualifier>

Following are a few examples of conditional SORT commands:

. SORT TO MALEPAY ON ANNUAL_PAY/D FOR MALE

. SORT TO FEMALES ON LAST_NAME FOR .NOT. MALE

. SORT TO FONELIST ON PHONE_NO/D FOR AREA_CODE="503"

.OR. AREA_CODE="206"

. SORT TO SORTED ON FIRST_NAME FOR AREA_CODE>="212"

When a subset is sorted, the target file contains only the records that meet the conditions specified in the qualifier (see fig. 5.7).

```
. USE EMPLOYEE
. SORT TO FEMALES ON LAST_NAME FOR .NOT. MALE
  100% Sorted          3 Records sorted
. USE FEMALES
. LIST ALL
Record#   FIRST_NAME    LAST_NAME   AREA_CODE  PHONE_NO  MALE  BIRTH_DATE  ANNUAL_PAY
      1   Tina B.       Baker       415        567-8967  .F.   10/12/56      25900.00
      2   Doris A.      Gregory     503        204-8567  .F.   07/04/62      16900.00
      3   Mary W.       Thompson    213        432-6782  .F.   06/18/55      24500.00
  .
```

Fig. 5.7. Sorting a subset of the file.

The sorted file FEMALES.DBF contains only three data records, each of which satisfies the condition of .NOT. MALE.

Sorting on Multiple Key Fields

Data records can also be sorted on the basis of several key fields. By specifying the names of the key fields, you can perform multiple sortings. The format of the SORT command is

. SORT TO <sorted file> ON <key field #1>,<key field #2>,FOR. . .

This command sorts the first key field in ascending order and temporarily stores the results in the sorted file. Then the contents of the sorted file are sorted again on the next key field, and the same sorting operation is repeated for each key field. After all the key fields are sorted, the results are saved in the sorted file.

With the multiple sorting procedure, you can arrange data records any way you desire. If you want to arrange telephone numbers in ascending order by area code, you can use the subset of phone numbers with the same area codes and order them alphabetically by last names.

To produce this type of phone list, sort EMPLOYEE.DBF with two key fields. The first key field to be sorted is AREA_CODE. LAST_NAME is the second key for the sorting process. Figure 5.8 shows the results of the multiple sorting operation.

```
. USE EMPLOYEE
. SORT TO FONELIST ON AREA_CODE,LAST_NAME
  100% Sorted          10 Records sorted
. USE FONELIST
. LIST ALL FIRST_NAME,LAST_NAME,AREA_CODE,PHONE_NO
Record#  FIRST_NAME    LAST_NAME   AREA_CODE  PHONE_NO
      1  Albert K.     Zeller      212        457-9801
      2  Mary W.       Thompson    213        432-6782
      3  Charles N.    Duff        216        456-9873
      4  Thomas T.     Hanson      216        573-5085
      5  James C.      Smith       216        123-4567
      6  Harry M.      Nelson      315        576-0235
      7  Tina B.       Baker       415        567-7777
      8  Doris A.      Gregory     503        204-8567
      9  Winston E.    Lee         503        365-8512
     10  Kirk D.       Chapman     618        625-7845
.
```

Fig. 5.8. Multiple sorting operations.

You can add a qualifier (FOR . . .) to a conditional SORT command that affects only a subset of the data records.

Some examples of conditional SORT commands with multiple key fields are

. SORT TO ROSTER ON ANNUAL_PAY/D, LAST_NAME FOR MALE

. SORT TO BDATES ON BIRTH_DATE, LAST_NAME FOR .NOT. MALE

. SORT TO LISTS ON ANNUAL_PAY, LAST_NAME FOR LAST_NAME<="Smith"

. SORT TO PAYLIST ON LAST_NAME,ANNUAL_PAY FOR MALE .AND. ANNUAL_PAY>=20000

Indexing a Database File

The SORT command creates a sorted file that contains the data fields of the ordered data records. If the number of data fields in each record is large, the sorting operation may be a long process. Another method used to organize data records is the operation of file indexing.

Single-Field Indexing

File indexing uses one or more data fields as key field(s) on which an index file can be generated. Then the index file is used to reorganize the contents of the database file.

INDEX ON TO

The indexing operation creates a target file in which data records are arranged in ascending order alphabetically, chronologically, or numerically, based on the key field specified.

The target file becomes an index file that is assigned a file identifier of .NDX by the INDEX ON TO command. The index file contains the entries of the key field and the corresponding record numbers. The names of the key indexing field and the target index file are specified in the INDEX ON TO command, such as

. INDEX ON <name of key field> TO <name of index file>

The key field can be a character/text field, a date field, or a numeric field. Logical and memo fields cannot be used as key fields in the indexing operation, however. The commands entered in figure 5.9 show how an indexing operation is performed.

```
. USE EMPLOYEE
. INDEX ON LAST_NAME TO LASTNAME
       10 records indexed
. DISPLAY ALL
Record#  FIRST_NAME  LAST_NAME  AREA_CODE  PHONE_NO  MALE  BIRTH_DATE  ANNUAL_PAY
      5  Tina B.     Baker      415        567-8967  .F.   10/12/56      25900.00
      6  Kirk D.     Chapman    618        625-7845  .T.   08/04/61      19750.00
      8  Charles N.  Duff       206        456-9873  .T.   07/22/64      13500.00
      3  Doris A.    Gregory    503        204-8567  .F.   07/04/62      16900.00
     10  Thomas T.   Hanson     206        573-5085  .T.   12/24/45      28950.00
      9  Winston E.  Lee        503        365-8512  .T.   05/14/39      34900.00
      4  Harry M.    Nelson     315        576-0235  .T.   02/15/58      29000.00
      1  James C.    Smith      206        123-4567  .T.   07/04/60      22000.00
      7  Mary W.     Thompson   213        432-6782  .F.   06/18/55      24500.00
      2  Albert K.   Zeller     212        457-9801  .T.   09/20/59      27950.00
.
```

Fig. 5.9. The INDEX ON TO command.

As you can see, the data records in EMPLOYEE.DBF have been arranged alphabetically by the employees' last names. This was done with the index file created by the INDEX command.

The INDEX command creates the index file LASTNAME.NDX that contains the entries in the LAST_NAME field and the corresponding record numbers. Because DISPLAY and LIST can show only the records of a database file (.DBF), the commands cannot be used to display the contents of an index file. The contents of the index file LASTNAME.NDX appear as the following:

FIRST_NAME	Record #
Baker	5
Chapman	6
Duff	8
Gregory	3
Hanson	10
Lee	9
Nelson	4
Smith	1
Thompson	7
Zeller	2

The record numbers in the index file are used to reorganize the data records. When you have indexed an active database file, the records are arranged in the order specified in the index file. The ordered data records remain active in RAM for further processing. However, if another database is activated with the USE command, the currently indexed database file will be lost. Because the contents of the file on disk are not affected by INDEX, you can reorganize the original file with the index file and the USE INDEX command.

USE INDEX

To organize the data records with the index file, you can use the following command:

. USE <database file> INDEX <name of an existing index file>

This command rearranges the data records in the order specified in the index file. In figure 5.10, the USE INDEX command rearranges EMPLOYEE.DBF by reactivating the index file LASTNAME.NDX.

As LASTNAME.NDX specifies, the records in the active database file have been arranged alphabetically.

SET INDEX TO

You can also reactivate an index file with a SET INDEX TO command. The format of this command is

. SET INDEX TO <name of an existing index file>

```
. USE EMPLOYEE INDEX LASTNAME
. DISPLAY ALL
Record#   FIRST_NAME    LAST_NAME   AREA_CODE  PHONE_NO  MALE  BIRTH_DATE  ANNUAL_PAY
      5   Tina B.       Baker       415        567-8967  .F.   10/12/56    25900.00
      6   Kirk D.       Chapman     618        625-7845  .T.   08/04/61    19750.00
      8   Charles N.    Duff        206        456-9873  .T.   07/22/64    13500.00
      3   Doris A.      Gregory     503        204-8567  .F.   07/04/62    16900.00
     10   Thomas T.     Hanson      206        573-5085  .T.   12/24/45    28950.00
      9   Winston E.    Lee         503        365-8512  .T.   05/14/39    34900.00
      4   Harry M.      Nelson      315        576-0235  .T.   02/15/58    29000.00
      1   James C.      Smith       206        123-4567  .T.   07/04/60    22000.00
      7   Mary W.       Thompson    213        432-6782  .F.   06/18/55    24500.00
      2   Albert K.     Zeller      212        457-9801  .T.   09/20/59    27950.00
.
```

Fig. 5.10. The USE INDEX command.

The SET INDEX TO command tells the computer to rearrange the data records with the index file already created. For example, to reactivate the index file LASTNAME.NDX, the command is

. SET INDEX TO LASTNAME

Figure 5.11 shows the results of the SET INDEX TO command.

```
. USE EMPLOYEE
. SET INDEX TO LASTNAME
. DISPLAY ALL
Record#   FIRST_NAME    LAST_NAME   AREA_CODE  PHONE_NO  MALE  BIRTH_DATE  ANNUAL_PAY
      5   Tina B.       Baker       415        567-8967  .F.   10/12/56    25900.00 .
      6   Kirk D.       Chapman     618        625-7845  .T.   08/04/61    19750.00
      8   Charles N.    Duff        206        456-9873  .T.   07/22/64    13500.00
      3   Doris A.      Gregory     503        204-8567  .F.   07/04/62    16900.00
     10   Thomas T.     Hanson      206        573-5085  .T.   12/24/45    28950.00
      9   Winston E.    Lee         503        365-8512  .T.   05/14/39    34900.00
      4   Harry M.      Nelson      315        576-0235  .T.   02/15/58    29000.00
      1   James C.      Smith       206        123-4567  .T.   07/04/60    22000.00
      7   Mary W.       Thompson    213        432-6782  .F.   06/18/55    24500.00
      2   Albert K.     Zeller      212        457-9801  .T.   09/20/59    27950.00
.
```

Fig. 5.11. The SET INDEX command.

Multiple-Field Indexing

Multiple keys are often used for sorting the data records in a database file. You can achieve the same results by using several data fields as a combined key field in the indexing operation. The multiple fields used as an indexing key in an INDEX ON command must be joined with plus signs, such as

. INDEX ON <field #1>+<field #2>+ . . . TO <index file>

For example, if two or more phone numbers in the
EMPLOYEE.DBF database file have the same area code, you may
need to index on both the AREA_CODE and the PHONE_NO
fields. This way, phone numbers with the same area code are
arranged in ascending order. Figure 5.12 shows an example.

```
. USE EMPLOYEE
. INDEX ON AREA_CODE+PHONE_NO TO PHONENOS
     10 records indexed
. LIST ALL AREA_CODE,PHONE_NO
Record#   AREA_CODE PHONE_NO
        1   206       123-4567
        8   206       456-9873
       10   206       573-5085
        2   212       457-9801
        7   213       432-6782
        4   315       576-0235
        5   415       567-8967
        3   503       204-8567
        9   503       365-8512
        6   618       625-7845
.
```

Fig. 5.12. Multiple field indexing.

As you can see, the data records are arranged first by area code and
then by phone number.

Searching Data in an
Indexed Database File

With an indexed database, you can search quickly for records that
share the same contents as the index key field. For example, if the
database file EMPLOYEE is indexed on the AREA_CODE field, all
the records with the same area code are ordered consecutively in
one block. By positioning the record pointer at the beginning of the
data block, you can access each record easily.

FIND

The FIND command positions the record pointer at the beginning of
a data block. If you specify the search key as an alphanumeric string,
the first data record that contains the key string is made the active
record, such as

. FIND <an alphanumeric string>

FIND searches the indexed database file for the first record with a character string that matches the contents of the key field. When a record with the specified string is found, the record pointer is set to that record. Then the contents of the record can be displayed. The FIND command works, however, only when locating a record in an indexed database file.

For example, the FIND command locates the first record in the indexed file EMPLOYEE that contains the character string *N* (see fig. 5.13).

```
. USE EMPLOYEE
. SET INDEX TO LASTNAME
. FIND "N"
. DISPLAY
Record#   FIRST_NAME    LAST_NAME   AREA_CODE  PHONE_NO  MALE  BIRTH_DATE  ANNUAL_PAY
      4   Harry M.      Nelson       315       576-0235  .T.   02/15/58     29000.00
.
```

Fig. 5.13. The FIND command.

The data record contains *Nelson* in the index field (LAST_NAME). The record was found because the character string that was specified in the FIND command matches the first character of *Nelson*. The items match if the key field contains the string specified in the command. Therefore, the same record will be found if any of the following FIND commands are used:

. FIND "Ne"
. FIND "Nel"
. FIND "Nelson"

However, the record *Nelson* will not be found with the following FIND commands used for the searching operation:

. FIND "nelson"
. FIND "elson"
. FIND "NELSON"

In a FIND operation, the characters in the string are compared with the beginning characters of the key field, so *nelson* or *elson* will not match *Nelson*. Because capital and lowercase letters are treated as unique characters, the string "NELSON" does not match "Nelson".

REINDEX

If the contents of the data records have been changed since the index files were created, the index files must be updated to reflect the changes. You can use the REINDEX command to rebuild all active index files when the contents of the database file have been modified. The format of this command is

. REINDEX

Before you enter the REINDEX command, however, the database file must be activated and referenced with the index file. To rebuild the index files LASTNAME.NDX and PHONENOS.NDX after EMPLOYEE.DBF has been changed, use the commands in figure 5.14.

```
. USE EMPLOYEE
. SET INDEX TO LASTNAME,PHONENOS
. REINDEX
Rebuilding index - B:LASTNAME.ndx
     10 records indexed
Rebuilding index - B:PHONENOS.ndx
     10 records indexed
.
```

Fig. 5.14. The REINDEX command.

Operations on an Index File

No more than seven index files can be created for a database file. You can use the DIR command to display a listing of all existing index files on the disk, such as

. DIR *.NDX

The asterisk (*) indicates that all files with the identifier (.NDX) are to be displayed in the directory. If you want to display all file types, you can enter the following command:

. DIR *.*

Like a database file, index files can be deleted, renamed, or copied with one of the following commands:

. ERASE <index file identification>
. RENAME <source index file> TO <destination index file>
. COPY FILE <source index file> TO <destination index file>

Some examples are

. ERASE PHONENOS.NDX
. RENAME ABC.NDX TO XYZ.NDX
. COPY FILE ABC.NDX TO XYZ.NDX

Before an index file can be erased, renamed, or copied onto another file, the file must be closed. Active index files can be closed by entering the following command:

. CLOSE INDEX

This command closes all the active index files as a group. The CLOSE INDEX command cannot be used selectively to close a single index file.

Counting and Summarizing Data Records

One of the most important dBASE III functions is the summarizing of data. For example, you may need to count in EMPLOYEE.DBF the number of employees whose annual salaries fall within a certain range. Or perhaps you need to find the average annual salary for all male employees. For this purpose, dBASE III provides the summary commands of COUNT, TOTAL, and AVERAGE.

COUNT, COUNT FOR

Data records in a database file can be tallied with a COUNT command. A conditional COUNT command can be used to count all the data records in the active file. You can use a conditional COUNT command to count records selectively. A COUNT command can be entered with or without a qualifier:

. COUNT
. COUNT <a qualifier>

The first command is an unconditional COUNT command that tallies the total number of data records in the active file. When an unconditional COUNT command is applied to the EMPLOYEE.DBF database file, the computer will tally all the data records currently stored in the file (see fig. 5.15).

To count the records selectively, you can add a qualifier to the command. The qualifier defines the condition to be met for the records to be counted. To count only the data records in the

```
. USE EMPLOYEE
. COUNT
      10 records
.
```

Fig. 5.15. The COUNT command.

EMPLOYEE.DBF database file with area code 206, you must define
the qualifier as shown in figure 5.16.

```
. USE EMPLOYEE
. COUNT FOR AREA_CODE="216"
      3 records
.
```

Fig. 5.16. The conditional COUNT command.

If several conditions need to be specified in the COUNT command,
you can define the conditions by using one or more of the .AND.,
.OR., and .NOT. relational operators. Figure 5.17 shows some of
these examples.

```
. USE EMPLOYEE
. COUNT FOR AREA_CODE="206".AND.MALE
      3 records
. COUNT FOR AREA_CODE="206".OR.AREA_CODE="503"
      5 records
. COUNT FOR ANNUAL_PAY>=20000.AND.ANNUAL_PAY<=30000
      6 records
. COUNT FOR .NOT. MALE .AND. ANNUAL_PAY>=25000
      1  record
.
```

Fig. 5.17. Relational operators.

SUM

You can sum and display with a conditional or unconditional SUM
command the contents of numeric fields in the active database file.
The formats of the SUM command, with or without a qualifier, are

. SUM <name of data field>
. SUM <name of data field> FOR <a qualifier>

The first command computes and displays the sum of all the values in the specified data field. With an unconditional SUM command, all the data records are included in the summing operation. The second command shows a conditional SUM command. By placing a qualifier in the command, you can ensure that only the data records which meet the condition are subjected to the summing operation. Figure 5.18 shows the results of the SUM commands.

```
. USE EMPLOYEE
. SUM ANNUAL_PAY
     10 records summed
   ANNUAL_PAY
     243350.00
. SUM ANNUAL_PAY FOR MALE
      7 records summed
   ANNUAL_PAY
     176050.00
. SUM ANNUAL_PAY FOR ANNUAL_PAY<=25000
      5 records summed
   ANNUAL_PAY
      96650.00
. SUM ANNUAL_PAY FOR .NOT. MALE .AND. ANNUAL_PAY>=20000
      2 records summed
   ANNUAL_PAY
      50400.00
.
```

Fig. 5.18. The SUM command.

AVERAGE

An average value (arithmetic mean) of the contents of a numeric field can be computed and displayed with the AVERAGE command. The averaging operation, using a conditional or unconditional AVERAGE command, may involve part or all of the records in the database. Figure 5.19 shows some of these examples.

TOTAL

Data records in an active file with the same key field contents may be combined in groups. Values stored in the numeric fields in those groups can be totaled and saved in another database file as summary statistics. The format of the TOTAL command is

. TOTAL ON <key field> TO <name of summary file>

The TOTAL command sums the numeric fields of the active database file and saves the results to the summary file. The numeric

```
. USE EMPLOYEE
. AVERAGE
     10 records averaged
ANNUAL_PAY
  24335.00
. AVERAGE ANNUAL_PAY FOR MALE
      7 records averaged
 ANNUAL_PAY
   25150.00
. AVERAGE ANNUAL_PAY FOR .NOT. MALE
      3 records averaged
ANNUAL_PAY
  22433.33
. AVERAGE ANNUAL_PAY FOR ANNUAL_PAY>=20000 .AND. ANNUAL_PAY<=30000
      6 records averaged
ANNUAL_PAY
   26383.33
.
```

Fig. 5.19. The AVERAGE command.

fields of the summary file contain the totals of all the data records that have the same key field contents. When you enter the TOTAL command, all the numeric fields in the database file are totaled unless you specify otherwise. The structure of the summary file is copied from the database file.

If the field size is not large enough for the total, an error message is displayed and an asterisk (*) is placed in the data field. Before you can enter TOTAL command, you must use a sorting or indexing command to arrange the database file in ascending or descending order.

A new database file, QTYSOLD.DBF, has been created to illustrate the totaling operation. The QTYSOLD.DBF database file contains the weekly sales figures of a small television store during December, 1984. The data structure and the data records are shown in figure 5.20.

```
. USE QTYSOLD
. DISPLAY STRUCTURE
Structure for database : B:QTYSOLD.dbf
Number of data records :      2
Date of last update    : 01/01/80
Field  Field name  Type      Width    Dec
    1  DATE        Date          8
    2  MODEL       Character    10
    3  UNITS_SOLD  Numeric       3
** Total **                     22
.
```

Fig. 5.20. Data structure of QTYSOLD.DBF.

The data records contained in the database file QTYSOLD.DBF are shown in figure 5.21.

```
. USE QTYSOLD
. LIST ALL
Record#   DATE     MODEL          UNITS_SOLD
      1   12/07/84 RCA-XA100               2
      2   12/07/84 RCA-XA200               5
      3   12/07/84 ZENITH-19P              4
      4   12/07/84 ZENITH-21C              3
      5   12/14/84 RCA-XA100               2
      6   12/14/84 RCA-XA200               4
      7   12/14/84 ZENITH-19P              3
      8   12/14/84 ZENITH-25C              4
      9   12/21/84 RCA-XA100               8
     10   12/21/84 RCA-XA200               6
     11   12/21/84 ZENITH-19P              6
     12   12/21/84 ZENITH-25C              7
     13   12/28/84 RCA-XA100               4
     14   12/28/84 RCA-XA200               5
     15   12/28/84 ZENITH-19P              4
     16   12/28/84 ZENITH-25C              2
.
```

Fig. 5.21. Data records in QTYSOLD.DBF.

As shown in figure 5.21, each data record in the database file contains a date (DATE), a model number (MODEL), and the quantity sold (UNITS_SOLD) during the week. To generate the weekly totals of televisions sold, you can enter the TOTAL command as shown in figure 5.22.

```
. USE QTYSOLD
. TOTAL ON DATE TO QTYWEEK
     16 Record(s) totalled
      4 Records generated
. USE QTYWEEK
. LIST DATE,UNITS_SOLD
Record#   DATE     UNITS_SOLD
      1   12/07/84         14
      2   12/14/84         13
      3   12/21/84         27
      4   12/28/84         15
.
```

Fig. 5.22. The TOTAL command.

All the units sold with the same date have been totaled and saved as one data record in the summary file QTYWEEK.DBF.

	In QTYSOLD.DBF			In QTYWEEK.DBF	
Record #	DATE	UNITS_SOLD	Record #	DATE	UNITS_SOLD
1	12/07/84	2	1	12/07/84	14
2	12/07/84	5	2	12/14/84	13
3	12/07/84	4	. . . . . .		. . .
4	12/07/84	3			
5	12/14/84	. . .			

To use TOTAL on a subset of the data records, you can add a qualifier that allows the totaling of only those data records that meet a certain condition. The format of a conditional TOTAL command is

. TOTAL ON <key field> TO <name of summary file> FOR <a qualifier>

The example in figure 5.23 contains a qualifier that totals only the data records that meet the condition FOR MODEL<ZENITH.

```
. USE QTYSOLD
. TOTAL ON DATE TO RCATOTAL FOR MODEL<"ZENITH"
        8 Record(s) totalled
        4 Records generated
. USE RCATOTAL
. LIST DATE,UNITS_SOLD
Record#    DATE        UNITS_SOLD
        1  12/07/84             7
        2  12/14/84             6
        3  12/21/84            14
        4  12/28/84             9
.
```

Fig. 5.23. The conditional TOTAL command.

The TOTAL command in the example totals by the date all the RCA television sets sold. The qualifier specifies that the TOTAL operation should be carried out FOR only the records whose MODEL is less than ZENITH. As a result, only those records containing RCA-XA100 or RCA-XA200 will be totaled.

The same logic can be used to generate a monthly summary of the television models sold. Before the database file QTYSOLD.DBF is totaled, however, you must arrange the data records in ascending or descending order with a SORT or INDEX command. Figure 5.24 shows how a monthly summary can be produced with INDEX and TOTAL.

The results of the TOTAL command show that each record in the summary file QTYMONTH.DBF contains the total number of television sets for each model sold during December, 1984. You can use the SUM command to find the monthly total for all television sets sold:

```
. USE QTYSOLD
. INDEX ON MODEL TO SORTMODEL
     16 records indexed
. TOTAL ON MODEL TO QTYMONTH
     16 Record(s) totalled
      5 Records generated
. USE QTYMONTH
. LIST MODEL,UNITS_SOLD
Record#   MODEL          UNITS_SOLD
      1   RCA-XA100             16
      2   RCA-XA200             20
      3   ZENITH-19P            17
      4   ZENITH-21C             3
      5   ZENITH-25C            13
.
```

Fig. 5.24. Producing a monthly summary with INDEX and TOTAL.

. SUM UNITS_SOLD

The SUM command can be applied to the original database file (QTYSOLD.DBF) or to any one of the summary files (QTYWEEK.DBF or QTYMONTH.DBF), and the same results will be achieved.

Chapter Summary

This chapter has introduced the two most useful dBASE III commands for rearranging data records. You can use the SORT command to sort in a specified order the data records of an active database file. The result of the SORT command is a target file that contains the ordered data records of the database file.

The INDEX command is similar to SORT, but the indexing operation is much faster than the sorting process. INDEX creates an index file that contains only the key fields. The index file is used to rearrange the data records in the active database file.

SORT and INDEX give you the option of accessing all or part of the data records in the database file. To select a subset of the data records for the sorting or indexing operation, add a qualifier clause (FOR . . .) to the SORT or INDEX command.

SORT and INDEX do not change the order of the data records in the file on disk. Target files are created to store the arranged data fields or records. If the contents of the database file have been changed, you must re-sort or reindex the database file.

The dBASE III commands used to generate summary statistics are SUM, AVERAGE, and TOTAL. With the SUM command, you can select and sum all the values in a numeric data field. The AVERAGE command can be used to compute the average for all the values in a chosen data field. The TOTAL command sums the numeric fields of the active database file and saves the results in a summary file. The numeric fields of the summary file contain the totals of all the data records with the same key field contents. Before using the TOTAL command, you must rearrange the data records in ascending or descending order.

6

Memory Variables, Expressions, and Functions

An Overview

In addition to data stored in the database, you often need to retain intermediate results of data manipulation procedures so that you can use these values for further processing. Instead of storing these results as records in a file, you can save the data in memory as variables. A *memory variable* is a specified amount of computer memory set aside to hold a given data element. Because a memory variable takes up little memory space and the variable's contents can be recalled almost instantly, memory variables are important in data manipulation. This chapter covers the way memory variables are defined and used in database management.

Also discussed in this chapter are the uses of expressions and functions in data manipulation. An *expression* is a combination of data records and memory variables. Expressions are used to define the operations performed on specified data elements. *Functions* are commands with which you perform certain predefined operations without specifying all the steps at the time of the operation. For example, you can use a function for finding square roots.

This chapter introduces the following commands, which are used for processing memory variables:

Commands	*Functions*
STORE =	Enter data into memory variables
? DISPLAY MEMORY	Display memory variables
SAVE TO	Saves memory variables to disk file
RELEASE ERASE	Discard memory variables
RESTORE	Retrieves memory variables from disk file

The following are built-in functions of dBASE III:

Functions	*For*
TIME(), DATE() CDOW, CMONTH, DOW DAY, MONTH, YEAR	Time and date processing
CTOD, VAL, DTOC, STR	Field/Variable conversion
UPPER, LOWER, ASC, CHR	String conversion
SPACE, TRIM, AT, SUBSTR	Character manipulation
INT, ROUND, SQRT, LOG, EXP	Mathematical operation
RECNO()	Pointing to a record
ROW(), COL(), PROW(), PCOL()	Displaying a location

Memory Variables

The term *variable* is used in algebra to mean a quantity that may assume different values. In dBASE III, *variable* is a name assigned to a memory location you can use to hold a data element. A memory variable can be a data field or a changeable data item. The contents of a memory variable can be an alphanumeric string, a value, or a date.

Memory variables are temporarily held in RAM during processing. Contents of memory variables are stored outside the structure of a database file and are not considered part of the database contents.

Memory variables are the major components of formulas. Intermediate results from computations or data manipulations are often stored in memory variables to be recalled and used for further calculation or for report generation.

Determining the Type of Memory Variable

dBASE III offers four types of memory variables: alphanumeric (character), numeric, date, and logical. The type is determined by the kind of data stored. An alphanumeric variable can store only an alphanumeric string. Similarly, you can store numbers or values for computations in numeric variables only. A date variable holds a date in the form mm/dd/yy, and a logical variable stores a logical True (T) or False (F). You can change the variable type by assigning a different kind of data. For instance, when an alphanumeric string is placed in a variable, that variable becomes an alphanumeric variable. If you later assign a numeric value to the same variable, it becomes a numeric variable.

Naming the Variable

Regardless of type, a memory variable can be assigned a name that consists of up to ten characters. As with field names, these ten characters may be a combination of letters, digits, and underscores. However, the first character of a memory variable name must be a letter. The following names are acceptable memory variable names:

SALES	Grosspay	DISCOUNT
SaleDate	WEEKLYHRS	PAY_RATE
ACCOUNTNO	UNITSSOLD	TAXRATE

The same name should not be used for a variable and a data field in the same application. If the same name is assigned to a variable and to a field, after the record containing the field is activated, the name is recognized only for the field. However, because a memory variable is often needed to retain the contents of a data field for further computation, you may want to assign a variable name that is related to the corresponding field name. For example, if the field name contains an underscore, such as ACCOUNT_NO, the name without the underscore, ACCOUNTNO, can be used for the variable. If the field name does not contain an underscore, you can use a letter M in front of the field name for the memory variable name. For instance, you can use the name MSALES for the memory variable to hold the contents of the data field SALES.

Entering Data in a Memory Variable

You can enter data in a memory variable in several ways: you can enter data from the keyboard, you can assign to a memory variable the contents of a data field of the active data record, or you can copy the contents of one memory variable to another memory variable.

The = Command

The equal sign (=) is a command entered from the keyboard. This command assigns an alphanumeric string, a value, or a logical state to a memory variable of the same type. Use the following form:

. <name of memory variable>=<data element>

The interpretation of the equal sign differs from the normal mathematical use. Instead of stating that two quantities are equal, in dBASE III the equal sign defines an action. The equal sign assigns to the memory variable on the left of the sign the data element on the right. The data element to be entered in the memory variable must be defined in a specified form depending on the kind of data element. To avoid ambiguity, an alphanumeric string must be enclosed in quotation marks. Contents of a logical variable must be specified in the form of .T. or .F. (or .Y. or .N.). Be sure to include the two periods. Numbers entered in numerical variables can be integers or decimal values (see fig. 6.1). A date cannot be entered in a date variable by the = command.

If the memory name is correctly defined and the data is correctly specified, the data element is assigned to the variable. The program

```
. TESTSTRING="This is a test string"
This is a test string
. MEMBERSHIP=.T.
.T.
. HOURS=32
32
. PAYRATE=7.50
7.50
.
```

Fig. 6.1. Assigning data to memory variables.

confirms the command by echoing the contents of the variable immediately after the = command is executed unless echoing has been turned off. If an error is made in the = command, the error message ***** Unrecognized command verb ***** is displayed.

Contents of a data field in the active data record (including character, numeric, logical, and date fields) can also be assigned to a memory variable with the = command. Use the following format:

. <name of memory variable>=<name of data field>

For example, you can assign the contents of the data fields of the EMPLOYEE database file to memory variables by using the = command (see fig. 6.2).

```
. USE EMPLOYEE
. GO TOP
. FIRSTNAME=FIRST_NAME
James C.
. MMALE=MALE
.T.
. BIRTHDATE=BIRTH_DATE
07/04/60
. ANNUALPAY=ANNUAL_PAY
22000.00
.
```

Fig. 6.2. Assigning the contents of a data field to a memory variable.

The STORE Command

The STORE command also assigns to a memory variable a data element or the contents of a data field of the active record. In fact, you can use the = and STORE commands interchangeably. The STORE command has the following formats:

. STORE <data element> TO <name of memory variable>
. STORE <name of data field> TO <name of memory variable>

The first format is used for entering data from the keyboard. This STORE command assigns alphanumeric, numeric, and logical memory variables but not dates (see fig. 6.3).

```
. STORE "This is a test string" TO TESTSTRING
This is a test string
. STORE .T. TO MEMBERSHIP
.T.
. STORE 32 TO HOURS
32
. STORE 7.5 TO PAYRATE
7.5
.
```

Fig. 6.3. The STORE command.

A STORE command in the second format assigns to a memory variable the content of a data field of the active record, regardless of the field type. The variable type becomes that of the data field when the STORE command is executed. The example in figure 6.4 illustrates assigning to corresponding variables the contents of data fields in the EMPLOYEE database file.

```
. USE EMPLOYEE
. LOCATE FOR FIRST_NAME="Doris"
Record =        3
. DISPLAY
Record#  FIRST_NAME    LAST_NAME   AREA_CODE PHONE_NO MALE BIRTH_DATE ANNUAL_PAY
      3  Doris A.      Gregory      503       204-8567 .F.  07/04/62    16900.00
. STORE FIRST_NAME TO FIRSTNAME
Doris A.
. STORE MALE TO MMALE
.F.
. STORE BIRTH_DATE TO BIRTHDATE
07/04/62
. STORE ANNUAL_PAY TO ANNUALPAY
16900.00
.
```

Fig. 6.4. A second form of the STORE command.

Displaying Memory Variables

As you enter data in memory variables, the variables are temporarily held in RAM. Therefore, at any time during data manipulation, you can display the contents of all the variables.

The DISPLAY MEMORY Command

You can use the DISPLAY MEMORY command to display detailed information about all the active memory variables. Simply enter the command as

. *DISPLAY MEMORY*

This command displays the names of all the active memory variables in the order in which they were last updated. The DISPLAY command also shows the type of data stored in each variable and the content of the variable (see fig. 6.5). The abbreviation **pub** following a variable name indicates that the variable is a public variable.

```
. DISPLAY MEMORY
TESTSTRING   pub   C   "This is a test string"
MEMBERSHIP   pub   L   .T.
HOURS        pub   N           32  (          32.00000000)
PAYRATE      pub   N          7.5  (           7.50000000)
FIRSTNAME    pub   C   "Doris A.       "
MMALE        pub   L   .F.
BIRTHDATE    pub   D   07/04/62
ANNUALPAY    pub   N       16900.00  (       16900.00000000)
      8 variables defined,       77 bytes used
    248 variables available,    5923 bytes available
.
```

Fig. 6.5. Results of the DISPLAY MEMORY command.

Memory variables are public or private. A *private variable* can be accessed only by a specified segment of a program. The contents of a *public variable* can be accessed by every part of the program. This distinction, however, is useful only for batch command processing (to be discussed in Chapter 11). All variables defined in the interactive mode are public variables.

The command also displays summary statistics regarding the number of variables defined, the amount of memory used, and the number of variables and bytes still available.

The ? Command

The DISPLAY MEMORY command displays all existing variables as a group. To display the contents of a single memory variable, you use the ? command in the following format:

. ? <name of the memory variable to be displayed>

Figure 6.6 shows how to use the ? command to display the contents of several different types of memory variables.

```
. ? TESTSTRING
This is a test string
. ? MEMBERSHIP
.T.
. ? HOURS
        32
. ? PAYRATE
       7.5
. ? FIRSTNAME
Doris A.
. ? BIRTHDATE
07/04/62
. ? ANNUALPAY
    16900.00

.
```

Fig. 6.6. The ? command.

Saving Memory Variables on Disk

Memory variables are temporarily held in RAM, and they can be accessed at any stage of the data manipulation process. However, when you leave dBASE III, the variables are erased (or released) from memory. Therefore, if you want to use these variables in different dBASE III applications, you must retain the variables in some permanent storage device. With the SAVE command, you can save on a floppy disk or a hard disk the contents of the active memory variables.

The SAVE command stores all or part of the current set of memory variables to a disk file. To save all the active memory variables, use the following form of the SAVE command:

. SAVE TO <name of memory file>

An example is

. SAVE TO VARLIST

This command instructs the computer to copy all the memory variables to a file with the name specified in the command (VARLIST). Unless otherwise designated, the file extension for the memory file created by this command is MEM (VARLIST.MEM).

You can also save only some of the variables. To select the memory variables you want to save, use a selection clause, such as ALL LIKE or ALL EXCEPT:

. SAVE ALL LIKE <variable description> TO <name of memory file>

. SAVE ALL EXCEPT <variable description> TO <name of memory file>

The phrase *variable description* means the skeleton of a variable name. dBASE III has two symbols (also called wild cards) that substitute for the characters in a variable name. The question mark (?) substitutes for a single character, and the asterisk (*) stands for a string of characters of any length. For instance, to save in the file NETVARS.MEM all the active memory variables with names beginning with the letters *NET* (NETREVENUE, NETCOST, NETPROFIT, etc.), you can specify the variables with an asterisk:

. SAVE ALL LIKE NET* TO NETVARS

The asterisk (*) in the variable description instructs the program to save every variable with *NET* as the first three characters of the variable name.

Suppose you want to save all the memory variables with six-character names containing *RATE* as the second through the fifth characters (WRATE1, MRATE2, YRATE3, etc.). You can use the ? as in the following command:

. SAVE ALL LIKE ?RATE? TO RATES

The question marks (?) in the variable name description ?RATE? instruct the computer to ignore the characters in the variable names at these positions.

You can also exclude specified variables from a memory disk file. For example, if you do not want to save the memory variables with names beginning with the letters *NET*, you can use the ALL EXCEPT clause in the SAVE command:

. SAVE ALL EXCEPT NET????? TO MEMVARS
. SAVE ALL EXCEPT NET* TO MEMVARS

The first command saves all memory variables whose names begin with *NE* followed by any five alphanumeric characters. The second command saves all memory variables to the file except those whose names begin with *NET* followed by any alphanumeric characters.

Deleting Memory Variables

Memory variables can be deleted from the active memory list. The RELEASE command permanently removes all or part of the active memory variables. As in the SAVE command, the clauses ALL, ALL LIKE, and ALL EXCEPT can be used to select the memory variables to be released:

. RELEASE ALL
. RELEASE ALL LIKE <variable name description>
. RELEASE ALL EXCEPT <variable name description>

The * and ? symbols can be used as they are used in the SAVE commands. Following are some examples:

. RELEASE ALL LIKE *NET
. RELEASE ALL LIKE ?RATE?
. RELEASE ALL EXCEPT *NET
. RELEASE ALL EXCEPT NET?????

The RELEASE command removes the specified active memory variables from RAM; however, the command does not delete memory variables from a memory file. To delete a memory file that has been saved on disk, you must use the ERASE command:

. ERASE <name of memory file to be erased>

For instance, the following command removes the memory file MEMVAR.MEM:

. ERASE MEMVAR.MEM

Loading Memory Variables from Memory Files

The memory variables that have been saved in a memory file can be copied back to RAM. The RESTORE command retrieves all the memory variables in a memory file and places them in the computer's memory. The format of this command is

. RESTORE FROM <name of the memory file>

An example is

. RESTORE FROM RATES.MEM

This RESTORE command erases all memory variables currently in RAM before the memory variables from RATES.MEM are restored.

To retain the current memory variables, you must combine the ADDITIVE clause with the RESTORE command:

. RESTORE FROM <name of the memory file> ADDITIVE

The command with the clause

. RESTORE FROM VARLIST.MEM ADDITIVE

retrieves all the variables in VARLIST.MEM and adds the variables to the current active memory list.

Expressions

Besides serving as temporary storage, memory variables can be used in processing operations. A memory variable can be specified in an expression to define a procedure, to describe a qualifier phrase in a command, or to serve as an output element.

Depending on the applications, different types of expressions can be used in dBASE III. An expression may include a data field, a memory variable, a constant, or a combination of these forms. However, all the elements in an expression must be the same type. An expression containing data elements of different types is not acceptable and results in a **Data type mismatch** error message.

Using Arithmetic Expressions

The most common expression is an arithmetic expression, which may contain

a value
a memory variable
a numeric data field
a combination of these joined by one or more arithmetic operators (+, -, *, /, etc.)

For instance, the following clauses are arithmetic expressions:

32
HOURS
ANNUAL_PAY
HOURS*PAYRATE
ANNUAL_PAY + 0.05*ANNUAL_PAY

HOURS and PAYRATE are names of memory variables, and * is the symbol for multiplication. HOURS*PAYRATE indicates that multiplication is to be performed on the two data elements (that is, the contents of the variables HOURS and PAYRATE).

Expressions are useful for arithmetic calculations. An expression can be used to assign a value to a memory variable or to replace the contents of a numeric data field with a new value. In the example in figure 6.7, the arithmetic expressions assign values to the memory variables listed to the left of the equal signs.

```
.  HOURS=32
32
.  PAYRATE=7.5
7.5
.  GROSSPAY=HOURS*PAYRATE
                240.0

 .
```

Fig. 6.7. Arithmetic expressions assign values to variables.

The multiplication symbol (*) in the arithmetic expression is called an arithmetic operator. Other arithmetic operators include +, -, /, and ^ for the operations of addition, subtraction, division, and raising the power, respectively. When more than one arithmetic operator is included in an expression, the expression is evaluated from left to right according to the following priority system:

Highest priority	^
Second priority	*, /
Lowest priority	+, -

You can use parentheses in an arithmetic expression to define the evaluation sequence and suppress the normal priority system. Material within parentheses is always evaluated first. When pairs of parentheses are nested in an arithmetic expression, the expression within the inner parentheses is evaluated first. Then the expressions within the outer parentheses are evaluated. Arithmetic operators within parentheses are evaluated from left to right following the normal priority system. As an example, the following arithmetic expression is evaluated in the steps listed.

(QTYA+QTYB)*PRICE*((1-DISCOUNT)/100)

1. Evaluate (1-DISCOUNT).

2. Evaluate (QTYA+QTYB).

3. Evaluate ((1-DISCOUNT)/100). [You are actually using the result of step 1 in this calculation.]

4. Evaluate (QTYA+QTYB)*PRICE. [This step uses the result of step 2.]

5. Evaluate the entire equation: (QTYA+QTYB)*PRICE*((1-DISCOUNT)/100). [This is the result of step 4 multiplied by the result of step 3.]

You can also use in an arithmetic expression numeric data fields in an active data record. As shown in figure 6.8, the numeric field UNITS_SOLD in QTYSOLD.DBF can be used in an arithmetic expression to compute the total price.

```
. USE QTYSOLD
. LOCATE FOR MODEL="RCA-XA200"
Record =            2
. DISPLAY
Record#  DATE       MODEL         UNITS_SOLD
     2  12/07/84 RCA-XA200               5
. UNITPRICE=495.90
495.90
. TOTALPRICE=UNITPRICE*UNITS_SOLD
          2479.50

.
```

Fig. 6.8. Numeric data field in an arithmetic expression.

Similarly, as shown in figure 6.9, an arithmetic expression can be used with a DISPLAY command to compute record totals for all the RCA-XA200 television sets listed as sold in QTYSOLD.DBF (UNITPRICE*UNITS_SOLD).

```
. USE QTYSOLD
. UNITPRICE=495.90
495.90
. DISPLAY DATE,UNITS_SOLD,UNITPRICE*UNITS_SOLD FOR MODEL="RCA-XA200"
Record#  DATE      UNITS_SOLD  UNITPRICE*UNITS_SOLD
     2  12/07/84        5              2479.50
     6  12/14/84        4              1983.60
    10  12/21/84        6              2975.40
    14  12/28/84        5              2479.50

.
```

Fig. 6.9. An arithmetic expression with the DISPLAY command.

Contents of the numeric fields in the active records can be adjusted by means of an arithmetic expression specified in a REPLACE command. For an example, see figure 6.10. To raise by 5 percent all the employees' annual salaries (in the numeric field, ANNUAL_PAY), you use the REPLACE command. As a result, every employee's annual salary (ANNUAL_PAY) is increased by 5 percent (ANNUAL_PAY*1.05).

```
. USE EMPLOYEE
. REPLACE ALL ANNUAL_PAY WITH ANNUAL_PAY*1.05
      10 records replaced
. LIST LAST_NAME,ANNUAL_PAY
Record#   LAST_NAME   ANNUAL_PAY
       1  Smith        23100.00
       2  Zeller       29347.50
       3  Gregory      17745.00
       4  Nelson       30450.00
       5  Baker        27195.00
       6  Chapman      20737.50
       7  Thompson     25725.00
       8  Duff         14175.00
       9  Lee          36645.00
      10  Hanson       30397.50
.
```

Fig. 6.10. An arithmetic expression with the REPLACE command.

Using Alphanumeric Expressions

Another frequently used expression in dBASE III is the alphanumeric expression (also called character expression). An alphanumeric expression may contain

an alphanumeric string enclosed in quotation marks
an alphanumeric memory variable
an alphanumeric data field
a combination of these joined by the + sign

For example, each of the following phrases is an alphanumeric expression:

"Employee's Name"
FIRST_NAME
LAST_NAME
"Employee's Name"+" is "+FIRST_NAME+LAST_NAME

One important use of an alphanumeric expression is to assign an alphanumeric data element to a memory variable. For instance, you can use either of the following commands to assign the contents of the alphanumeric expression to an alphanumeric variable:

. LONGSTRING=STRING A+STRING B+STRING C
. STORE STRING A+STRING B+STRING C TO LONGSTRING

You can also combine data fields in the records of the active database file and form an alphanumeric expression that can be used as the object of a DISPLAY or LIST command. For example, in figure 6.11 the name of an employee is displayed with an alphanumeric expression that consists of two fields: FIRST_NAME and LAST_NAME.

```
. USE EMPLOYEE
. DISPLAY FIRST_NAME+LAST_NAME FOR MALE
Record#  FIRST_NAME+LAST_NAME
      1  James C.    Smith
      2  Albert K.   Zeller
      4  Harry M.    Nelson
      6  Kirk D.     Chapman
      8  Charles N.  Duff
      9  Winston E.  Lee
     10  Thomas T.   Hanson
. LIST LAST_NAME+","+FIRST_NAME FOR .NOT. MALE
Record#  LAST_NAME+","+FIRST_NAME
      3  Gregory    ,Doris A.
      5  Baker      ,Tina B.
      7  Thompson   ,Mary W.
  "
```

*Fig. 6.11. An alphanumeric expression with the DISPLAY and
        LIST commands.*

In addition, you can use the REPLACE command to replace the contents of a field in the active records of a file with the contents of an alphanumeric expression. In figure 6.12 the contents of the data

```
. USE EMPLOYEE
. NEWCODE="513"
513
. REPLACE AREA_CODE WITH NEWCODE FOR AREA_CODE="503"
      2 records replaced
. LIST ALL LAST_NAME, AREA_CODE
Record#  LAST_NAME  AREA_CODE
      1  Smith      216
      2  Zeller     212
      3  Gregory    513
      4  Nelson     315
      5  Baker      415
      6  Chapman    618
      7  Thompson   213
      8  Duff       216
      9  Lee        513
     10  Hanson     216
  .
```

Fig. 6.12. An alphanumeric expression with the REPLACE command.

field AREA_CODE in the database file EMPLOYEE.DBF have been replaced with the contents of the variable NEWCODE.

Displaying Expressions

Contents of alphanumeric and numeric expressions can be displayed in a number of ways. For example, you can use a DISPLAY or a LIST command to display the name of an employee with an alphanumeric expression that contains the memory variable IDLABEL (see fig. 6.13).

```
. USE EMPLOYEE
. LOCATE FOR LAST_NAME="Gregory"
Record =        3
. DISPLAY
Record#  FIRST_NAME    LAST_NAME   AREA_CODE PHONE_NO MALE BIRTH_DATE ANNUAL_PAY
       3 Doris A.      Gregory       513       204-8567 .F.  07/04/62    17745.00
. IDLABEL="Employee's Name ..... "
Employee's Name .....
. DISPLAY IDLABEL+FIRST_NAME+LAST_NAME
Record#   IDLABEL+FIRST_NAME+LAST_NAME
       3  Employee's Name ..... Doris A.      Gregory
. LIST IDLABEL+LAST_NAME+", "+FIRST_NAME
Record#   IDLABEL+LAST_NAME+", "+FIRST_NAME
       1  Employee's Name ..... Smith      , James C.
       2  Employee's Name ..... Zeller     , Albert K.
       3  Employee's Name ..... Gregory    , Doris A.
       4  Employee's Name ..... Nelson     , Harry M.
       5  Employee's Name ..... Baker      , Tina B.
       6  Employee's Name ..... Chapman    , Kirk D.
       7  Employee's Name ..... Thompson   , Mary W.
       8  Employee's Name ..... Duff       , Charles N.
       9  Employee's Name ..... Lee        , Winston E.
      10  Employee's Name ..... Hanson     , Thomas T.
.
```

Fig. 6.13. Displaying alphanumeric and numeric expressions.

You can also use the ? command to display the contents of a specific alphanumeric expression (see fig. 6.14). Note that in the ? command the alphanumeric string "Total Sale . . . " is separated by a comma from the numeric expression UNITS_SOLD*UNITPRICE. Therefore, each is considered a separate expression.

An expression must contain only data elements of the same type. An alphanumeric expression and a numeric expression cannot be joined with a plus sign. The expression

   ? "Total Sale . . . "+UNITS_SOLD*UNITPRICE

will result in the error message **Data type mismatch.**

```
. USE QTYSOLD
. LOCATE FOR MODEL="ZENITH-19P"
Record =        3
. DISPLAY
Record#  DATE      MODEL        UNITS_SOLD
      3  12/07/84 ZENITH-19P            4
. UNITPRICE=259.5
259.5
. ? "Total Sale ....... ",  UNITS_SOLD*UNITPRICE
Total Sale .......              1038.0

.
```

*Fig. 6.14. Displaying the contents of an alphanumeric expression
by using the ? command.*

Functions

Functions in dBASE III are special operations for mathematical or string manipulations. You can apply functions to data fields or expressions. Mathematical functions can involve rounding a decimal number to its integer, computing the square root of a value, and many other actions. In data manipulation, you can use string functions that isolate parts of an alphanumeric string to be used in searching, sorting, and indexing operations. With other string functions, you can insert blank spaces in an alphanumeric string or trim off unwanted blank spaces. Functions for data type conversion change data elements from one type to another. For instance, with a data type conversion function, you can convert a date to an alphanumeric string, a numeric field to an alphanumeric string, or the contents of an alphanumeric variable to a numeric value. The time/date functions display date and time in a number of formats used in business data processing applications.

Format of a Function

A function, which is designed to perform a special operation, must also have a function name. The object of the function is called an argument; in the command, the argument is specified within parentheses. The format of a function is

. <name of function>(<an argument>)

In the example

. INT(3.7415)

the function, INT, finds the integer of the decimal value (3.7415), which is the argument of the function. The result of the function INT(3.7415) is returned as a numeric data element that is the integer portion of the value, 3. As shown in figure 6.15, the function may be used as an expression in a display command or as part of an arithmetic expression.

```
. ? INT(3.7415)
    3
. ANSWER=1200/INT(3.7415)
    400.00
.
```

Fig. 6.15. The INT function.

Many functions are available for manipulating data elements of different types. These functions are summarized by their operations in the following sections.

Mathematical Functions

As stated earlier, a mathematical function performs a mathematical operation on a numeric date element, which is given as the argument in the function command. The argument is in the form of a numeric expression and may consist of numeric values or numeric data fields. The results of a mathematical function are always returned as numeric data. In addition to INT (explained in the preceding section), the types of mathematical functions supported by dBASE III are ROUND, SQRT, LOG, and EXP.

The ROUND Function

A decimal value can be rounded to a specified number of decimal places (n) by the ROUND function. The decimal value can be the results of a numeric expression. The format of a ROUND function is

. ROUND(<a numeric expression>,<n>)

Note that the number of places shown after the decimal point for the value returned by the function is always the same as in the original value (see fig. 6.16). That is, the command

. ?ROUND(3.7415.3)

rounds the value to three places after the decimal point.

```
.  ? ROUND(3.7415,0)
 4.0000
.  ? ROUND(3.7415,1)
 3.7000
.  ? ROUND(3.7415,3)
 3.7420
.  HOURS=39.5
39.5
.  PAYRATE=9.75
9.75
.  ? HOURS*PAYRATE
                    385.125
.  ? ROUND(HOURS*PAYRATE,2)
                      385.130

.
```

Fig. 6.16. The ROUND function.

The SQRT Function

The SQRT function computes the square root of a value in the argument. The argument may be specified as an arithmetic expression

. SQRT(<a numeric expression>)

The square root returned by the function has a minimum of two decimal places. The maximum number of decimal places in the square root is the same as the number of decimal places in the number in the argument. Therefore, if more decimal places are desired, extra zeros must be added to the end of the value (see fig. 6.17).

```
.  ? SQRT(100)
       10.00
.  ? SQRT(2)
        1.41
.  ? SQRT(2.00)
        1.41
.  ? SQRT(2.00000000)
1.41421356
.  A=3.125
3.125
.  B=1567.89
1567.89
.  ? SQRT(A*B)
   69.99754

.
```

Fig. 6.17. The SQRT function.

The LOG Function

Two types of logarithms are used in mathematics and statistics. One is the base 10 common logarithm, which is denoted as $\log_1/10 \; x$. The other is the base e (where e = 2.71828183 . . .) natural logarithm, which is denoted by the ln x symbol. In dBASE III, only the natural logarithm (LOG) is available, but you can easily calculate the common logarithm of a value by the LOG function. To calculate the natural logarithm of a value, just specify the value in the argument as a numeric expression:

    . LOG(<a numeric expression>)

See figure 6.18 for examples.

```
 .  ?LOG(2.71828183)
1.00000000
 .  ?LOG(10)
        2.30
 .  ?LOG(10.000000)
    2.302585
 .
```

Fig. 6.18. The LOG function.

The natural LOG function can also be used to compute the common logarithm of a value with the following conversion formula:

$$\text{Log}_{10} \; x = \frac{\ln x}{\ln 10} = (\ln x)/(\ln 10)$$

Therefore, to compute the common logarithm of the value of 1,000, use the following LOG function:

    LOG(1000)/LOG(10)

The EXP Function

EXP is the exponential function. By specifying a value, x, in the argument, the function returns the exponent of e/sx:

    . EXP(<a numeric expression)

Figure 6.19 shows some examples. In the figure, the command ?EXP(1.00) yields the value of e^1 = 2.72. Because the argument of the function is in 2 decimal places (1.00), the result returned from

```
.  ?EXP(1.00)
        2.72
.  ?EXP(1.00000000)
2.71828183
.  A=2
2
.  B=4
4
.  ?EXP(A*B)
     2980.96
.
```

Fig. 6.19. The EXP function.

the function will also be in 2 decimal places. If you set the argument in more decimal places, as in the command ?EXP(1.00000000), you'll get a more accurate answer. You can also use a numeric expression as the argument for the EXP function, as shown in the third command, ?EXP(A*B).

String Manipulation Functions

An alphanumeric string can be manipulated by several functions, which produce specific results. For instance, characters in an alphanumeric string can be converted from capital letters to lowercase letters. Blank spaces in a character field can be removed. Extra blank spaces can be added to an alphanumeric string. Any character in an alphanumeric string can be isolated for display or for sorting or indexing operations.

The LOWER Function

The LOWER function converts to lowercase characters all the capital letters in an alphanumeric string; the function does not change numeric digits and symbols. The argument of the function is in the form of an alphanumeric expression, which may consist of a combination of alphanumeric strings in quotation marks and character data fields:

. LOWER(<an alphanumeric expression>)

See figure 6.20 for examples.

The LOWER function is effective for searching. For example, to locate the record that contains a specific character field, use LOWER to convert all contents of that character field into lowercase letters. In this way, regardless of how the actual string is stored in the field,

```
. ?LOWER("THIS IS A SAMPLE PHRASE IN CAPITAL LETTERS")
this is a sample phrase in capital letters
. USE EMPLOYEE
. ?LOWER(FIRST_NAME)
james c.
. ?LOWER(LAST_NAME+", "+FIRST_NAME)
smith      ,james c.
.
```

Fig. 6.20. The LOWER function.

you can find the string by specifying the search key in all lowercase letters (see fig. 6.21). The LOCATE command with the LOWER function finds the records that contain a last name in the forms of *SMITH*, *Smith*, *smith*, or any other combination of upper- and lowercase letters.

Without the LOWER function, the LOCATE command

. LOCATE FOR LAST_NAME="smith"

finds only records with *smith* in the LAST_NAME field.

```
. USE EMPLOYEE
. LOCATE FOR LOWER(LAST_NAME)="smith"
Record =       1
. DISPLAY LAST_NAME, FIRST_NAME
Record#  LAST_NAME  FIRST_NAME
      1  Smith      James C.
.
```

Fig. 6.21. The LOWER function with the LOCATE command.

The UPPER Function

The UPPER function performs a string conversion opposite to that of the LOWER function. UPPER converts to capital letters the lowercase letters in the alphanumeric string (see fig. 6.22). The format of an UPPER function is

. UPPER(<an alphanumeric expression>)

Figure 6.22 shows that by using UPPER(LAST_NAME) in the LOCATE command, you can convert to capital letters the alphabetic string in the field. Consequently, you can use *SMITH* as the search key for locating the data record.

```
. ?UPPER("This is an alphanumeric string!")
THIS IS AN ALPHANUMERIC STRING!
. USE EMPLOYEE
. LOCATE FOR UPPER(LAST_NAME)="SMITH"
Record =        1
. DISPLAY LAST_NAME+", "+FIRST_NAME
Record#  LAST_NAME+", "+FIRST_NAME
     1   Smith     , James C.
. ?UPPER(LAST_NAME+", "+FIRST_NAME)
SMITH     , JAMES C.
.
```

Fig. 6.22. The UPPER function.

The TRIM Function

The TRIM function removes the trailing spaces from a character string. The argument of the function is an alphanumeric expression, which may contain a combination of alphanumeric strings and character/text data fields. The format of the TRIM function is

    . TRIM(<an alphanumeric expression>)

Because the width of a character/text field is always preset by the structure, trailing blank spaces are automatically added to the end of any character string shorter than the preset width. As a result, when strings are displayed together, the blank spaces may make the display too wide. For instance, when the contents of the fields FIRST_NAME and LAST_NAME are displayed on the same line, several spaces are shown between the two fields. When you use the TRIM function to remove the trailing spaces from the first field, FIRST_NAME, the display looks more attractive (see fig. 6.23).

As shown in figure 6.23, the TRIM function is used to remove all those blank spaces in FIRST_NAME before it is linked to LAST_NAME as an alphanumeric expression.

```
. USE EMPLOYEE
. LOCATE FOR FIRST_NAME="Doris"
Record =       3
. ?FIRST_NAME+LAST_NAME
Doris A.    Gregory
. ?TRIM(FIRST_NAME)+LAST_NAME
Doris A.Gregory
. ?TRIM(FIRST_NAME)+" "+LAST_NAME
Doris A. Gregory
.
```

Fig. 6.23. The TRIM function.

The SPACE Function

An alphanumeric string with a specified number of blank spaces can be created by the SPACE function. The argument of the function specifies the number of spaces. The format of the function is

. SPACE(<number of blank spaces>)

The SPACE function may be used to create a memory variable for containing a specified number of spaces. You can also use the SPACE command to insert a specified number of spaces between the data elements to be displayed (see fig. 6.24).

```
. STORE "ABC" TO STRINGA
ABC
. STORE "XYZ" TO STRINGB
XYZ
. STORE SPACE(10) TO TENBLANKS

. ?STRINGA + TENBLANKS + STRINGB
ABC          XYZ
.
```

Fig. 6.24. The SPACE function.

The SUBSTR Function

The SUBSTR (substring) function extracts a specified part of an alphanumeric string. The argument of the function specifies in the following format the alphanumeric string, the starting position of the substring, and the number of characters to be extracted:

. SUBSTR(<alphanumeric expression>,<starting position>,<number of characters>)

In the example in fig. 6.25, the first SUBSTR function returns a substring CD by extracting two characters, beginning from the third character of the string ABCDEFG.

```
. ?SUBSTR("ABCDEFG",3,2)
CD
. ?SUBSTR("ABCDEFG",2,4)
BCDE
.
```

Fig. 6.25. The SUBSTR function.

As shown in figure 6.26, the SUBSTR function can extract a part of an alphanumeric string from a data field and assign the substring to a memory variable. You store the substring (the first three characters of PHONE_N0) to the memory variable PREFIX before using it as an alphanumeric expression in the ? command.

```
. USE EMPLOYEE
. GOTO 5
. DISPLAY PHONE_NO
Record#   PHONE_NO
       5  567-7777
. STORE SUBSTR(PHONE_NO,1,3) TO PREFIX
567
. ?"The telephone prefix is "+PREFIX
The telephone prefix is 567
.
```

Fig. 6.26. The SUBSTR function assigned to a memory variable.

With SUBSTR functions, you can rearrange characters in an alphanumeric string. Figure 6.27 shows an example that rearranges the characters in the variable XSTRING by moving the last three characters to the beginning of the string.

The example in figure 6.27 combines two substrings, SUBSTR(XSTRING,4,3) and SUBSTR(XSTRING,1,3), to form an alphanumeric expression that assigns the combined string to the variable XSTRING.

```
. XSTRING="ABCDEFG"
ABCDEFG
. XSTRING=SUBSTR(XSTRING,4,3)+SUBSTR(XSTRING,1,3)
DEFABC
. ?XSTRING
DEFABC
.
```

Fig. 6.27. The SUBSTR function to rearrange characters.

With the SUBSTR function, a part of an alphanumeric data field can be used for locating, sorting, or indexing operations. For example, if the database file EMPLOYEE.DBF is the active file, the following commands illustrate how you can use SUBSTR functions for the LOCATE, DISPLAY, LIST, SORT, and INDEX operations:

. LOCATE FOR SUBSTR(PHONE_NUMBER,5,4)="5085"

. DISPLAY LAST_NAME FOR SUBSTR(LAST_NAME,1,1)="G"

. LIST AREA_CODE, PHONE_NO FOR
SUBSTR(PHONE_NO,1,3)="123"

. SORT ON SUBSTR(PHONE_NO,1,3) TO SORTPRFX

. INDEX ON SUBSTR(PHONE_NO,1,3) TO INDXPRFX

In the first three commands, a substring—for example,
(PHONE_NUMBER,5,4) or (LAST_NAME,1,1)—is used for
specifying the condition in the qualifying clause (FOR . . .) of a
LOCATE, DISPLAY, or LIST command. The last two commands
use a substring, such as (PHONE_NO,1.3), as the key data field in
the sorting and indexing operations.

The AT Function

AT is a function you can use to search for an alphanumeric string for
a specified substring. If it is found, the function returns a number
that indicates the starting position of the substring in the searched
string. If the alphanumeric string does not contain the substring, the
function returns a zero. The format of the AT function is

. AT(<key substring >,<the alphanumeric string>)

See figure 6.28 for an example. The number returned by the first
AT function, 7, indicates that the substring *M.* begins at the seventh
position in the alphanumeric string *Harry M. Nelson*. Using the
same logic, you can locate the names of all the employees with *M.*
as the middle initial (see fig. 6.29).

```
. ? AT("M.", "Harry M. Nelson")
        7
. ? AT("son", "Harry M. Nelson")
          13
.
```

Fig. 6.28. The AT function.

```
. USE EMPLOYEE
. LOCATE FOR AT("M.",FIRST_NAME)<>0
Record =       4
. ?"The name found is "+TRIM(FIRST_NAME)+" "+LAST_NAME
The name found is Harry M. Nelson
.
```

Fig. 6.29. The AT function with the LOCATE command.

Data Type Conversion Functions

Data type conversion functions in dBASE III change data elements from one type to another. For instance, you can convert a numeric value or the contents of a numeric field to a character string. Similarly, contents of a date field can be converted to a character string, which may then be used in searching or indexing.

The VAL Function

The VAL function converts an alphanumeric string of digits to a numeric value. You specify the alphanumeric string of digits in the argument, and the function returns a numeric value. If the alphanumeric string contains nonnumeric characters, however, the VAL function returns a zero. The format of the function is

. VAL(<an alphanumeric string>)

By using the VAL function, you can enter the contents of an alphanumeric string of digits in a numeric variable or use these contents as part of a numeric expression (see fig. 6.30). If a string containing a decimal number, such as 123.789, is converted to a value by the VAL function, only the rounded integer portion of the string, 124, is returned (see fig. 6.31).

```
. XSTRING="1234"
1234
. VALUEX=VAL(XSTRING)
       1234
. VALUEY=VALUEX+VAL("2345")
       3579
.
```

Fig. 6.30. The VAL function.

```
. ?VAL("123.456")
       123
. ?VAL("123.789")
       124
. ?VAL("1995.95")
      1996
.
```

Fig. 6.31. The VAL function with decimal numbers.

The STR Function

To convert numeric data to an alphanumeric string, you use the STR function. When you specify the numeric value as the argument, the STR function returns an alphanumeric string (see fig. 6.32). The format of the function is

. STR(<a numeric expression>)

```
.  ?STR(1234)
       1234
.  ASTRING=STR(5678)
      5678
.  ?"The converted string is "+ASTRING
The converted string is        5678

.
```

Fig. 6.32. The STR function.

In figure 6.32, the STR converts the numeric value (5678) to the alphanumeric string "5678". As a result, the alphanumeric string is combined with a label ("The converted string is ") to form an alphanumeric expression in a ? command.

As the argument for the STR function, you can also use numeric data fields in a numeric expression. By this process, the contents of alphanumeric fields and numeric fields can be combined as an alphanumeric string to be displayed with a ? command (see fig. 6.33).

```
. USE EMPLOYEE
. LOCATE FOR LAST_NAME="Thompson"
Record =        7
. ?TRIM(FIRST_NAME)+" "+TRIM(LAST_NAME)+"'s salary is "+STR(ANNUAL_PAY)
Mary W. Thompson's salary is        25725

.
```

Fig. 6.33. The STR function with the ? command.

The STR function is important in data manipulation because you cannot mix numeric fields with alphanumeric fields in commands. For instance, if you do not convert the numeric field ANNUAL_PAY to an alphanumeric string and issue the ? command

. ?TRIM(FIRST_NAME)+" "+TRIM(LAST_NAME)+"'s salary
is "+ANNUAL_PAY

you get an error message.

The DTOC Function

Dates are stored in date fields in dBASE III, and many restrictions
are imposed on the way dates can be used for data manipulation. For
example, a date field cannot be used as a key field in the LOCATE
FOR, DISPLAY FOR, and LIST FOR commands. You cannot mix
dates or date variables with alphanumeric strings for displaying.
However, you can use a DTOC (date-to-character) function to
convert a date into a character string. Then the character string can
be used to perform operations that can be carried out only with an
alphanumeric string. The format of the DTOC function is

. DTOC(<a date>)

The date specified in the argument of the function must be the
contents of a date variable or a date field. For instance, if you enter
the command

. ?DTOC("03/08/85")

you will get an **Invalid function argument** error message
because the argument "03/08/85" is an alphanumeric string.

To see how to display a date with an alphanumeric string (such as a
label) by using the DTOC function, refer to figure 6.34.

As shown in figure 6.34, the contents of the date data field
BIRTH_DATE are first assigned to a date variable (BIRTHDATE).
The contents of either the data field or the variable can be converted
to an alphanumeric string to be included in an alphanumeric
expression.

```
. USE EMPLOYEE
. GO BOTTOM
. STORE BIRTH_DATE TO BIRTHDATE
12/24/45
. ?"Contents of the date field is "+DTOC(BIRTH_DATE)
Contents of the date field is 12/24/45
. ?"Contents of the date variable is "+DTOC(BIRTHDATE)
Contents of the date variable is 12/24/45
.
```

Fig. 6.34. The DTOC function.

After converting a date field into a character string, you can use all or a part of the character string to carry out different searching operations. For example, to search for all the employees who were born before 1960, you can use the SUBSTR function to select a substring of the character string DTOC(BIRTH_DATE) for the LIST operation (see fig. 6.35).

As seen in the LIST command in figure 6.35, the DTOC function converts the date field BIRTH_DATE (mm/dd/yy) to an alphanumeric string (mm/dd/yy). The substring that contains the seventh and eighth characters of the alphanumeric string (yy) is extracted by the SUBSTR function and used as a qualifier for the selective LIST operation.

```
. USE EMPLOYEE
. LIST LAST_NAME,BIRTH_DATE FOR SUBSTR(DTOC(BIRTH_DATE),7,2)<="60"
Record#   LAST_NAME   BIRTH_DATE
        1   Smith       07/04/60
        2   Zeller      09/20/59
        4   Nelson      02/15/58
        5   Baker       10/12/56
        7   Thompson    06/18/55
        9   Lee         05/14/39
       10   Hanson      12/24/45
.
```

Fig. 6.35. The DTOC function with the LIST command.

The CTOD Function

Dates can be entered in a date field only as part of the APPEND, BROWSE, or EDIT operations. A date cannot be entered in a date variable with a STORE or an = command. Any one of the following commands results in an error:

. STORE 01/25/85 TO ADATE
. STORE "01/25/85" TO ADATE
. ADATE=01/25/85
. ADATE="01/25/85"

These commands cause confusion for the program because the type of data element you intend to assign to a date variable has not been clearly identified. When you put quotation marks around the date, the data is treated as a character string. On the other hand, without the quotation marks, the date may be misinterpreted as an arithmetic operation (dividing the value of 01 by 25, for instance).

Fortunately, the CTOD (character-to-date) function solves some of these problems. The CTOD function converts an alphanumeric string to a date before the value is entered in a date variable. The format of a CTOD function is

. CTOD(<an alphanumeric string>)

For instance, the following STORE command with a CTOD function enters a date (01/25/85) in the date variable ADATE:

. STORE CTOD("01/25/85") TO ADATE

Similarly, as shown in figure 6.36, you can replace the contents of a date field (BIRTH_DATE) in the active record by a date that is converted from an alphanumeric string (such as 10/10/60).

```
. USE EMPLOYEE
. LOCATE FOR LAST_NAME="Zeller"
Record =      2
. DISPLAY BIRTH_DATE
Record#   BIRTH_DATE
      2  09/20/59
. REPLACE BIRTH_DATE WITH CTOD("10/10/59")
      1  record replaced
. DISPLAY BIRTH_DATE
Record#   BIRTH_DATE
      2  10/10/59

.
```

Fig. 6.36. The CTOD function with the REPLACE command.

The CHR Function

The CHR function returns an ASCII character (see Appendix A) when that character's numeric code is specified in the argument of the function. The format of the function is

. CHR(<numeric code of an ASCII character>)

You can display the ASCII characters by simply specifying their numeric codes as the arguments of the CHR functions (see fig. 6.37).

ASCII characters include control characters, letters, numbers, and symbols. You use a control character, such as CHR(12), to perform a "form feed" operation that ejects a page on the printer. Most ASCII characters are invisible when you enter them at the keyboard. Some require multiple keystrokes. In such cases, the ASCII numeric code for the control character can be printed with a ? command to

```
.  ?CHR(83)
S
.  ?CHR(109)
m
.  ?CHR(105)
i
.  ?CHR(116)
t
.  ?CHR(104)
h
.  ?CHR(83),CHR(109),CHR(105),CHR(116),CHR(104)
S m i t h
.
```

Fig. 6.37. The CHR function.

perform the control operation. For instance, if the printer is activated, the command . *?CHR(12)* will cause the printer to eject the paper to the top of the next page.

The ASC Function

The CHR function shows the ASCII character when you supply the numeric code in the argument; ASC does the reverse. When you specify the ASCII character in the argument, the ASC function returns the corresponding numeric code for the character (see fig. 6.38). The format of the function is

. ASC(<an ASCII character>)

```
.  ?ASC("S")
   83
.  ?ASC("S"),ASC("m"),ASC("i"),ASC("t"),ASC("h")
   83   109   105   116   104
.
```

Fig. 6.38. The ASC function.

Time/Date Functions

dBASE III has a set of functions for processing dates and time. Some of these functions require an argument, but others do not. Although the input data type is a date, the data elements returned by these functions may be numeric values or alphanumeric strings. The date/time functions include TIME, DATE, CDOW, CMONTH, DOW, DAY, MONTH, and YEAR.

The TIME and DATE functions always use as input the current time and date stored in the internal system clock and therefore do not need an argument in the function. The formats are

TIME()
DATE()

The other functions require arguments in the form of a date data field or a date memory variable:

<name of function>(<a date field/variable>)

Descriptions of these functions are given in table 6.1. The BIRTH_DATE date field of the data record of Smith is used as the sample date.

Table 6.1
Summary of Time/Date Functions

Function	Example	Returned Data Element	Returned Data Type
TIME( )	. ?TIME( )	Current system time	Alphanumeric
DATE( )	. ?DATE( )	Current system date	Alphanumeric
CDODW	. ?CDOW(BIRTH_DATE)	Character date of the week	Alphanumeric
CMONTH	. ?CMONTH(BIRTH_DATE)	Character month of the year	Alphanumeric
DOW	. ?DOW(BIRTH_DATE)	Numeric code for day of the week	Alphanumeric
DAY	. ?DAY(BIRTH_DATE)	Numeric code for day of the month	Numeric
MONTH	. ?MONTH(BIRTH_DATE)	Numeric code for month of the year	Numeric
YEAR	. ?YEAR(BIRTH_DATE)	Numeric code for year	Numeric

The ROW( ), COL( ), PROW( ), PCOL( ) Functions

dBASE III has four other functions that find the current cursor position on the screen and the printing position on the printer: ROW(), COL(), PROW(), and PCOL(). When ROW() and COL() are invoked, the respective row and column positions of the cursor are returned. Similarly, the current printing position on the printer can be found by invoking the PROW() and PCOL() functions. These functions are often used in the batch processing mode for controlling the output position on the screen or on the printer; therefore, these functions are discussed in later chapters.

A Summary Example

Functions play an important part in data manipulation. As a summary of the frequently used functions, figure 6.39 provides an example that calculates the ending balance of a beginning principal of $10,000.

```
. DATE1=CTOD("01/25/85")
01/25/85
. DATE2=CTOD("01/25/86")
01/25/86
. DAYS=DATE2-DATE1
       365
. YEARRATE=0.12000000
0.12000000
. DAILYRATE=YEARRATE/365
          0.00032877
. PRINCIPAL=10000
10000
. ENDBALANCE=PRINCIPAL*(1+DAILYRATE)^DAYS

                    11274.74615638
. ?"Ending Balance = ",ROUND(ENDBALANCE,2)
Ending Balance =          11274.75000000
.
```

Fig. 6.39. A summary example.

The example computes the ending balance on 01/25/86 (DATE2) of a savings account that begins with a deposit of $10,000 (PRINCIPAL) on 01/25/85 (DATE1). The annual interest rate (YEARRATE) is assumed to be 12 percent, or 0.12 in decimal form.

Interest earned by the account is computed by compounding daily at the rate of 0.032877 percent (DAILYRATE, determined by dividing the annual rate of 12 percent by 365 days). The number of days elapsed between 01/25/85 and 01/25/86 (DAYS) is computed by taking the difference between the following two dates:

DAYS = DATE2 - DATE1

The ending balance (ENDBALANCE) is then computed with the following formula:

ENDBALANCE = PRINCIPAL x (1 + DAILYRATE)/sD/sA/sY/sS

Chapter Summary

This chapter introduces the concept of memory variables. A memory variable is a name assigned to a memory location for temporarily holding a data element. Four types of memory variables can be used: alphanumeric, numeric, date, and logical. The type of memory variable is determined by the data element stored in the variable. The name of a memory variable can be up to 10 characters long, the first of which must be a letter. The other characters can be letters, digits, or the underscore (_).

Data elements can be entered in alphanumeric, numeric, and logical memory variables with the STORE or = command. However, you cannot assign a string like "03/08/85" to a date variable with the STORE or = command. The date must be converted from an alphanumeric string with the CTOD function before the date can be assigned to a date variable or a date field.

All or part of the active memory variables can be permanently saved in a memory file by the SAVE command. Contents of a memory file can be recalled in part or in whole with the RESTORE command. Active memory variables can be deleted from the memory by the RELEASE command.

Expressions in dBASE III define the operations to be carried out on specified data elements. dBASE III has two types of expressions. An arithmetic expression contains one or more numeric variables or data fields joined by one or more arithmetic operators (+, -, *, /, ^). An arithmetic expression is often used to assign a value to a memory variable or to replace the contents of a numeric data record. An alphanumeric expression consists of one or more alphanumeric strings, alphanumeric variables, or data records joined by plus signs. An alphanumeric expression is used to enter an alphanumeric string in an alphanumeric variable or to replace the contents of a character data field.

This chapter also introduces all the dBASE III functions that you use to convert data elements from one type to another, to manipulate character strings, and to perform mathematical operations. The basic form of a function consists of the name of the function followed by a pair of parentheses. The content within the parentheses is called an argument and supplies the necessary information for the function's operation. Some functions, such as DATE(), TIME(), RECNO(), ROW(), COL(), PROW(), and PCOL(), do not require an argument. Other functions usually require that an argument be specified within the parentheses.

7

Generating Reports

An Overview

In the preceding chapters, you have seen how contents of a data record or a memory variable can be displayed on the screen or printed. This chapter shows two ways to produce custom labels and reports. One method is to display the label or report by issuing one of the following dBASE III commands:

```
?
@ . . . SAY
SET PRINT ON/OFF
SET DEVICE TO PRINT/SCREEN
```

Producing custom labels and reports by these commands can be a tedious process. With the label and report generators provided by dBASE III, however, you can easily produce sophisticated and detailed report forms. The commands used by the label and report generators are the following:

CREATE LABEL
MODIFY LABEL
LABEL FORM
CREATE REPORT
MODIFY REPORT
REPORT FORM

Displaying Data on the Screen

The ? command is one means for displaying items on the screen and sending them to the printer. This command can be used to display one or more data items of different types. Because each item can be a memory variable, a data record, or an expression, you can display a label containing an alphanumeric string, a character data field, a numeric memory variable, and a date field (see fig. 7.1).

```
. SET PRINT OFF
. USE EMPLOYEE
. STORE ANNUAL_PAY TO YEARLYPAY
23100.00
. ?"Employee's last name is ",LAST_NAME,BIRTH_DATE,YEARLYPAY
Employee's last name is  Smith       07/04/60       23100.00
.
```

Fig. 7.1. Displaying a label with the ? command.

You must use commas to separate data items of different types. Data items of different types cannot be displayed with a + sign or a space as the separator, as shown in figure 7.2. The first error message,

```
. USE EMPLOYEE
. STORE ANNUAL_PAY TO YEARLYPAY
23100.00
. ?"Annual salary is "+YEARLYPAY
Data type mismatch
                              ?
?"Annual salary is "+YEARLYPAY
Do you want some help? (Y/N) No
. ?"Employee's birth date is " BIRTH_DATE
Unrecognized phrase/keyword in command
                              ?
?"Employee's birth date is " BIRTH_DATE
Do you want some help? (Y/N) No
.
```

Fig. 7.2. Incorrect label entry without commas to separate items.

Data type mismatch, results from combining an alphanumeric string ("Annual Salary is ") with a numeric variable (YEARLYPAY). The second error message, **Unrecognized phrase/keyword in command** is caused by the space instead of a separator between the label "Employee's Birth Date is " and the date field BIRTH_DATE.

Because the ? command always displays the data items immediately below the command line, this command lacks flexibility: you cannot position the display at a specific screen location. Another type of display command is needed to select a particular screen location for data or results. The dBASE III command for this function is the @..SAY command. The @..SAY command displays a data item of a given type at a given location on the screen or the printed copy.

The format of an @ . . . SAY command is

.@<row>,<column> SAY <the data item to be displayed>

The screen location is specified by a row number and a column number. A screen is divided into 25 rows and 80 columns. Row 1 starts from the top of the screen, and column 1 begins from the farthest left position in a row. Row 1, column 1, refers to the upper left corner of the screen; and the lower right corner of the screen is identified as row 25, column 80.

An example of the @ . . . SAY command is

.@5,10 SAY LAST_NAME

Unlike the ? command, which can display multiple data items, the @ . . . SAY command displays only one data item. The data item in an @ . . . SAY command must be in one of the following forms:

1. An alphanumeric expression, which may consist of one alphanumeric variable or character field or several alphanumeric variables and/or character fields joined by plus signs. (FIRSTNAME is a character variable.)

    @5,10 SAY LAST_NAME+FIRST_NAME+AREA_CODE
    @10,5 SAY LAST_NAME+FIRSTNAME

2. A numeric variable, a numeric data field, or an expression involving more than one numeric variable and/or data field. (YEARLYPAY and UNITPRICE are numeric variables; ANNUAL_PAY and QTY_SOLD are numeric data fields.)

    @5,5 SAY ANNUAL_PAY
    @10,10 SAY YEARLYPAY*1.10
    @7,5 SAY QTY_SOLD*UNITPRICE

3.   A date field or a date variable (BILLDATE)

   @5,10 SAY BIRTH_DATE
   @10,5 SAY BILLDATE

4.   A logical data field or a logical variable (MEMBERSHIP)

   @10,10 SAY MALE
   @5,5 SAY MEMBERSHIP

Row and column numbers in the @ . . . SAY command can also be arithmetic expressions. Using a memory variable as a row number, for example, causes the output to be displayed at different locations when the value of the variable changes:

. STORE 5 TO ROW
. STORE 10 TO COLUMN
. @ROW,COLUMN SAY . . .

The row and column positions for the cursor are stored in the system variables ROW() and COL(), respectively. The information in these two variables does not play a significant role in interactive processing, but these variables provide great flexibility in output placement during batch processing.

An @ command followed by a row and column number without the SAY clause can be used to erase part of a screen display. For instance, the following command erases the fifth line, beginning at column 10:

. @5,10

Another important feature of the @..SAY command is its capability to employ a user-defined template to display output. The template defines which types of characters or symbols are to be displayed and how they should appear. You define the template by adding a PICTURE clause after the output element specified in the @ . . . SAY command:

. @5,10 SAY ANNUAL_PAY PICTURE "$##,###.##"

The string "$##,###.##" following the word PICTURE is a template; it "draws a picture" of the way the value in ANNUAL_PAY is to appear when the number is displayed. The $ and # symbols determine the type of character. The $, for example, tells the program to display dollar signs in place of leading zeros. The # symbols indicate that only digits, spaces, and signs of a value can appear at the positions marked with these symbols. The comma and decimal point instruct the program to place these symbols at the corresponding positions. Assume that the value in the data field ANNUAL_PAY is 28950.95; the number is printed differently when different pictures are given in the @ . . . SAY commands. The following list provides some examples.

If the PICTURE is defined as	*The printed number is*
"$##,###.##"	$28,950.95
"$##,###.#"	$28,950.9
"$##,###"	$28,950
"$###,###.##"	$$28,950.95

Note that "$##,###" produces an integer ($28,950) by ignoring the digits after the decimal point. The string does not round the value to its integer. If you want to round the value of ANNUAL_PAY to its integer ($28,951), you must use one of the following commands:

@5,10 SAY ANNUAL_PAY+0.5 PICTURE "$##,###"
@5,10 SAY ROUND(ANNUAL_PAY,0) PICTURE
"$##,###"

Be sure to enter enough symbols (#) for the total number of digits in a value. Otherwise, ********** is displayed.

Other symbols can also be used in a template. Most of the symbols are for specifying a picture of an input command, but the following symbols are used for displaying output in an @ . . . SAY command:

!   Displays lowercase letters as capital letters.

9   Displays signs and digits in a value.

*   Displays an asterisk in front of a value when the asterisk is followed by 9s; displays asterisks in place of leading zeros when the asterisk is followed by # symbols.

To see how these symbols are used in a template to produce custom formatted output, assume that the following string and value are assigned to the memory variables:

ASTRING="ABCxyz"
BALANCE=-1345.87

In the following examples, the output produced by the sample @ . . . SAY commands is shown next to the corresponding command.

Command	Output
@ . . . SAY ASTRING PICTURE "!!!!!!"	ABCxyz
@ . . . SAY BALANCE PICTURE "99999"	-1345
@ . . . SAY BALANCE PICTURE "999,999.9"	-1,345.8
@ . . . SAY BALANCE PICTURE "*99,999.99"	* -1,345.87
@ . . . SAY BALANCE PICTURE "*##,###.##"	*-1,345.87

Because the @ . . . SAY command can display an alphanumeric expression, @ . . . SAY can show a data element with a label, which is enclosed in quotation marks in the command (see fig. 7.3). However, in the @ . . . SAY command, an alphanumeric string cannot form a label for a numeric or a date variable or data field. Numeric data must be converted to an alphanumeric string by the STR function and then displayed as an alphanumeric expression with the label:

@5,10 SAY "Annual Salary is "+STR(ANNUAL_PAY)

```
. USE EMPLOYEE
. LOCATE FOR LAST_NAME="Nelson"
Record =        4
. @8,5 SAY "Employee's last name is "+LAST_NAME


    Employee's last name is Nelson

.
```

Fig. 7.3. Displaying a label by using the @ . . . SAY command.

Similarly, the DTOC function can be used to convert a date field or variable to an alphanumeric string and display the field or variable in an @ . . . SAY command with a label:

@5,10 SAY "The birth date is "+DTOC(BIRTH_DATE)

Contents of a logical variable or data field cannot be converted to an alphanumeric string because dBASE III lacks a built-in function for this conversion. As a result, an @ . . . SAY command cannot display contents of logical fields with a label.

Printing Data on a Printer

With the ? and @ . . . SAY commands, results are displayed on the screen, but the data can be sent also to a printer. The commands to activate the printer are SET PRINT ON and SET DEVICE TO PRINTER. The two commands are used differently and produce different results.

The SET PRINT ON/OFF Commands

The printer must first be turned on and connected to the computer. Failure to do so results in the computer's locking. In most cases, connecting and turning on the printer unlocks the computer; otherwise, you must restart the computer and reinitiate the dBASE III program.

The SET PRINT ON command activates the printer and directs to the printer and the screen all output that has not been formatted by the @ . . . SAY command. The printer remains activated until it is turned off by the SET PRINT OFF command (see fig. 7.4). The output printed includes the results of the ? command and all the commands entered after the printer is activated:

```
. ?"Employee's name is "+TRIM(FIRST_NAME)+"
"+LAST_NAME
Employee's name is Thomas T. Hanson
. SET PRINT OFF
```

```
. USE EMPLOYEE
. GO BOTTOM
. SET PRINT ON
. ?"Employee's name is "+TRIM(FIRST_NAME)+" "+LAST_NAME
Employee's name is Thomas T. Hanson
. SET PRINT OFF
.
```

Fig. 7.4. Using the SET PRINT ON/OFF commands.

When the printer is activated by the SET PRINT ON command, whatever you enter from the keyboard is reproduced by the printer. As a result, corrections (such as using the Backspace key to delete and reenter characters) appear on the printed copy.

To begin a new page on the printer paper, add an EJECT command before the ? command:

. SET PRINT ON

. EJECT

. ?"Employee's name is "+TRIM(FIRST_NAME)+
" "+LAST_NAME

The SET PRINT ON command is used mainly for directing to the printer the output generated by a ? command. A different command must be used to display output produced by an @ . . . SAY command.

The SET DEVICE TO PRINT/SCREEN Commands

The SET DEVICE TO PRINT command is designed primarily to route to the printer all output generated by @ . . . SAY commands. With the SET DEVICE TO PRINT command, the output elements specified in an @ . . . SAY command are sent to the printer but not to the screen.

The program treats the printed page as if it were a screen: the first print line corresponds to the first row on the screen, and the horizontal printing position is the same as a column. When SET DEVICE TO PRINT is first invoked, the printer automatically ejects the paper enough to begin from the top of a page. In the example in figure 7.5, the output generated by the @ . . . SAY command is printed on the fifth line from the top of the page beginning at the tenth position on the line. The commands are not printed. The printer is deactivated by the command SET DEVICE TO SCREEN.

Creating and Using Custom Labels

With the ? and @ . . . SAY command, designing a label for displaying the contents of data records requires several commands and can be a tedious process. Fortunately, dBASE III provides a tool for creating a custom label, which can be saved in a label file (.LBL) on the disk. The label file can be recalled whenever you want to display the contents of a data record in an active database file. You create a custom label by using the CREATE LABEL command.

```
. USE EMPLOYEE
. LOCATE FOR PHONE_NO="432-6782"
Record =        7
. SET DEVICE TO PRINT
. @5,10 SAY "Phone no."+PHONE_NO+" belongs to "+TRIM(FIRST_NAME)+" "+LAST_NAME
. SET DEVICE TO SCREEN
.
```

Fig. 7.5. Using the SET DEVICE TO commands.

The CREATE LABEL Command

The CREATE LABEL command creates a label file with .LBL as its file identifier. The file contains a two-page form for specifying the design details of a custom label. On the first page of the form, you set the width, height, and spacing of a label. On the second page, you select the data field to be used with the label. The format of the command is

. CREATE LABEL <name of label file>

An example is

. CREATE LABEL EMPLOYEE

The active database file, EMPLOYEE.DBF, and the label file, EMPLOYEE.LBL, have the same name. Because the files have different file extensions, however, the files are treated as unique disk files, and the similar names should not cause any problem. In fact, unless you have more than one label file for a database file, using the same file name may provide clearer reference than using an entirely different name.

In response to the CREATE LABEL command, the first page of a label design form is displayed. All the data fields of the current data record in the active database file are shown at the top of the form (see fig. 7.6).

Below the data field description is a menu to use for defining the format of the label. The default values are given for each choice. **Width of label** indicates the maximum number of characters per line. The total number of lines reserved for a label is specified as **Height of label. Left margin** determines the beginning position of the label line. Because the label can be used for displaying multiple data records, the space (in lines) between labels must also be defined. Multiple labels can be displayed or printed horizontally, so

```
Structure of file B:EMPLOYEE.dbf

FIRST_NAME C  12    MALE       L   1
LAST_NAME  C  10    BIRTH_DATE D   8
AREA_CODE  C   3    ANNUAL_PAY N   8  2
PHONE_NO   C   8


                    Width of label:        35
                    Height of label:        5
                    Left margin:            0
                    Lines between labels:   1
                    Spaces between labels:  0
                    Number of labels across: 1

Remarks:
```

Fig. 7.6. First page of a label design form.

the total number of labels to be displayed across the screen or page
can also be set. The **Remarks** line at the bottom of the screen is
reserved for your notes; the remarks are not displayed as part of the
label. When a label design form is displayed, you can use the arrow
keys to select the menu items for entering new values (see fig. 7.7).

```
Structure of file B:EMPLOYEE.dbf

FIRST_NAME C  12    MALE       L   1
LAST_NAME  C  10    BIRTH_DATE D   8
AREA_CODE  C   3    ANNUAL_PAY N   8  2
PHONE_NO   C   8


                    Width of label:        45
                    Height of label:        4
                    Left margin:           10
                    Lines between labels:   1
                    Spaces between labels:  0
                    Number of labels across: 1

Remarks:  Custom label for an employee's record in EMPLOYEE.dbf file
```

Fig. 7.7. Completed first page of a label design form.

After all the new values have been entered, use the down-arrow key or the RETURN key to move the cursor past the last menu item (the remarks line). The second page of the design form is displayed (see fig. 7.8).

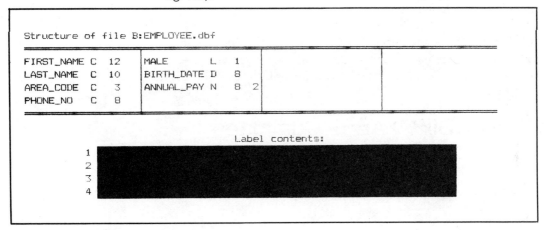

Fig. 7.8. Second page of a label design form.

On the second page of the label design form, you specify the data fields to be displayed on each label line. The format of the label has been determined by the parameters entered on the first page of the design form. On each label line an alphanumeric expression can be specified as the contents of the label. Numeric expressions or dates must be converted to character strings before they can be included in the alphanumeric expression (see fig. 7.9).

```
Structure of file B:EMPLOYEE.dbf

FIRST_NAME C  12    MALE       L   1
LAST_NAME  C  10    BIRTH_DATE D   8
AREA_CODE  C   3    ANNUAL_PAY N   8   2
PHONE_NO   C   8

                        Label contents:
  1 "        Employee:  "+TRIM(FIRST_NAME)+" "+TRIM(LAST_NAME)
  2 "     Telephone No:  "+"("+AREA_CODE+") "+PHONE_NO
  3 "       Birth Date:  "+DTOC(BIRTH_DATE)
  4 "    Annual Salary: $"+STR(ANNUAL_PAY,8,2)
```

Fig. 7.9. Specifying the content of a label.

After all the label lines have been defined, save the label. With the down-arrow key or the RETURN key, move the cursor past the last label line. During the design stage, the up-arrow (or PgUp) and down-arrow (or PgDn) keys can be used to move from one page of the design form to the other. However, when the cursor moves to a position before the first item on the first page or after the last item on the second page, the label is saved on the disk, and the program exits to the dot prompt. If you accidentally exit while designing, you can easily return to the same label by using the MODIFY LABEL command.

The MODIFY LABEL Command

The MODIFY LABEL command returns you to a label file that has already been designed. The format of this command is

. MODIFY LABEL <name of the label file>

For example, when the command

. MODIFY LABEL EMPLOYEE

is invoked, the label design form in EMPLOYEE.LBL is displayed. At this point, you can modify the design form by using the same procedures you used creating the label.

The LABEL FORM Command

The custom label can be used to display or print the contents of the data records. The LABEL FORM command selects the label file with the form for displaying one or more data records in the active database file. The format of the command is

. LABEL FORM <name of the label file>

When the commands

. USE EMPLOYEE
. LABEL FORM EMPLOYEE

are entered, all the data records in the active file (EMPLOYEE.DBF) are displayed according to the label design. A partial display of these data records may look like figure 7.10. You can display selected data records by using a qualifier (FOR . . .) in the LABEL FORM command (see fig. 7.11).

The custom label stored in the label file can also be used to print the contents of data records. You use the LABEL FORM command with

```
. USE EMPLOYEE
. LABEL FORM EMPLOYEE
             Employee: James C. Smith
          Telephone No: (216) 123-4567
            Birth Date: 07/04/60
         Annual Salary: $23100.00

             Employee: Albert K. Zeller
          Telephone No: (212) 457-9801
            Birth Date: 10/10/59
         Annual Salary: $29347.50

             Employee: Doris A. Gregory
          Telephone No: (513) 204-8567
            Birth Date: 07/04/62
         Annual Salary: $17745.00

             Employee: Harry M. Nelson
          Telephone No: (315) 576-0235
            Birth Date: 02/15/58
         Annual Salary: $30450.00

*** INTERRUPTED ***
.
```

Fig. 7.10. Displayed labels from a database file.

```
. USE EMPLOYEE
. LABEL FORM EMPLOYEE FOR AREA_CODE="216"
             Employee: James C. Smith
          Telephone No: (216) 123-4567
            Birth Date: 07/04/60
         Annual Salary: $23100.00

             Employee: Charles N. Duff
          Telephone No: (216) 456-9873
            Birth Date: 07/22/64
         Annual Salary: $14175.00

             Employee: Thomas T. Hanson
          Telephone No: (216) 573-5085
            Birth Date: 12/24/45
         Annual Salary: $30397.50

.
```

Fig. 7.11. Selected records displayed as labels.

a TO PRINT clause added at the end. For instance, the output is directed to the printer by the following command:

. LABEL FORM EMPLOYEE FOR AREA_CODE="206" TO PRINT

Creating and Using the Custom Report Form

A complete report form can also be created and saved in a report form file (.FRM). The report form specifies the details of the headings and their locations in the report. A report form is created with the CREATE REPORT command. For illustrating the creation of a custom report form, the database file QTYSOLD.DBF is used. A listing of the data records in this database file is given in figure 7.12.

The final sales report follows. This sales summary is produced by showing the weekly subtotal for the units sold; the subtotal is identified by the end-of-week date (12/07/84, 12/14/84, etc.).

SUPER STEREO AND TELEVISION STORE
WEEKLY SALES SUMMARY
For the Month of December, 1984

T.V. MODEL	Units Sold
** Week of 12/07/84	2
RCA-XA100	
RCA-XA200	5
ZENITH-19P	4
ZENITH-21C	3
** Subtotal **	
	14
** Week of 12/14/84	2
RCA-XA100	
RCA-XA200	4
ZENITH-19P	3
ZENITH-25C	4
** Subtotal **	
	13
** Week of 12/21/84	8
RCA-XA100	
RCA-XA200	6
ZENITH-19P	6
ZENITH-25C	7
** Subtotal **	
	27

```
** Week of 12/28/84      4
RCA-XA100
RCA-XA200                5
ZENITH-19P               4
ZENITH-25C               2
** Subtotal **

                        15

*** Total ***

                        69
```

```
. USE QTYSOLD
. LIST ALL
Record#   DATE      MODEL        UNITS_SOLD
       1  12/07/84  RCA-XA100             2
       2  12/07/84  RCA-XA200             5
       3  12/07/84  ZENITH-19P            4
       4  12/07/84  ZENITH-21C            3
       5  12/14/84  RCA-XA100             2
       6  12/14/84  RCA-XA200             4
       7  12/14/84  ZENITH-19P            3
       8  12/14/84  ZENITH-25C            4
       9  12/21/84  RCA-XA100             8
      10  12/21/84  RCA-XA200             6
      11  12/21/84  ZENITH-19P            6
      12  12/21/84  ZENITH-25C            7
      13  12/28/84  RCA-XA100             4
      14  12/28/84  RCA-XA200             5
      15  12/28/84  ZENITH-19P            4
      16  12/28/84  ZENITH-25C            2
```

Fig. 7.12. Listing of data records in QTYSOLD.DBF.

The CREATE REPORT Command

Use the CREATE REPORT command to display the report design form. The report form is saved in a disk file after the form is created. The format of the CREATE REPORT command is

. CREATE REPORT <name of report form file>

You can create a custom report form (WEEKLY.FRM) for generating a weekly sales summary from the data records in the active database file QTYSOLD.DBF. Use the following commands:

. USE QTYSOLD
. CREATE REPORT WEEKLY

In response to the CREATE REPORT command, the first page of the
report design form is displayed (see fig. 7.13).

```
Structure of file B:QTYSOLD.dbf

DATE       D   8
MODEL      C  10
UNITS_SOLD N   3



                        Page heading:




             Page width (# chars):          80
             Left margin (# chars):          8
             Right margin (# chars):         0
             # lines/page:                  58
             Double space report? (Y/N):     N
```

Fig. 7.13. First page of a report design form.

At the top of the form, the names of the data fields are shown with
their data types and field widths. Four blank lines are provided for
entering the heading. The lower part of the form is a menu to use
for entering information about the page format. To generate the
sales summary shown previously, enter the information given in
figure 7.14.

When the first page of the design form has been completed, you can
go to the next page of the form design by using the down-arrow key
or the RETURN key to move the cursor beyond the last item on the
screen. (Pressing PgDn does the same thing.) The next page is used
for selecting the numeric data field on which the subtotal is to be
carried out (see fig. 7.15).

In the space after **Group/subtotal on**, enter an arithmetic
expression. Because you want to total all the units sold in a week,
use the DATE field (end-of-the-week date) as the object of the
subtotal operation. The summary report should list all the models

```
Structure of file B:QTYSOLD.dbf

DATE       D    8
MODEL      C   10
UNITS_SOLD N    3
```

```
                          Page heading:

SUPER STEREO AND TELEVISION STORE
WEEKLY SALES SUMMARY
For the Month of December, 1984
```

```
              Page width (# chars):        80
              Left margin (# chars):        8
              Right margin (# chars):       0
              # lines/page:                58
              Double space report? (Y/N):   N
```

Fig. 7.14. Information for generating the sales summary report.

and units sold for each week. Select N to answer the question **Summary report only? (Y/N)**. Otherwise, only the subtotal figures will be displayed with no list of the models and units sold. An answer of N to the question **Eject after each group/ subtotal? (Y/N)** instructs the computer to print all the subtotals on the same page. The heading for the subgroup in the example is *Week of*; enter the heading in the space provided. Because you do not have a second level of subtotals within a week, you can ignore the lower portion of the design form. Figure 7.16 shows the completed second page of the design form.

The next phase of the report form design process is specifying the data fields to be displayed within each subgroup. The sales summary example shows the models and units sold each week. Therefore, in the next part of the design form, you need to specify the field names for the models and units. A field definition form is required for each data field selected. The first field definition form is displayed as soon as you move beyond the second page of the report design form (see fig. 7.17).

In the space for **Field contents**, you can enter one or more data fields as a report field. If only one data field is used, enter the name

```
Structure of file B:QTYSOLD.dbf

DATE        D   8
MODEL       C  10
UNITS_SOLD  N   3

Group/subtotal on:



Summary report only? (Y/N): N      Eject after each group/subtotal? (Y/N): N

Group/subtotal heading:



Subgroup/sub-subtotal on:



Subgroup/subsubtotal heading:
```

Fig. 7.15. Second page of a report design form.

of the data field. Multiple data fields may be combined as an alphanumeric or a numeric expression. If the field contains a numeric data element, specify the number of decimal places to be displayed. If the contents are to be totaled, answer Y to the question **Total? (Y/N)**: .

In the lower portion of each form, four display lines are reserved for the label of data field. After defining the first data field, you can display another form to specify the next data field. To move from one definition form to another, use the up-arrow (or PgUp) key or the down-arrow (or PgDn) key.

The following keystrokes can be used to edit the field selection:

Ctrl-U   Delete the current field shown.

Ctrl-N   Insert a new field.

Ctrl-End   Leave the form design process and save
                  the designed form in the disk file.

```
Structure of file B:QTYSOLD.dbf

DATE       D   8
MODEL      C  10
UNITS_SOLD N   3


Group/subtotal on:              DATE




Summary report only? (Y/N): N         Eject after each group/subtotal? (Y/N): N

Group/subtotal heading:         Week of:




Subgroup/sub-subtotal on:




Subgroup/subsubtotal heading:
```

Fig. 7.16. Completed second page of a report design form.

For the sales summary report, the two fields selected are MODEL and UNITS_SOLD. The fields can be defined with the forms shown in figures 7.18 and 7.19.

Figure 7.18 shows the design form that can be used to specify the first data field (MODEL) to be included in the report. In the space for **Field header**, you enter the desired label for the data field specified. If that data field is a numeric field, you can select the number of decimal places required for the value to be displayed. Furthermore, if you want to display at the bottom of the report the total for the data field, you can enter a Y to the prompt **Total? (Y/N):** . The width of the field is set either to the field width that is specified in the data structure or to the anticipated maximum digits of a value (for a numeric data field), whichever is greater. The field width can also be entered at the keyboard. Figure 7.19 displays the design form for specifying the second data field (UNITS_SOLD); the procedure is the same as that for specifying the first data field (MODEL).

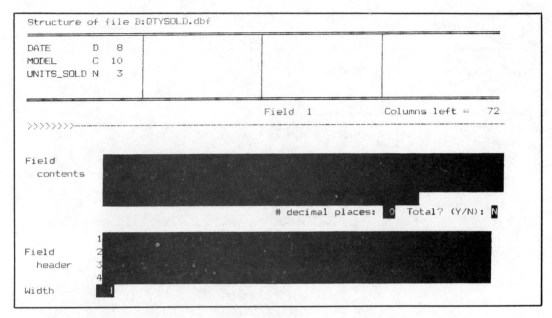

Fig. 7.17. First field definition form in a report design form.

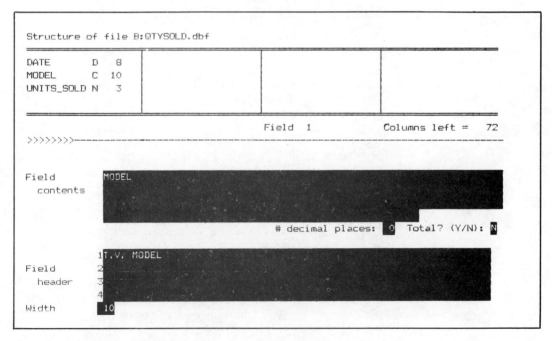

Fig. 7.18. Defining the first fields for the sales summary report.

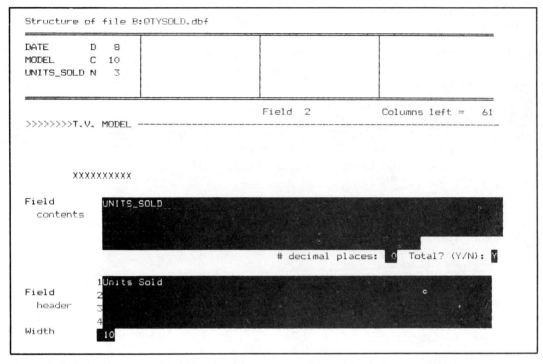

Fig. 7.19. Defining the second field for the sales summary report.

A Sample Custom Report

The sample sales report can be displayed on the screen (if the report is not too long) or printed. Use the report form in WEEKLY.FRM and use QTYSOLD.DBF as the active database file. To use the report form, invoke one of the following commands:

```
. REPORT FORM WEEKLY
. REPORT FORM WEEKLY TO PRINT
```

The first command uses all the data records in the active database file to compile a sales summary report in the format defined in WEEKLY.FRM. The second command routes the same report to the printer. You can also select data records in the database file by including a FOR qualifier in the command.

Two examples are

```
. REPORT FORM WEEKLY FOR MODEL="RCA-XA100" .OR.
MODEL="RCA-XA200"
```

. REPORT FORM WEEKLY FOR DTOC(DATE)<="12/21/84"
TO PRINT

The second command selects in QTYSOLD.DBF the records dated
before 12/21/84. Because the last two digits of all the date fields
in the database file are 84, only the first five characters (mm/dd)
determine the chronological order of the data records. A problem
is that a date like 01/01/85 is considered earlier than 12/01/84.
Because dBASE III compares the strings from left to right, the string
01/01/85 is less than the string 12/01/84. You can solve this
problem by changing the dates to the form yy/mm/dd; 85/01/01
is not considered less than 84/12/01.

After you have designed the report form and saved it to a disk file
(for example, WEEKLY.FRM), if needed, you can use the MODIFY
REPORT command to recall the report for editing or modification.
The format of the command is

. MODIFY REPORT <name of the report form file>

Examples are

. MODIFY REPORT WEEKLY.FRM
. MODIFY REPORT WEEKLY

For the MODIFY REPORT command, the file extension of the file is
automatically assumed to be .FRM. When invoked, the command
retrieves the contents of the report file and displays them on the
screen in the same page sequence as that of the file when it was last
created. At this point, you can modify the contents of the report
form by using the set of editing keystrokes discussed previously.
Afterward, you press Ctrl-End, and the modified report form will be
saved to disk, replacing the original version of the report form. If
you don't make any modifications, you press the Esc key, and the
program will return to the dot prompt.

The preceding example generated custom reports by using single
data fields as report columns (DATE and UNITS_SOLD in the
WEEKLY.FRM). However, you can combine several data fields in an
expression for the field contents. For instance, by using multiple data
fields to produce one report column, you can use the report
generator to create an employee roster from EMPLOYEE.DBF (see
fig. 7.20).

The name of the report form is ROSTER.FRM. The design forms
used to generate the employee roster are displayed in figures 7.21
through 7.26. In figure 7.23, you combine the data fields

```
.  REPORT FORM ROSTER
    Page No.       1
    03/18/85
                              SUPER STEREO AND TELEVISION STORE
                                    Employee Roster


      Employee's Name           Telephone Number Birth Date Annual Salary


        Smith, James C.           (216)  123-4567    07/04/60       23100.00
        Zeller, Albert K.         (212)  457-9801    10/10/59       29347.50
        Gregory, Doris A.         (513)  204-8567    07/04/62       17745.00
        Nelson, Harry M.          (315)  576-0235    02/15/58       30450.00
        Baker, Tina B.            (415)  567-7777    10/12/56       27195.00
        Chapman, Kirk D.          (618)  625-7845    08/04/61       20737.50
        Thompson, Mary W.         (213)  432-6782    06/18/55       25725.00
        Duff, Charles N.          (216)  456-9873    07/22/64       14175.00
        Lee, Winston E.           (513)  365-8512    05/14/39       36645.00
        Hanson, Thomas T.         (216)  573-5085    12/24/45       30397.50


    .
```

Fig. 7.20. Employee Roster report.

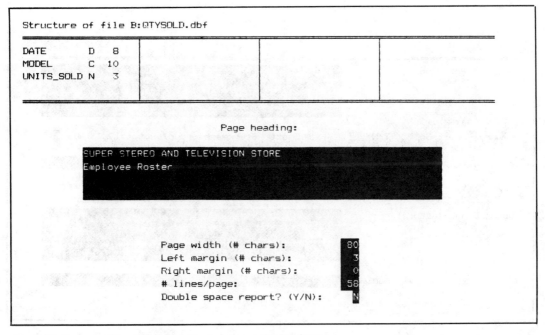

Fig. 7.21. Page 1 of the Employee Roster report design form.

LAST_NAME and FIRST_NAME as an alphanumeric expression that forms the contents of the report field labeled Employee's Name:

. TRIM(LAST_NAME)+", "+TRIM(FIRST_NAME)

Similarly, AREA_CODE and PHONE_NO are included as the contents of the report field Telephone Number (see fig. 7.24).

You can use an alphanumeric expression to define a report field and include a numeric expression as the contents of the report field. For instance, you can generate a salary projection. Using an assumed inflation rate of 5 percent for computing the pay raises for the employees, you can define the projected 1986 salaries by multiplying 1985 salaries (ANNUAL_PAY) by a factor of 1.05:

ANNUAL_PAY*1.05

The salary projection report shown in figure 7.27 can be generated with the report form PROJECTN.FRM. Report fields have been defined with the definition forms shown in figures 7.28 through 7.33.

```
Structure of file B:EMPLOYEE.dbf

FIRST_NAME C  12     MALE       L   1
LAST_NAME  C  10     BIRTH_DATE D   8
AREA_CODE  C   3     ANNUAL_PAY N   8   2
PHONE_NO   C   8

Group/subtotal on:




Summary report only? (Y/N): N        Eject after each group/subtotal? (Y/N): N

Group/subtotal heading:




Subgroup/sub-subtotal on:




Subgroup/subsubtotal heading:
```

Fig. 7.22. Page 2 of the Employee Roster report design form.

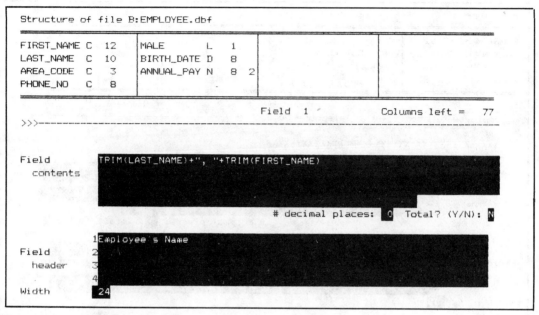

Fig. 7.23. Combining data fields as an alphanumeric expression.

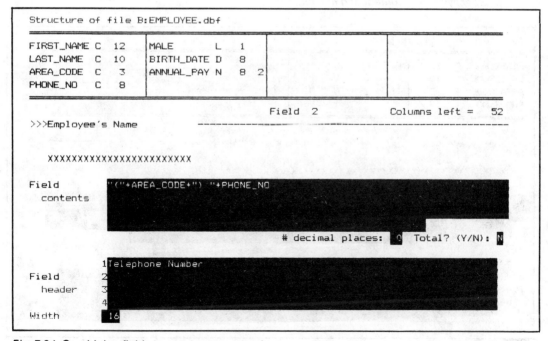

Fig. 7.24. Combining fields to create a report column.

```
Structure of file B:EMPLOYEE.dbf

FIRST_NAME C  12    MALE       L   1
LAST_NAME  C  10    BIRTH_DATE D   8
AREA_CODE  C   3    ANNUAL_PAY N   8   2
PHONE_NO   C   8
```

Field 3   Columns left =   35

>>>Employee's Name   Telephone Number ─────────────────────────

XXXXXXXXXXXXXXXXXXXXXXX XXXXXXXXXXXXX

Field   BIRTH_DATE
contents

decimal places: 0 Total? (Y/N): N

          1 Birth Date
Field   2
header   3
          4
Width   10

Fig. 7.25. Specifying field content and header.

```
Structure of file B:EMPLOYEE.dbf

FIRST_NAME C  12    MALE       L   1
LAST_NAME  C  10    BIRTH_DATE D   8
AREA_CODE  C   3    ANNUAL_PAY N   8   2
PHONE_NO   C   8
```

Field 4   Columns left =   24

>>>Employee's Name   Telephone Number Birth Date ───────────────

XXXXXXXXXXXXXXXXXXXXXXX XXXXXXXXXXXXX   xx/xx/xx

Field   ANNUAL_PAY
contents

decimal places: 2 Total? (Y/N): N

          1 Annual Salary
Field   2
header   3
          4
Width   13

Fig. 7.26. Specifying field content and header.

```
. REPORT FORM PROJECTN
  Page No.       1
  03/18/85

                        SUPER STEREO AND TELEVISION STORE
                              Salary Projections
                          For the Years of 1986-1987
                      (Annual: Annual Inflation Rate = 5%)


  Name of Employee              1985            1986            1987


  James C. Smith              23100.00        24255.00        25467.75
  Albert K. Zeller            29347.50        30814.88        32355.62
  Doris A. Gregory            17745.00        18632.25        19563.86
  Harry M. Nelson             30450.00        31972.50        33571.12
  Tina B. Baker               27195.00        28554.75        29982.49
  Kirk D. Chapman             20737.50        21774.38        22863.09
  Mary W. Thompson            25725.00        27011.25        28361.81
  Charles N. Duff             14175.00        14883.75        15627.94
  Winston E. Lee              36645.00        38477.25        40401.11
  Thomas T. Hanson            30397.50        31917.38        33513.24
  *** Total ***
                             255517.50       268293.38       281708.04

  .
```

Fig. 7.27. Salary projection report.

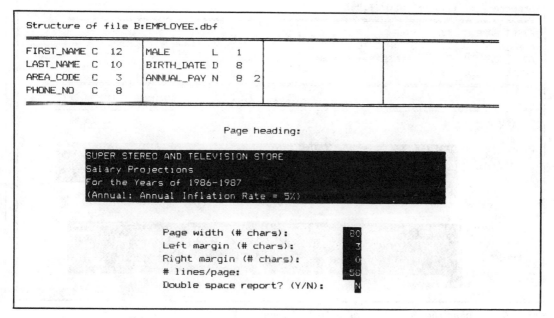

Fig. 7.28. Page 1 of report design form for salary projections report.

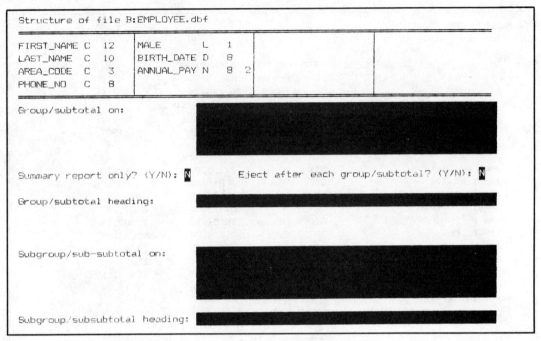

Fig. 7.29. Page 2 of report design form for salary projections report.

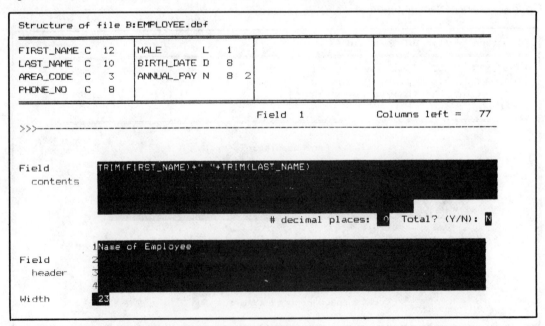

Fig. 7.30. Combining fields for content of a report column.

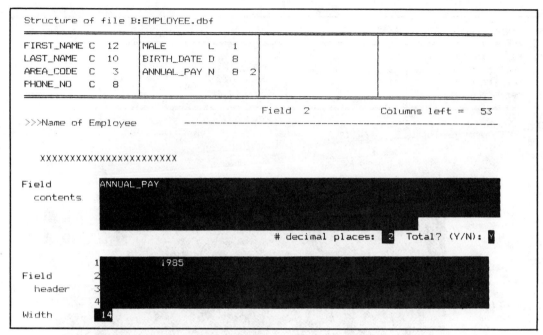

Fig. 7.31. Specifying content and header of a report column.

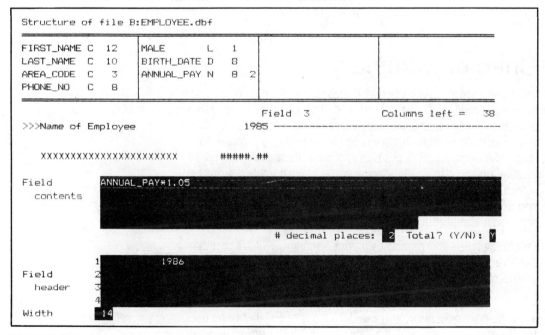

Fig. 7.32. Specifying column content and header.

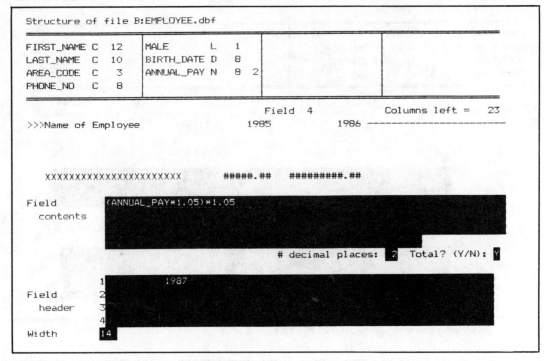

Fig. 7.33. Specifying projection column content.

Chapter Summary

You have learned how to display the contents of a data record or a
memory variable with the ? command. This command, even though
powerful, always begins the display from the farthest left position
and so lacks flexibility. One solution to the problem is to use the
@ . . . SAY command to position an output item at a specified
location on the display. By specifying the row and column on the
screen or the printer, you can place an output element anywhere
you desire. As a result, with the ? and @ . . . SAY commands, you
can design and produce custom labels and reports.

Producing labels and reports using the ? and @ . . . SAY commands,
however, can be tedious. Instead, you can use the label and report
generators in dBASE III to generate with ease custom labels and
reports.

With the label generator, you can design a specific label to be used
for displaying the contents of a data field. With the report generator,

you can design the complete report form, including the labels and data fields. Label and report designs created with these generators can be saved on disk as label and report files. The files can be recalled for displaying data records in an active database file during processing.

8

Fundamentals of Command File Programming

An Overview

You have been using dBASE III commands in the interactive mode. This mode of processing, even though easy to use, is not efficient for repetitive tasks. This chapter presents command file programming, the batch processing mode of data manipulation. Because the scope of command file processing is broad, this chapter begins by introducing the fundamentals of creating and processing a command file. Next, the text covers how a program can be created and edited in the dBASE III text editor and then saved on a disk file. The dBASE III commands discussed in this chapter include the following:

MODIFY COMMAND
DO

SET PRINT ON/OFF
TYPE
TYPE TO PRINT
COPY FILE
ERASE
SET TALK ON/OFF
SET ECHO ON/OFF

Defining a Program

A dBASE III program is a set of dBASE III commands designed to perform a specific task.

As demonstrated in the preceding chapters, dBASE III is an effective program for database management applications. Data in a database file can be manipulated or processed with the dBASE III commands in the interactive mode. The commands required for performing a data management task are entered from the keyboard and executed one by one in sequence. You can monitor your results as the command is being executed. This mode of processing, however, can be tedious, time-consuming, and inefficient for a repetitive task.

You can solve some problems by switching to the batch processing mode. Batch processing involves the creation of a file that contains all the dBASE III commands for a particular task. The collection of commands becomes a program, which is saved on the disk as a command file (or program file). The whole program can then be executed at any time.

A Sample Program

In the interactive mode, you can enter the commands you need to search the EMPLOYEE database file for an employee whose phone number has an area code of 206 (see fig. 8.1). The results of each command are shown as the commands are executed.

```
. USE EMPLOYEE
. LOCATE FOR AREA_CODE="216"
Record =      1
. ? "Employee's Name ........ ", FIRST_NAME, LAST_NAME
Employee's Name ........  James C.     Smith
. ? "Area Code, Phone Number. ", AREA_CODE, PHONE_NO
Area Code, Phone Number.  216 123-4567
.
```

Fig. 8.1. Commands entered in the interactive mode.

.The same set of commands can be entered in a command, or program, file, which looks like the following:

```
***** Program: SAMPLE.PRG *****
* This is a sample program
* Activate the database file
USE EMPLOYEE
* Search for the employee record with "206" as the area code
LOCATE FOR AREA_CODE="206"
* Display the first record found
? "Employee's Name . . . ", FIRST_NAME, LAST_NAME
? "Area Code, Phone Number. ", AREA_CODE, PHONE_NO
* Exit to the dot prompt
RETURN
```

When you execute this set of commands as a batch (or a program file), you see the output shown in figure 8.2.

```
. DO SAMPLE
Record =        1
Employee's Name ........   James C.     Smith
Area Code, Phone Number.   216 123-4567
.
```

Fig. 8.2. Output from a program file.

Program Format

A program consists of lines, each of which instructs the computer to perform a specific operation. The operation may be as simple as displaying a data field or as complicated as performing complex mathematical calculations. The instructions given by the programmer must be "understood" by the computer. To avoid ambiguity, each instruction must follow the specific syntax rules that govern legitimate programming format and the semantic rules that determine the meaning of a command. The syntax rules for dBASE III commands are discussed in the preceding chapters. In most cases, the semantic rules of a dBASE III instruction follow the rules of the English language.

Program Lines

Unlike other computer programming languages, the format for a command line in dBASE III is relatively free with few restrictions. For instance, you may separate words within an instruction line with at least one space. However, dBASE III has one important requirement: Every instruction line must end with a RETURN.

You have two types of instruction lines in a dBASE III program. Comment lines may be used for remark statements that describe the nature of the program and the procedures involved. Using remarks to document the program and make the program more readable is always a good practice. A comment line can consist of any information, but the comment line must always begin with an asterisk (*). The following line is a comment line:

***** Program: SAMPLE.PRG *****

Because comment lines do not play any part in manipulating the database, they are ignored by the computer when the program is executed.

Command lines make up the other type of program lines. Command lines instruct the computer to carry out specific operations. The syntax rules of dBASE III require that each command line begin with a verb, which can be a word (USE, LOCATE) or a symbol (?). The following lines are examples of command lines:

USE EMPLOYEE
LOCATE FOR AREA_CODE = "206"
?"Employee's Name . . . ", FIRST_NAME, LAST_NAME

The line can begin at the first position on the line or be indented for easier reading. You can use both capital and lowercase letters in an instruction line. The maximum length of an instruction line is 256 characters, and spaces are treated as characters.

Creating a Program with MODIFY COMMAND

You can create a program by using the text editor provided by dBASE III. With the text editor, you type the command lines one at a time and simultaneously display the lines on the screen. Information can then be edited or modified before it is saved as a program file on the disk.

To create a new program file with the text editor, use MODIFY COMMAND. Enter the command and the program name at the dot prompt the same way you have been entering other commands:

. MODIFY COMMAND <name of program file>

The file created by MODIFY COMMAND is a command file with PRG as the file identifier. For example, to create a new program, SAMPLE.PRG, which consists of the instruction lines shown previously, you first invoke the text editor by typing

. *MODIFY COMMAND SAMPLE*

The file extension is automatically made PRG when you use MODIFY COMMAND, but you can also create or modify different types of files with this command. In these cases, you must include the file identifier in the file name.

In response to MODIFY COMMAND, the text editor is invoked, and you see the following message displayed at the top of the screen:

dBASE Word Processor

You can immediately start entering the first instruction line of your program. The line begins at the cursor position. When you press the RETURN key at the end of the line, the cursor moves to the beginning of the next line so that you can enter the next program line. Each time you press RETURN, a < symbol, indicating the end of a program line, is displayed at the right edge of the screen. Each program line must end with a RETURN (also called a carriage return or a line feed). When you have a program line longer than 80 characters, keep typing; press RETURN only at the end of the program line. In this case, the line you type may be wrapped around. Even though the wrapped line may not look neat, the content of the line is not affected. The maximum number of characters for one program line is 256; but to make a program more readable, you should write short program lines unless long lines are absolutely necessary. When you must write long program lines, enter a semicolon at the end of the screen line.

During the process of entering program lines, you can use the arrow keys to move the cursor anywhere on the screen so that you can edit the lines. Pressing the Ins (insert) key toggles between the insert and overwrite modes. When you are in insert mode, anything you type is inserted at the cursor position. When the insert mode is off, typed characters overwrite the characters at the cursor position.

In addition, you can use the Del key to delete characters. You can scroll the screen up or down one section at a time with the PgDn or the PgUp keys, respectively. A summary of the functions of the keys that can be used for cursor movements and screen editing is given in table 8.1.

Users who are familiar with WordStar may be glad to learn that they can use that word processor to create and edit a dBASE III program

Table 8.1
Keystrokes Used for Editing under MODIFY COMMAND

Keystroke	Function
Left arrow (←)	Moves cursor left one character
Right arrow (→)	Moves cursor right one character
Up arrow (↑)	Moves cursor up one line
Down arrow (↓)	Moves cursor down one line
Home	Moves cursor to previous word
End	Moves cursor to next word
Ins	Toggles between insert and overwrite modes
Backspace (←)	Deletes character to left of cursor
Del	Deletes character at cursor
Ctrl-Y (^Y)	Deletes line at cursor
Ctrl-T (^T)	Deletes from cursor to next word
PgUp	Scrolls screen down 18 lines
PgDn	Scrolls screen up 18 lines
Esc	Exits from text editor without saving file
Ctrl-W (^W)	Writes (saves) contents on disk and exits to dot prompt
Ctrl-KR (^KR)	Reads another text file into file at cursor position
Ctrl-KW (^KW)	Writes (saves) file to another file

as a nondocument file. Most of the editing commands used by WordStar can be applied to the dBASE III text editor.

Saving a Program

After you have all the program lines entered in the form you want, press Ctrl-W to save the listing in a program file. The message **File is being saved** appears in the top left corner of the screen while the program is being saved. The program file is saved under the name specified by MODIFY COMMAND. The file created with the command, MODIFY COMMAND SAMPLE, for example, is named SAMPLE.PRG.

Executing a Program with the DO Command

After the program has been saved on the disk, you can recall the program for modification or for processing. To execute a program that is saved as a program file, use the DO command.

The DO command instructs the computer to "do" a certain task by following the steps specified in a program file. The object of a DO command must be a program file. The format of the command is

. DO <name of the program file to be executed>

To process the program named SAMPLE.PRG, which was created earlier, enter

.DO SAMPLE

Because the DO command is reserved for program files, you do not need to specify the file extension .PRG in the command. The DO command retrieves and places in RAM the correct program file. The processor is then invoked to interpret and execute each instruction line in the file. The output displayed on the screen when the program SAMPLE.PRG is executed by DO is shown in figure 8.2.

Displaying and Printing a Program Directory

To verify the existence of the program files currently saved on the disk, use the DIR or TYPE command. A DIR command displays a directory of the files on the default disk. For example, the command

. DIR *.PRG

produces a directory of all the program (.PRG) files on the default disk. The asterisk (*), which is also called a wild card, serves as an all-inclusive phrase in the command (see fig. 8.3). dBASE III displays a directory of the program files with information about the total disk memory used and the total number of files.

```
. DIR *.PRG
SAMPLE.PRG

   512 bytes in     1 files.
 49152 bytes remaining on drive.
.
```

Fig. 8.3. Display of a directory.

Printing a Directory

To obtain a printed copy of the displayed directory, you have several alternatives. One way to produce a hard copy of the screen display is to use the "print screen" (PrtSc) key. Make sure that the printer is turned on; then press and hold down the Shift key while you press also the PrtSc key. This keystroke combination reproduces through the printer the screen display (except for some special symbols or lines). This process is called *doing a screen dump*.

Using the SET PRINT ON/OFF Commands

Another way to obtain a hard copy of the program file directory is to use the SET PRINT ON command to activate the printer before you enter the DIR command.

When dBASE III is first brought up, the printer is usually not activated, and the displays are directed only to the screen, or monitor. However, you can choose to have the results of dBASE III commands sent to both the printer and the screen. You can activate the printer with the SET PRINT ON command at any time, and the printer remains on until it is turned off with the SET PRINT OFF command.

To produce a hard copy of the program file directory shown in the last section, use the following commands:

. SET PRINT ON
. DIR *.PRG

When you enter these two commands, the file directory generated by DIR *.PRG is displayed on the screen and printed at the same time. After printing the directory, enter the SET PRINT OFF command at the dot prompt to turn off the printer.

Displaying the Contents of Program Files

After you have written a program and saved it in a program file, you may want to display the file's contents for verification. The DIR command displays only the file directory, but you have several ways to display the actual contents of the files. A program file can be displayed for verification or modification with MODIFY COMMAND. You can also display the contents of a program file with a TYPE command, but you can do no editing. The TYPE command is entered at the dot prompt in the following format:

. TYPE <name of program file>

As shown in figure 8.4, the TYPE command produces on the screen the complete listing of SAMPLE.PRG.

```
***** Program: SAMPLE.PRG *****
* This is a sample program
* Activate the database file
USE EMPLOYEE
* Search for the employee with "206" as his/her area code
LOCATE FOR AREA_CODE="206"
* Display the first record found
? "Employee's Name ........ ", FIRST_NAME, LAST_NAME
? "Area code, Phone Number: ", AREA_CODE, PHONE_NO
* Exit to the dot prompt
RETURN
```

Fig. 8.4. Listing of SAMPLE.PRG after the TYPE command.

Printing the Contents of a Program File

A printed copy of the program listing can be obtained in several ways. You can print portions of a program with Shift-PrtSc while the program is displayed on the screen during the MODIFY COMMAND process. You can also activate the printer with the SET PRINT ON command before you invoke MODIFY COMMAND.

After the printer is activated, the program can be simultaneously displayed on the screen and printed. During editing with the text editor, only one section of the program can be displayed at a time. Therefore, you must scroll the screen to list a program that takes more than one screen to display. As a result, using Shift-PrtSc or SET PRINT ON to obtain a printed copy of the program may not produce a complete listing of the program. To produce the entire listing of a program, use the TYPE TO PRINT command. The command's format is

. TYPE <name of program> TO PRINT

For example, the command

. TYPE SAMPLE.PRG TO PRINT

prints a complete listing of the program SAMPLE.PRG. Other effects of the TYPE TO PRINT and the SET PRINT ON commands are significantly different. The latter command activates the printer and keeps it ON until the printer is turned off by the SET PRINT OFF command. The TYPE TO PRINT command, however, activates the printer during the printing process and automatically deactivates the printer after the program is printed.

Modifying a Program

Program files can be easily modified. To recall a program from the disk, use MODIFY COMMAND. The program file is retrieved and displayed in the text editor. To modify an existing program file, just type the name of the program file in the command. The format of the command is

. MODIFY COMMAND <name of the existing program file>

For example, when the command

. MODIFY COMMAND SAMPLE

is invoked, the program named SAMPLE (the file extension .PRG again is assumed) is displayed in the text editor. After examining the program listing, if you want no changes, you can exit from the text editor by pressing the Esc key. However, if modifications are necessary, edit the program. Use the keystrokes summarized in table 8.1. After making all the necessary changes, press Ctrl-W. The version of the file currently displayed in the text editor replaces the version that was saved on the disk.

Copying a Program

You have seen that a program can be modified and saved with MODIFY COMMAND. However, the original program is lost when the new version is saved on the disk file under the same file name. Therefore, if you need to retain a copy of the original version of the program, you need a different approach. You can create a duplicate copy of the program under a new file name. Then, without disturbing the contents of the original program, you can make the modifications on the duplicate copy.

To copy a program file to another file with a new name, you can use the COPY FILE command (introduced in Chapter 4):

. COPY FILE <existing program name> TO <new program name>

An example of the command is

. COPY FILE SAMPLE.PRG TO SAMPLE1.PRG

To use the COPY FILE command, you must include the file identifiers (.PRG) for the program names in the command. Making the new program the same type as the original program helps to avoid confusion (although this step is not mandatory). The new program, SAMPLE1.PRG, is treated as if it had been created in the text editor and can be examined or modified with MODIFY COMMAND.

Deleting a Program

You can delete a program file from the disk with the ERASE command (see Chapter 4):

. \ERASE <name of program>

When the command

. ERASE SAMPLE1.PRG

is executed, for example, the following message is displayed to indicate that the program has been permanently deleted from the disk:

File has been deleted

Remember that the ERASE command is irreversible. Once erased, a program cannot be recovered.

Controlling Program Output

As you have seen from the screen displays, two types of results are displayed in response to the command DO SAMPLE. The first type consists of interactive messages between dBASE III and the programmer. These messages provide detailed information about a program step. For instance, the message

```
Record =          1
```

is an interactive message that describes the current contents of the record pointer.

The second type of result is generated by the instructions specified in the program. These messages include lines like the following:

Employee's Name . . . James C. Smith
Area Code, Phone Number. 206 123-4567

See figure 8.5 for other examples of interactive messages that result from executing the program. For instance, the two values (38 and 9.5) are interactive messages that describe the values assigned to the two memory variables (HOURS and PAYRATE). This kind of message, although useful for tracing programming steps, can be distracting. Therefore, in most cases during batch processing, the messages should be removed to make the program results more readable. The command to suppress these interactive messages is the SET TALK OFF command.

Note that in this and following figures, the purpose of the screen print is to show the listing of the program but not the steps to create the program.

```
. TYPE SAMPLE1.PRG
*****    Program: SAMPLE1.PRG    *****
*  Program to illustrate interactive messages
HOURS=38
PAYRATE=9.5
?"GROSS PAY =",HOURS*PAYRATE
RETURN

. DO SAMPLE1
38
9.5
GROSS PAY =                    361.0
.
```

Fig. 8.5. File with interactive messages displayed.

Using the SET TALK OFF/ON Commands

The SET TALK OFF command eliminates all the interactive messages during the processing stage. Only the results produced by the display commands (such as DISPLAY, LIST, and ?) are shown as output. You can enter the command at the dot prompt or as an instruction line within a program. To illustrate the effect of the SET TALK OFF command, you can use SAMPLE1.PRG revised as SAMPLE2.PRG (see fig. 8.6).

The only output displayed is that produced by the ? command. All the interactive messages have been eliminated by the inclusion of a SET TALK OFF command. When it is invoked, it remains in effect until a SET TALK ON command is entered. A SET TALK ON command instructs the computer to display all the interactive messages during the processing stage. SET TALK ON is usually the default setting for dBASE III.

```
. TYPE SAMPLE2.PRG
*****    Program: SAMPLE2.PRG    *****
* Show effects of SET TALK OFF
SET TALK OFF
HOURS=38
PAYRATE=9.5
?"GROSS PAY =",HOURS*PAYRATE
RETURN

. DO SAMPLE2
GROSS PAY =                   361.0
.
```

Fig. 8.6. Effect of the SET TALK OFF command.

Tracing Program Errors during Execution

Some interactive messages are undesirable and should be removed by the SET TALK OFF command, but other interactive messages are helpful for locating program errors during program execution. You can display these messages by using the SET ECHO ON command.

The SET ECHO ON command displays each command line as it is executed. These interactive messages leave a trail by which you can locate a program error in a specific command line. To illustrate the usefulness of this command, two errors are intentionally incorporated in the program shown in figure 8.7.

```
. TYPE SAMPLE3.PRG
*****   Program: SAMPLE3.PRG   *****
* A sample program with two errors
SET TALK OFF
HOURS-38
PAYRATE=9.5
? "GROSS_PAY = "; HOURS*PAYRATE
RETURN

.
```

Fig. 8.7. Program with errors.

The two errors introduced to instruction lines in the program are the following:

1. A minus sign (-) is used for assigning a value (38) to the memory variable HOURS in the instruction, as in the following:

    HOURS-38

    An equal sign (=) should be used instead of the minus sign.

2. A semicolon (;) is used to separate the string "GROSS PAY = " from the results of the formula HOURS*PAYRATE:

    ? "GROSS PAY = "; HOURS*PAYRATE

    A comma (,) should be used instead of the semicolon.

When you execute the program with the DO SAMPLE3 command, you see the results shown in figure 8.8.

```
. DO SAMPLE3
*** Unrecognized command verb
Called from - B:SAMPLE3.prg
Terminate command file? (Y/N)
```

Fig. 8.8. First error message.

The first error message *** Unrecognized command verb is displayed when the first error is encountered. The line

Called from - B:SAMPLE3. PRG

indicates that the error came from the program SAMPLE3.PRG on the default disk drive, B. When an error in the program is encountered, you can skip that command line by typing N in response to the question

Terminate command file ? (Y/N)

When you type N, the next program line will be executed. The first error message does not show the program line where the error was detected. As a result, the message **Unrecognized command verb** does not provide enough information as to what verb and which command line are involved. Therefore, you may need to use the SET ECHO ON command to display each command line as it is executed. If an error is found, the command line is displayed with the error message. To illustrate this application, a SET ECHO ON command is added to the beginning of the program SAMPLE4.PRG (see fig. 8.9).

```
. TYPE SAMPLE4.PRG
*****    Program: SAMPLE4.PRG    *****
* Show effects of SET ECHO ON
SET TALK OFF
SET ECHO ON
HOURS-38
PAYRATE=9.5
? "GROSS_PAY = "; HOURS*PAYRATE
RETURN

.
```

Fig. 8.9. File with SET ECHO ON.

When you execute the program, you see the results shown in figure 8.10. Each command line is displayed as it is executed. As a result, the program execution can be monitored step by step. For instance, the first error message ***** Unrecognized command verb** is shown immediately after the command line HOURS-38, so you can tell where the error is.

The information contained in the second error message is far more precise in pointing to the exact location of the error found in a command line. The second error message **Unrecognized phrase/keyword in command** is displayed with a question mark (?) above the line where the error is found. The question mark points to the character (space) following the semicolon (the error in this example).

```
. DO SAMPLE4
SET TALK OFF
SET ECHO ON
HOURS-38
*** Unrecognized command verb
Called from - B:SAMPLE4.prg
Terminate command file? (Y/N) No
PAYRATE=9.5
? "GROSS_PAY = "; HOURS*PAYRATE
Unrecognized phrase/keyword in command
                    ?
? "GROSS_PAY = "; HOURS*PAYRATE
Called from - B:SAMPLE4.prg
Terminate command file? (Y/N) No
RETURN
.
```

Fig. 8.10. Results of SET ECHO ON.

Chapter Summary

This chapter introduces another approach to data manipulation with dBASE III commands. Instead of using the interactive mode of processing, you can perform data processing tasks by collecting all the necessary commands to form a command, or program, file. The program file, as a batch, is then executed with a DO command.

To create a new program file, you begin by invoking the dBASE III text editor with MODIFY COMMAND. You can use the same command for editing existing program files. After a program has been edited, you can save the program on the disk file. The program can later be recalled for further modifications or for processing.

This chapter introduces a number of ways in which a program file can be displayed or printed. You can print a hard copy of the program file by using the TYPE TO PRINT command. The SET PRINT ON command activates the printer, and SET PRINT OFF turns off the printer. A hard copy of the screen display can also be made by doing a screen dump. To provide intermediate monitoring of the execution process, you can use the SET TALK ON command. To trace a program error during execution, use the SET ECHO ON command.

9

Programming Input and Output Operations

An Overview

This chapter explains how to use input commands to enter and modify data. The new commands are the following:

    CLEAR
    ACCEPT TO
    INPUT TO
    WAIT TO
    APPEND BLANK
    @ . . . SAY . . . GET
    READ

The two basic commands for displaying output (? and @ . . . SAY) were introduced in Chapter 7. This chapter explains how to print custom reports by using these commands with the SET PRINT ON and SET DEVICE TO PRINT commands.

Entering Data in Memory Variables

Memory variables are important in data manipulation. Variables are often used to store the results of a calculation that will be used again. Memory variables can also store data that will replace the contents of another data record. In some cases, a set of memory variables can even be used as a small database file.

Data is entered in memory variables many different ways. The STORE and = commands assign a value or an alphanumeric string to a numeric, character/text, or logical variable, such as

```
. STORE 123.45 TO VALUEX
VALUEX=123.45
. STORE "Mary J. Smith" TO BUYERNAME
BUYERNAME="Mary J. Smith"
. STORE .T. TO MEMBERSHIP
MEMBERSHIP=.T.
```

To enter data in these variables with the STORE or = commands, you must specify the values in the command lines. For example, the program in figure 9.1 assigns an alphanumeric string ("206") to the memory variable AREACODE. The variable AREACODE is used later as a search key in the LOCATE command line.

```
.TYPE AREACODE.PRG
***** Program: AREACODE.PRG *****
* Find the first record with area code of "206"
SET TALK OFF
SET ECHO OFF
* Specify the area code to be located
AREACODE="206"
* Select the database file
USE EMPLOYEE
* Search for such an area code
LOCATE FOR AREA_CODE=AREACODE
* Show the data record found
DISPLAY
RETURN
.
```

Fig. 9.1. Using memory variables.

The output from this program is shown in figure 9.2.

Every time the program is executed, the alphanumeric string "206" is assigned to the memory variable. To search for a data record with

```
. DO AREACODE
Record# FIRST_NAME LAST_NAME AREA_CODE PHONE_NO MALE BIRTH_DATE ANNUAL_PAY
      1   James C.   Smith      206     123-4567 .T.  07/04/60    22000.00
.
```

Fig. 9.2. Output generated by the memory variable program.

the area code 415, you need to change the command line that assigns the alphanumeric string to the memory variable AREACODE:

AREACODE="415"

After entering the change, you must use the text editor to modify the program and then reexecute it. Because you must change the alphanumeric string whenever you search for a new area code, this kind of data search operation is inefficient. However, with the ACCEPT command, the same program can search for different area codes.

ACCEPT TO

With the ACCEPT TO command, you can assign an alphanumeric string to a memory variable outside the program. ACCEPT TO enters the string in an alphanumeric memory variable and can be used with or without a prompting message. The prompt must be enclosed in quotation marks, such as

. ACCEPT <prompt> TO <name of alphanumeric memory variable>

For example, you could enter the following commands:

. ACCEPT TO AREACODE

. ACCEPT "Enter the area code to be searched . . . " TO AREACODE

Figure 9.3 shows an example of an ACCEPT command.

When the program is executed, the prompt and a blinking cursor appear. At this point, you can enter the answer to the prompt. As soon as the RETURN key is pressed, the data element is assigned to the memory variable AREACODE. Then the memory variable is used as a search key for the LOCATE command. This program produces the output shown in figure 9.4.

```
. TYPE PROMPT.PRG
*****   Program: PROMPT.PRG   *****
* Find the first record with an area code keyed in
SET TALK OFF
SET ECHO OFF
* Prompt for the area code to be located
ACCEPT "Enter the area code to be searched .... " TO AREACODE
USE EMPLOYEE
LOCATE FOR AREA_CODE=AREACODE
DISPLAY
RETURN

.
```

Fig. 9.3. The ACCEPT command.

```
. DO PROMPT
Enter the area code to be located .... 415
Record#  FIRST_NAME   LAST_NAME   AREA_CODE  PHONE_NO  MALE  BIRTH_DATE  ANNUAL_PAY
     5   Tina B.      Baker       415        567-7777  .F.   10/12/56     27195.00
. DO PROMPT
Enter the area code to be located .... 212
Record#  FIRST_NAME   LAST_NAME   AREA_CODE  PHONE_NO  MALE  BIRTH_DATE  ANNUAL_PAY
     2   Albert K.    Zeller      212        457-9801  .T.   10/10/59     29347.50
. DO PROMPT
Enter the area code to be located .... 513
Record#  FIRST_NAME   LAST_NAME   AREA_CODE  PHONE_NO  MALE  BIRTH_DATE  ANNUAL_PAY
     3   Doris A.     Gregory     513        204-8567  .F.   07/04/62     17745.00
 .
```

Fig. 9.4. Output from a program with ACCEPT.

When you enter a different area code, you do not need to modify the program PROMPT.PRG to display another data record. With an ACCEPT command, only an alphanumeric string can be assigned to a character variable. The ACCEPT command cannot be used to enter data in numeric or logical variables.

A value can be entered in a numeric variable with the ACCEPT command, however, if the value is treated as an alphanumeric string. After the value is entered, the alphanumeric variable can be converted to a numeric variable with the VAL function (see Chapter 6).

The program shown in figure 9.5 is an example. The values (123 and 234) are assigned to the variables X and Y as alphanumeric strings. Then the alphanumeric variables are converted to numeric variables with the VAL function:

```
. TYPE XPLUSY.PRG
*****  Program: XPLUSY.PRG  *****
* A program to add X and Y
* Prompt for values of variables X and Y
ACCEPT "Enter value for X =" TO X
ACCEPT "      value for Y =" TO Y
* Convert strings X and Y to numeric values
X=VAL(X)
Y=VAL(Y)
? "Sum of X and Y =",X+Y
RETURN

. DO XPLUSY
Enter value for X =123
      value for Y =234
Sum of X and Y =          357
.
```

Fig. 9.5. Converting to a numeric variable.

$$X=VAL(X)$$
$$Y=VAL(Y)$$

The VAL function converts the alphanumeric string to a numeric value and assigns that value to the variable X. VAL rounds the decimal value of an alphanumeric string to the integer. However, even though the decimal point and the digits to the right of the decimal point are not shown, VAL retains the digits in the variable (see fig. 9.6).

```
. TYPE VALUEOFX.PRG
*****   Program: VALUEOFX.PRG   *****
* Illustrate effects of VAL function
X="123.85"
* X is an alphanumeric string
? VAL(X)
? VAL(X)+200
? VAL(X)*100
RETURN

. DO VALUEOFX
      124
      324
      12385
.
```

Fig. 9.6. The results of a VAL function.

The first ? command displays the contents of the alphanumeric string X. The second and third ? commands show that the value returned by the VAL function is 124 (123.85 rounded to the integer). The fourth ? command, which displays the results of multiplying VAL(X) by 100, shows that the original digits have been retained. With the help of the VAL function, the ACCEPT command can be used to assign a decimal value to a numeric variable. For instance, the following instruction lines can be used to assign the value of 123.85 to the numeric variable X:

```
. ACCEPT "Enter a value for X . . . " TO X
  X=VAL(X)*100/100
```

The value of VAL(X)*100 is 12385. The value is then divided by 100, and the result (123.85) is entered in the variable X.

As you can see, entering a value in a numeric variable is a lengthy procedure with ACCEPT. Fortunately, another command can be used to enter numeric data or an alphanumeric string in a memory variable. This command is the INPUT command.

INPUT TO

INPUT assigns a data element to a memory variable in the following form:

. INPUT "<a prompting message>" TO <name of the memory variable>

An example of the INPUT command is

. INPUT "Enter Employee's Last Name : " TO LASTNAME

The INPUT command was designed for programs that request data from the keyboard during execution. The prompt asks you to enter and label the data element. Possible data elements include

an alphanumeric string enclosed in quotation marks
a numeric value
a date
a logical state (T or F)

The variable type is determined when you enter the data element. If the data element is an alphanumeric string, you must enclose it in quotation marks. To enter a date to a memory variable, you must convert the date from a character string, using the DTOC function. A logical field requires an answer in the form of .T. or .F. (including the periods). The program in figure 9.7 shows how to enter various data elements in different memory variables.

```
*****    Program: INPUTING.PRG    *****
* A program show how to use an INPUT command
SET TALK OFF
SET ECHO OFF
?
?
?
INPUT "  Enter:        Today's Date .... " TO DATE
?
INPUT "              Customer's Name .... " TO CUSTOMER
?
INPUT "            Amount of Purchase ... " TO AMOUNT
?
INPUT "    Cash Purchase (.T. or .F.)? " TO CASH
?
?
?
? "      Contents of variables:"
? "         DATE ="+DTOC(DATE)
? "     CUSTOMER ="+CUSTOMER
? "       AMOUNT = "+STR(AMOUNT,5,2)
? "         CASH = ",CASH
RETURN
```

Fig. 9.7. Entering data elements to memory variables with the
INPUT TO command.

After you answer the input statements, the prompt appears (see fig. 9.8). Then you can enter the data elements in the memory variables.

An alphanumeric string must be enclosed in quotation marks before being assigned to a variable. A date entered as "03/15/85" is an alphanumeric string.

WAIT TO

With the WAIT command, you can enter a single character to an alphanumeric variable. The format of WAIT is

. WAIT "<a prompting message>" TO <name of memory variable>

as in

. WAIT "Do You Want to Continue (Y/N)?" TO CHOICE

```
. DO INPUTING


Enter:      Today's Date .... CTOD("03/15/85")

          Customer's Name .... "Adam S. Smith"

        Amount of Purchase ... 95.55

    Cash Purchase (.T. or .F.)? .T.



    Contents of variables:
        DATE =03/15/85
    CUSTOMER =Adam S. Smith
      AMOUNT = 95.55
        CASH =  .T.
  .
```

Fig. 9.8. Contents of memory variables.

The WAIT command is similar to the ACCEPT command except for minor differences. With the WAIT command, you can enter only one character to a variable, whereas the ACCEPT command assigns alphanumeric strings of any size. The ACCEPT command requires that you end the data element by pressing RETURN, but the RETURN keystroke is not necessary with the WAIT command.

WAIT is often used in programs that prompt for the answer to a decision variable. The answer is applied to conditional transfer commands, such as IF . . . ENDIF and DO CASE. The next chapter explains more uses of the WAIT command.

Editing Data Records

The ACCEPT command can also be used in a program to locate a specific data record. By using a number of ACCEPT commands, you can enter multiple search keys in several memory variables. Then the search keys are used in a LOCATE command as conditional qualifiers. The data record that meets the conditions will be displayed for editing. For example, suppose that you need to modify a specific data record in the EMPLOYEE.DBF database file. To find the data record for the employee, use FIRSTNAME and LASTNAME as the memory variables for the search keys (see fig. 9.9).

When the program is executed, a prompt appears for the variables FIRSTNAME and LASTNAME (see fig. 9.10).

```
. TYPE EDITIT.PRG
*****   Program: EDITIT.PRG   *****
* Program to edit an employee's record
SET TALK OFF
SET ECHO OFF
*  Clear the screen
CLEAR
USE EMPLOYEE
*  Get the employee's name
ACCEPT "Enter Employee's First Name .... " TO FIRSTNAME
ACCEPT "              Last Name ..... " TO LASTNAME
*  Search for the employee's record
LOCATE FOR LAST_NAME=LASTNAME .AND. FIRST_NAME=FIRSTNAME
*  Edit current record
EDIT RECNO()
RETURN

.
```

Fig. 9.9. Using memory variables as search keys with the EDITIT.PRG.

```
Enter Employee's First Name .... Doris
              Last Name ..... Gregory
```

Fig. 9.10. Results of the editing program.

After you enter the data elements, the program finds the record that meets the conditional qualifier (FOR LAST_NAME=LASTNAME .AND. FIRST_NAME=FIRSTNAME). You can display and edit the contents of the record with the following command:

    . EDIT RECNO()
    . EDIT

RECNO() contains the number of the current data record. If record 4 is found, for example, the command EDIT RECNO() is the same as EDIT 4. With EDIT RECNO(), you can display and edit the current record (see fig. 9.11).

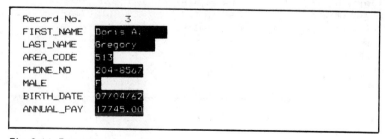

Fig. 9.11. Record to be edited.

Then you can edit the displayed record (see Chapter 4). After you have finished editing, you can press Ctrl-End to save the edited record and exit the program.

As you can see in figure 9.11, the data fields are labeled with the field names specified in the data structure. Because a data field name is limited to ten characters, the name may not provide a clear description of the data field. To solve the problem, you can use a set of custom labels defined with @ . . . SAY commands (see Chapter 7). The @ . . . SAY command specifies the row and column number of the label to be displayed. The label is enclosed in quotation marks, following the word SAY. Then a GET clause links the label with a specific data field in the record to be edited, such as

@5,10 SAY "Employee's First Name : " GET FIRST_NAME

When the command is executed, the label "Employee's First Name:" is displayed at row 5, column 10. Following the label, blank spaces are displayed for you to enter the FIRST_NAME field. The number of blank spaces depends on the length of the data field. The program in figure 9.12 shows how to design a custom form.

```
. TYPE EDITIT1.PRG
*****    Program: EDITIT1.PRG    *****
* Another program to edit an employee's record
* using custom labels for data fields
SET TALK OFF
SET ECHO OFF
CLEAR
USE EMPLOYEE
ACCEPT "Enter Employee's First Name .... " TO FIRSTNAME
ACCEPT "            Last Name ..... " TO LASTNAME
LOCATE FOR LAST_NAME=LASTNAME .AND. FIRST_NAME=FIRSTNAME
* Create custom labels for data fields
@5,10  SAY "Employee's First Name : " GET FIRST_NAME
@7,10  SAY "            Last Name : " GET LAST_NAME
@9,10  SAY "           Area Code : " GET AREA_CODE
@11,10 SAY "           Phone No. : " GET PHONE_NO
@13,10 SAY "          Male?(T/F) : " GET MALE
@15,10 SAY "          Birth Date : " GET BIRTH_DATE
@17,10 SAY "        Annual Salary : $" GET ANNUAL_PAY
READ
RETURN

.
```

Fig. 9.12. Creating custom labels.

After you enter the data for the variables (FIRSTNAME, LASTNAME), the editing screen is displayed (see fig. 9.13).

```
Enter Employee's First Name .... Harry
                  Last Name ..... Nelson


              Employee's First Name :  Harry M.

                         Last Name :  Nelson

                         Area Code :  315

                         Phone No. :  576-0235

                      Male?(T/F) :  T

                        Birth Date :  02/15/58

                     Annual Salary : $ 30450.00
```

Fig. 9.13. The editing screen.

The cursor is positioned at the first data field, which is a result of the READ command.

When a READ command is encountered in a program, the cursor is positioned at the first field specified in the @ . . . GET instruction line. Then the program waits for you to enter a new data element in the data field. Arrow keys can be used to move the cursor to another data field for editing. However, you should not move the cursor off the screen before all the data elements have been entered. When the cursor is moved off screen, the program saves the entered data and returns to the dot prompt.

The set of @ . . . SAY commands in the program EDITIT1.PRG can be saved as a template in a format file (.FMT) and used again in other programs. A format file can be created with the text editor, using the command

. MODIFY COMMAND <name of format file>

as in

. MODIFY COMMAND EDITFORM.FMT

To avoid confusion, the file extension of a format file (.FMT) should be attached to the file name. When the text editor is invoked, the set of @ . . . SAY commands can be entered (see fig. 9.14).

```
dBASE Word Processor
*****    A Format File : EDITFORM.FMT    *****
*  Create a format file for editing an employee's record
@5,10   SAY "Employee's First Name : " GET FIRST_NAME
@7,10   SAY "          Last Name : " GET LAST_NAME
@9,10   SAY "          Area Code : " GET AREA_CODE
@11,10  SAY "          Phone No. : " GET PHONE_NO
@13,10  SAY "         Male?(T/F) : " GET MALE
@15,10  SAY "         Birth Date : " GET BIRTH_DATE
@17,10  SAY "      Annual Salary : $" GET ANNUAL_PAY
```

Fig. 9.14. A format file with @ . . . SAY commands.

Adding New Data Records

New data records can be added to a database file with a program that defines the necessary steps. For example, the following program adds a new data record to EMPLOYEE.DBF with an APPEND command (see fig. 9.15).

```
. TYPE APENDIT.PRG
*****    Program: APENDIT.PRG    *****
*  Program to append an employee's record
SET TALK OFF
SET ECHO OFF
*  Clear the screen
CLEAR
*  Select the database file
USE EMPLOYEE
*  Append new record to active database file
APPEND
RETURN

.
```

Fig. 9.15. Program to append record.

When you execute the program, the data entry form is displayed (see fig. 9.16).

At this point, you can enter a new set of data elements. As soon as the data record is added, you can press the Ctrl-End key combination to save the new record and exit from the program.

Fig. 9.16. Data entry form.

APPEND BLANK

An APPEND BLANK command displays and appends a data entry form without data field labels. You can attach custom labels to data fields to provide detailed descriptions. Labels can be defined by @ . . . SAY commands and can be used either as a part of the program or to format a file that has been saved on disk. Figure 9.17 shows how to design a custom screen to append a new record to EMPLOYEE.DBF with @ . . . SAY commands.

```
. TYPE APENDIT1.PRG
*****    Program: APENDIT1.PRG    *****
*   Another program to append an employee's record
SET TALK OFF
SET ECHO OFF
USE EMPLOYEE
CLEAR
*   Append new record with custom labels
APPEND BLANK
*   Show current record number
? "Enter Data for Record No.", RECNO()
@5,10   SAY "Employee's First Name : " GET FIRST_NAME
@7,10   SAY "          Last Name : " GET LAST_NAME
@9,10   SAY "          Area Code : " GET AREA_CODE
@11,10  SAY "          Phone No. : " GET PHONE_NO
@13,10  SAY "         Male?(T/F) : " GET MALE
@15,10  SAY "         Birth Date : " GET BIRTH_DATE
@17,10  SAY "      Annual Salary : $" GET ANNUAL_PAY
READ
RETURN
.
```

Fig. 9.17. Designing a custom screen with @ . . . SAY.

When the program is executed, the custom labels for the new record appear (see fig. 9.18).

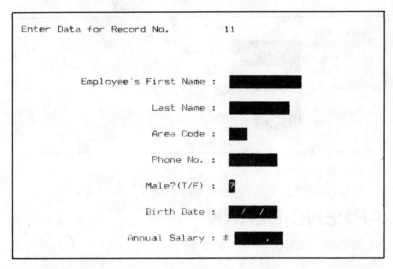

```
Enter Data for Record No.        11



        Employee's First Name :  ████████████

                   Last Name :  ██████████

                   Area Code :  ███

                   Phone No. :  ██████████

                 Male?(T/F) :  ▓

                 Birth Date :  ████ /  /

               Annual Salary :  $ ████████ .
```

Fig. 9.18. Custom labels of data field.

You can also use the format file EDITFORM.FMT to create custom labels (see fig. 9.19).

```
. TYPE APENDIT2.PRG
*****  Program: APENDIT2.PRG  *****
*   Aappend employee's record with a format file
SET TALK OFF
SET ECHO OFF
USE EMPLOYEE
*   Append new record with custom labels in EDITFORM.FMT
SET FORMAT TO EDITFORM.FMT
APPEND BLANK
READ
RETURN

.
```

Fig. 9.19. Using EDITFORM.FMT.

The results of APENDIT2.PRG (fig. 9.17) are identical to the results of APENDIT1.PRG (fig. 9.18).

In the preceding examples, the entry form for editing a data field has been displayed in reverse video. The data field on the entry form is shown by a shaded block. For example, a data entry form on an IBM monochrome monitor will show black characters on a bright green background, while other text is displayed as green characters on a black background. dBASE III displays the data field in reverse video by default. However, you can change the display mode with the SET DELIMITER command.

SET DELIMITER ON/OFF

With the SET DELIMITER ON/OFF command, you can use a pair of symbols to indicate the width of a data field on the data entry form. To set the delimiter, use the following two commands:

. SET DELIMITER ON
. SET DELIMITER TO <delimiter symbol(s)>

An example of the command is

. SET DELIMITER TO "[]"

When dBASE III is started, the delimiter is *off* and uses reverse video to mark a data field. To choose a different delimiter, you must activate the delimiter with the SET DELIMITER ON command. When the delimiter is set to *on*, you can specify the symbol to mark a data field. Symbols such as [], { }, or quotation marks can be used to mark the beginning and end of a data field. You can also specify only one symbol (such as #) as the delimiter. In this case, the same symbol will be used to mark the beginning and the end of the data field. For example, the following program uses the symbols [] to mark the data fields for the editing operation (see fig. 9.20).

```
. TYPE APENDIT3.PRG
***** Program: APENDIT3.PRG  *****
*  Another program to append an employee's record
SET DELIMITER ON
*  Set brackets [] as delimiter
SET DELIMITER TO "[]"
USE EMPLOYEE
CLEAR
*  Append new record with custom labels
APPEND BLANK
*  Show current record number
? "Enter Data for Record No.", RECNO()
@5,10  SAY "Employee's First Name : " GET FIRST_NAME
@7,10  SAY "           Last Name : " GET LAST_NAME
@9,10  SAY "           Area Code : " GET AREA_CODE
@11,10 SAY "           Phone No. : " GET PHONE_NO
@13,10 SAY "          Male?(T/F) : " GET MALE
@15,10 SAY "         Birth Date : " GET BIRTH_DATE
@17,10 SAY "      Annual Salary : $" GET ANNUAL_PAY
READ
RETURN

.
```

Fig. 9.20. Setting the delimiter with [ ].

When you execute the program, the following entry form is
displayed.

```
Enter Data for Record No.          11



            Employee's First Name :   [              ]

                     Last Name :   [           ]

                     Area Code :   [   ]

                     Phone No. :   [        ]

                   Male?(T/F) :   [?]

                   Birth Date :   [  /  /  ]

                  Annual Salary :  $ [      .  ]
```

Fig. 9.21. Results of APPENDIT3.PRG.

If you are using a monitor with a graphics interface card, you should
see the display shown in figure 9.21. With an IBM monochrome
monitor, you may need to enter SET INTENSITY OFF before the
SET DELIMITER ON command to eliminate the reverse video.

Deleting Data Records

As you have seen, programs can be used to edit and append data
records. You can also write a program to delete data records. The
following program shows how to delete a data record of the
EMPLOYEE.DBF file by identifying the employee's first and last
names (see fig. 9.22).

After you enter the first and last names, the record is deleted. Then
the database file is rewritten by the PACK command (see fig. 9.23).

Displaying Output

The dBASE III display commands ? and @ . . . SAY were
introduced in the preceding chapters. The @ . . . SAY command
(see Chapter 7) displays an output element at a specific location on
the display medium. The screen is divided in a format of 25 rows by
40 columns, where a row equals one print line, and a column equals
one character. The print line on most printers ranges from 40 to 80

```
. TYPE DELETEIT.PRG
*****    Program: DELETEIT.PRG    *****
*  Program to delete an employee's record
SET TALK OFF
SET ECHO OFF
*  Clear the screen
CLEAR
*  Select the database file
USE EMPLOYEE
*  Get the employee's name
ACCEPT "Enter Employee's First Name .... " TO FIRSTNAME
ACCEPT "               Last Name ..... " TO LASTNAME
*  Search for the employee's record
LOCATE FOR LAST_NAME=LASTNAME .AND. FIRST_NAME=FIRSTNAME
*  Delete the current record
DELETE
PACK
RETURN


.
```

Fig. 9.22. Deleting a data record.

```
Enter Employee's First Name .... Doris
                Last Name ..... Gregory
. LIST
Record#   FIRST_NAME   LAST_NAME   AREA_CODE PHONE_NO MALE BIRTH_DATE ANNUAL_PAY
    1     James C.     Smith       206       123-4567 .T.  07/04/60    22000.00
    2     Albert K.    Zeller      212       457-9801 .T.  10/10/59    27950.00
    3     Harry M.     Nelson      315       576-0235 .T.  02/15/58    29000.00
    4     Tina B.      Baker       415       567-8967 .F.  10/12/56    25900.00
    5     Kirk D.      Chapman     618       625-7845 .T.  08/04/61    19750.00
    6     Mary W.      Thompson    213       432-6782 .F.  06/18/55    24500.00
    7     Charles N.   Duff        206       456-9873 .T.  07/22/64    13500.00
    8     Winston E.   Lee         503       365-8512 .T.  05/14/39    34900.00
    9     Thomas T.    Hanson      206       573-5085 .T.  12/24/45    28950.00

.
```

Fig. 9.23. File repacked after delete command.

characters, although some printers can print up to 132 characters on a line. dBASE III is often used with an 80-column matrix or letter-quality printer.

A PICTURE clause can be added to the @ . . . SAY command to generate a special output format. A collection of @ . . . SAY commands can be used in a program to display an employee's personal file (see fig. 9.24).

After you enter the first and last names, you see the output shown in figure 9.25.

```
. TYPE CARDFILE.PRG
*****   Program: CARDFILE.PRG   *****
* Produce an employee's personnel file
SET TALK OFF
SET ECHO OFF
* Get employee's name
CLEAR
@5,1 SAY " Enter Name of the Employee:"
@7,1 SAY " "
ACCEPT "                   Last Name ...... " TO LASTNAME
ACCEPT "                   First Name ..... " TO FIRSTNAME
* Find the employee's record
USE EMPLOYEE
LOCATE FOR FIRST_NAME=FIRSTNAME .AND. LAST_NAME=LASTNAME
* Display output on screen
CLEAR
@5,7 SAY "EMPLOYEE'S PERSONAL DATA SHEET"
@7,5  SAY "Name (Last, First) : "+TRIM(LAST_NAME)+", "+TRIM(FIRST_NAME)
@9,5  SAY "Home Telephone No. : ("+AREA_CODE+") "+PHONE_NO
@11,5 SAY "        Birth Date : "+DTOC(BIRTH_DATE)
@13,5 SAY "     Annual Salary : "
@13,26 SAY ANNUAL_PAY PICTURE "$##,###.##"
RETURN

.
```

Fig. 9.24. Using the @ . . . SAY command to display output.

```
     EMPLOYEE'S PERSONAL DATA SHEET

  Name (Last, First) : Nelson, Harry M.

  Home Telephone No. : (315) 576-0235

          Birth Date : 02/15/58

       Annual Salary : $30,450.00

.
```

Fig. 9.25. Output from @ . . . SAY commands.

To obtain a printed copy of the report, add the commands SET DEVICE TO PRINT and EJECT at the beginning of the program (see fig. 9.26).

The SET DEVICE TO PRINT command sends the output to the printer. The EJECT command sends a form feed instruction to the printer to advance the paper by one page. As a result, the report generated by the @ . . . SAY commands is printed at the top of a

```
*****    Program: PRNTCARD.PRG    *****
* Print an employee's personnel file on printer
 SET TALK OFF
 SET ECHO OFF
CLEAR
@5,1 SAY " Enter Name of the Employee:"
@7,1 Say " "
ACCEPT "                Last Name ...... " TO LASTNAME
ACCEPT "                First Name ..... " TO FIRSTNAME
USE EMPLOYEE
LOCATE FOR FIRST_NAME=FIRSTNAME .AND. LAST_NAME=LASTNAME
CLEAR
* Activate the printer and go to a new page
SET DEVICE TO PRINT
EJECT
@5,7 SAY "EMPLOYEE'S PERSONAL DATA SHEET"
@7,5  SAY "Name (Last, First) : "+TRIM(LAST_NAME)+", "+TRIM(FIRST_NAME)
@9,5  SAY "Home Telephone No. : ("+AREA_CODE+") "+PHONE_NO
@11,5 SAY "         Birth Date : "+DTOC(BIRTH_DATE)
@13,5 SAY "      Annal Salary : "
@13,26 SAY ANNUAL_PAY PICTURE "$##,###.##"
SET DEVICE TO SCREEN
RETURN
```

Fig. 9.26. Printing a hard copy with PRINTCARD.PRG.

new page. The SET DEVICE TO SCREEN redirects the output to the screen.

The ? Command

The ? command is used to display one or more output elements in a command. If the elements are separated by commas, mixed types of output elements can be included in the same command, such as

. ?"Name of Employee ",FIRST_NAME+
LAST_NAME,BIRTH_DATE,ANNUAL_PAY

When a ? command is entered, the output is displayed on the screen because the monitor is the default display medium used by dBASE III. If the printer has been activated with the SET PRINT ON command, the output is printed as well.

The ? command displays the output elements from left to right on a new display line. The display position of an output element depends on the type of element involved (see fig. 9.27).

The output of the program is displayed in figure 9.28.

As you can see, the contents of the first alphanumeric string on the ? command (ABCDE) are displayed on the far left position of the

```
. TYPE PRINT1.PRG
*****    Program: PRINT1.PRG    *****
* A program to show the printing positions
SET TALK OFF
SET ECHO OFF
ASTRING="ABCDE"
BSTRING="XYZ"
VALUEX=-123.45
VALUEY=0.6789
VALUEZ=98765
DATE1=CTOD("03/08/85")
LOGIC=.T.
* Display a ruler
?"12345678901234567890123456789012345678901234567890"
?ASTRING,BSTRING
?VALUEX,VALUEY,VALUEZ
?DATE1,LOGIC
RETURN
```

Fig. 9.27. Showing different display positions with PRINT1.PRG.

```
. DO PRINT1
12345678901234567890123456789012345678901234567890
ABCDE XYZ
        -123.45            0.6789        98765
03/08/85 .T.
.
```

Fig. 9.28. The output of PRINT1.PRG.

display line. The comma used to separate the alphanumeric strings inserts a blank space between the strings ABCDE and XYZ on the display line. The comma separating a date variable and a logical variable also inserts a blank space. However, the same spacing rules do not apply to numeric output. Figure 9.29 shows how numeric values are displayed with a ? command.

When you execute the program, the following results are displayed (see fig. 9.30).

The output of the program shows some interesting results. With a ? command, the decimal point of the first numeric variable is always displayed at the eleventh column. Commas do not provide the same consistent spacing with the ? command, and, as a result, positioning numeric values can be difficult. To solve the spacing problem, you can convert the output elements to alphanumeric strings with the STR function. For example, to convert the value of VALUEX (-123.45) to an alphanumeric string, you enter

STR(VALUEX,7,2)

```
. TYPE PRINT2.PRG
*****   Program: PRINT2.PRG   *****
* Show printing position of numeric variables
SET TALK OFF
SET ECHO OFF
VALUEX=-123.45
VALUEY=0.6789
VALUEZ=98765
* Display a ruler
?"12345678901234567890123456789012345678901234567890"
?VALUEX
?VALUEY
?VALUEZ
?VALUEX,VALUEY,VALUEZ
?VALUEY,VALUEX,VALUEZ
?VALUEZ,VALUEX,VALUEY
RETURN

.
```

Fig. 9.29. Positioning numeric variables with PRINT2.PRG.

```
. DO PRINT2.PRG
12345678901234567890123456789012345678901234567890
      -123.45
          0.6789
     98765
      -123.45              0.6789        98765
          0.6789      -123.45            98765
     98765          -123.45              0.6789
.
```

Fig. 9.30. Results of PRINT2.PRG.

The result is a string of seven characters with two decimal places. Figure 9.31 shows how to set equal lengths for numeric values and to position numeric output.

The decimal points are aligned vertically because the length of the return strings were set to 15 characters (see fig. 9.32).

As you have seen, a comma separating alphanumeric strings inserts blank space between elements. What if you do not want a space between elements? To solve the problem, you can use arithmetic operators between elements to specify the string as an expression. For example, to display the contents of the strings ASTRING and BSTRING without space separating the strings, use a plus sign, as in the following:

. ?ASTRING+BSTRING

```
.  TYPE PRINT3.PRG
*****    Program: PRINT3.PRG    *****
* Show effect of STR on printing position
SET TALK OFF
SET ECHO OFF
VALUEX=-123.45
VALUEY=0.6789
VALUEZ=98765
* Display a ruler
?"123456789012345678901234567890123456789012345678901234567890"
?STR(VALUEX,15,4),STR(VALUEY,15,4),STR(VALUEZ,15,4)
?STR(VALUEY,15,4),STR(VALUEX,15,4),STR(VALUEZ,15,4)
?STR(VALUEZ,15,4),STR(VALUEX,15,4),STR(VALUEY,15,4)
RETURN



.
```

Fig. 9.31. The STR function with PRINT3.PRG.

```
.  DO PRINT3
123456789012345678901234567890123456789012345678901234567890
     -123.4500         0.6789       98765.0000
        0.6789      -123.4500       98765.0000
    98765.0000      -123.4500           0.6789

.
```

Fig. 9.32. Results of STR.

Because of erratic spacing, you may wish to avoid placing commas in the ? command line. The following program converts data fields to alphanumeric strings, then displays the strings as alphanumeric expressions without commas (see fig. 9.33).

The output produced by the program is shown in figure 9.34.

To print a copy of the program, add the SET PRINT ON command to the beginning of the program. After printing the report, you can use SET PRINT OFF to deactivate the printer and return the display to the screen.

The ?? Command

Because the ? command has a built-in line feed instruction, output elements are always displayed on a new line. A line feed operation is the same as a carriage return on a typewriter and generally works well for most output displays. However, in some cases, you may

```
. TYPE PRINT4.PRG
*****   Program: PRINT4.PRG   *****
* A program to display an employee's record
USE EMPLOYEE
CLEAR
?"Employee's Name:  "+TRIM(FIRST_NAME)+" "+LAST_NAME
?"Telephone No:     ("+AREA_CODE+") "+PHONE_NO
?"Birth Date:       "+DTOC(BIRTH_DATE)
?"Annual Salary:    "+STR(ANNUAL_PAY,8,2)
RETURN


.
```

Fig. 9.33. ? without commas.

```
Employee's Name: James C. Smith
Telephone No:    (206) 123-4567
Birth Date:      07/04/60
Annual Salary:   22000.00
.
```

Fig. 9.34. The output of PRINT4.PRG.

need to display an element directly following the last element position. To avoid a line feed operation, you can use the ?? command.

The only difference between the ? and ?? commands is that the ?? command does not begin a new display line. The ?? command displays the output element after the last element position. Figure 9.35 shows an example of the ?? command.

As you can see, the print command ??STRINGB positions the string immediately after the output from the print command ?STRINGA.

Chapter Summary

This chapter introduced the ACCEPT, INPUT, and WAIT commands that are used to assign a data element to a memory variable. Although each of these commands is an input command, ACCEPT, INPUT, and WAIT have different functions. ACCEPT assigns only alphanumeric strings to alphanumeric variables, whereas INPUT enters alphanumeric, numeric, date, or logical data in different variables. However, an alphanumeric string must be enclosed in quotation marks when used with the INPUT command. With the INPUT command, you can enter a date in a date variable by using

```
. TYPE PRINT5.PRG
*****    Program: PRINT5.PRG    *****
* Show the effects of ??
STRINGA="This is the first string"
STRINGB="This is the second string"
?STRINGA
?STRINGB
?STRINGA
??STRINGB
RETURN

. DO PRINT5
This is the first string
This is the second string
This is the first stringThis is the second string
.
```

Fig. 9.35. The ?? command.

the CTOD conversion function. Logical data must include two periods (for example, .T. or .F.) when entered to the logical variable. The WAIT command assigns only one character to an alphanumeric variable.

The two basic output commands discussed in this chapter are the @ . . . SAY and ? commands. With @ . . . SAY, you can position the output element at a specific location on the screen or printer. However, @ . . . SAY can display only one output element in the form of an alphanumeric or numeric expression. The ? command can display one or more different output elements separated by commas. The ?? command is similar to the ? command, except that ? positions the output on a new line, but ?? displays output wherever the last element ended. With proper use of the printing commands in this chapter, you can design custom forms for editing, appending, and displaying data records.

10

Conditional Branching and Program Loops

An Overview

Up to this point, the program examples you have seen have been processed in a logical sequence. That is, the processing started at the first instruction line and continued until the last command was executed.

This chapter shows how to change the normal processing sequence by using conditional branching and program loops. Conditional branching is one of dBASE III's most powerful tools. The dBASE III commands used in conditional branching are the following:

```
IF . . . ENDIF
IF . . . ELSE . . . ENDIF
DO CASE . . . ENDCASE
DO CASE . . . OTHERWISE . . . ENDCASE
```

Another command introduced in this chapter, the WAIT TO command, enables you to select the processing path during the conventional branching operation.

Program loops are also explained in this chapter. A program loop is an efficient way to repeat a program segment and can be used to process each data record in a database file. The following dBASE III commands are used in program loop operations:

DO WHILE . . . ENDDO
LOOP
EXIT

Conditional Branching

While sequential processing is adequate for simple data processing tasks, you need more flexibility to perform advanced data manipulations. In many data manipulations, you need to provide different processing avenues to meet varying types of computational conditions.

For example, to compute wages, you would multiply the total number of hours by the hourly wage. If there is overtime involved, however, you must compute the wage differently. For this reason, you need to provide a formula to compute the wage, depending on the data condition involved. If forty hours is a normal work week, and overtime is figured at one and one-half times the normal hourly rate, the computational logic is as follows:

For a normal work week,

calculate: Regular Pay = Hours x Wage Rate
Overtime Pay = 0

If overtime is involved,

calculate: Regular Pay = 40 x Wage Rate
Overtime Pay = (Hours - 40) x Wage Rate x 1.5

If you were writing a program to compute the weekly wage, you would create two different sections in your program; one for each type of condition involved. When the program is executed, the computer processes one of the two sections, depending on the data condition. This is called the method of conditional branching. Each branch represents a program section that is executed when a specific condition is met.

IF . . . ENDIF

With an IF . . . ENDIF command, you can designate the program section to be executed when the condition is met. The condition is defined in a clause following the IF command, and the program section is enclosed between the IF command line and the ENDIF command:

IF <condition>

    <program section for the condition being true>

ENDIF

An example of the IF . . . ENDIF command is

```
IF HOURS>40
   REGULARPAY=40*RATE
   OVERTIME=(HOURS-40)*RATE*1.5
ENDIF
```

If the condition is true (if HOURS > 40), the program section between IF and ENDIF is processed. If the condition is false, the section is skipped. The condition in the IF clause can be one of the following:

A logical variable or data record, such as

```
IF MALE
   ? "This is a male employee"
   . . .
   . . .
ENDIF
```

A simple numeric or alphanumeric relation, such as

```
IF ANNUAL_PAY>25000
. . .
. . .
ENDIF
IF AREACODE="206"
. . .
. . .
ENDIF
```

A compound relation, such as

    IF LAST_NAME="Smith" .AND. FIRST_NAME="James"
    . . .
    . . .
    ENDIF
    IF MALE .AND. AREA_CODE="503"
    . . .
    . . .
    ENDIF
    IF SUBSTR(BIRTHDATE,7,2)="60" .OR.
    SUBSTR(BIRTH_DATE,7,2)
    . . .
    . . .
    ENDIF
    IF .NOT. MALE .AND. ANNUAL_PAY>=25000
    . . .
    . . .
    ENDIF

To illustrate conditional branching, you can use the hourly wage example converted to a program (see fig. 10.1).

```
*****  Program: PAYROLL.PRG   *****
* A simplified payroll program
SET TALK OFF
SET ECHO OFF
* Get hours and rate
?
?
INPUT "        Enter Number of Hours Worked .... " TO HOURS
INPUT "                  Hourly Wage Rate .... " TO RATE
* Start computing wage
REGULARPAY=HOURS*RATE
OVERTIME=0
IF HOURS>40
   REGULARPAY=40*RATE
   OVERTIME=(HOURS-40)*RATE*1.5
ENDIF
?
?
? "        Regular Pay ........ "+STR(REGULARPAY,7,2)
? "        Overtime Pay ........ "+STR(OVERTIME,7,2)
? "        Total Gross Pay ..... "+STR(REGULARPAY+OVERTIME,7,2)
?
?
.RETURN
```

Fig. 10.1. Using IF . . . ENDIF.

When you execute the program, you see the output shown in figure 10.2.

```
. DO PAYROLL

        Enter Number of Hours Worked .... 38
                    Hourly Wage Rate .... 7.50


            Regular Pay ........  285.00
            Overtime Pay ........    0.00
            Total Gross Pay .....  285.00

.
```

Fig. 10.2. Output from IF . . . ENDIF program.

As you can see, the wage is computed according to the number entered in the variable HOURS. The memory variable HOURS defines the relation that specifies the condition for the branching operation. Conditional branching can also be used to process data records. To illustrate the operation, a new database file named WAGES.DBF has been created. The structure of WAGES.DBF is shown in figure 10.3.

```
. USE WAGES
. DISPLAY STRUCTURE
Structure for database : B:WAGES.dbf
Number of data records :      16
Date of last update    : 03/04/85
Field  Field name  Type       Width   Dec
    1  FIRST_NAME  Character     10
    2  LAST_NAME   Character      8
    3  DEPT        Character      1
    4  HOURS       Numeric        2
    5  RATE        Numeric        5       2
    6  GROSS_PAY   Numeric        6       2
    7  DEDUCTIONS  Numeric        6       2
    8  NET_PAY     Numeric        6       2
** Total **                     45

.
```

Fig. 10.3. The structure of WAGES.DBF.

Figure 10.4 displays the data records in WAGES.DBF.

Each data record contains the worker's name and wage parameters (hours worked, wage rate, etc.). To compute the wage, you can use a program similar to PAYROLL.PRG. By modifying PAYROLL.PRG, you can use a data field to specify the condition and locate an employee's record (see fig. 10.5).

Figure 10.6 shows the output of PAYROLL1.PRG.

```
. USE WAGES
. LIST
Record#   FIRST_NAME LAST_NAME DEPT HOURS   RATE GROSS_PAY DEDUCTIONS NET_PAY
      1   Cindy T.   Baker     B     38   7.50     0.00      0.00      0.00
      2   William B. Davison   A     41  11.50     0.00      0.00      0.00
      3   Floyd C.   Fuller    C     40   7.50     0.00      0.00      0.00
      4   Bob R.     Hill      A     42   7.75     0.00      0.00      0.00
      5   Mike D.    James     B     38   6.50     0.00      0.00      0.00
      6   David F.   Larson    C     38  11.00     0.00      0.00      0.00
      7   Alice G.   Miller    A     45   8.50     0.00      0.00      0.00
      8   Peter A.   Morrison  A     48   8.25     0.00      0.00      0.00
      9   Ellen F.   Norton    B     58   7.50     0.00      0.00      0.00
     10   Charlie H. Olson     A     36   9.25     0.00      0.00      0.00
     11   Tony W.    Palmer    A     37   7.25     0.00      0.00      0.00
     12   Grace S.   Porter    B     40  12.25     0.00      0.00      0.00
     13   Howard G.  Rosen     C     36   8.00     0.00      0.00      0.00
     14   Geroge D.  Stan      A     39  10.95     0.00      0.00      0.00
     15   Tamie K.   Tower     C     36   9.50     0.00      0.00      0.00
     16   Albert L.  Williams  B     43   8.50     0.00      0.00      0.00
.
```

Fig. 10.4. Data records in WAGES.DBF.

```
*****  Program: PAYROLL1.PRG   *****
* A payroll program for processing the WAGES.DBF
SET TALK OFF
SET ECHO OFF
* Get worker's name
?
ACCEPT "    Enter Worker's First Name .... " TO FIRSTNAME
ACCEPT "                    Last Name ..... " TO LASTNAME
USE WAGES
LOCATE FOR LAST_NAME=LASTNAME.AND.FIRST_NAME=FIRSTNAME
* Start computing wage
REGULARPAY=HOURS*RATE
OVERTIME=0
IF HOURS>40
   REGULARPAY=40*RATE
   OVERTIME=(HOURS-40)*RATE*1.5
ENDIF
?
? "    Worker's Name : "+TRIM(FIRST_NAME)+" "+TRIM(LAST_NAME)
?
? "         Regular Pay ......... "+STR(REGULARPAY,7,2)
? "         Overtime Pay ........ "+STR(OVERTIME,7,2)
? "         Total Gross Pay ..... "+STR(REGULARPAY+OVERTIME,7,2)
?
RETURN
```

Fig. 10.5. Program to process WAGES.DBF.

```
. DO PAYROLL1

    Enter Worker's First Name .... Cindy
                    Last Name ..... Baker

    Worker's Name : Cindy T. Baker

            Regular Pay ......... 285.00
            Overtime Pay ........   0.00
            Total Gross Pay .....  285.00

  .
```

Fig. 10.6. The output of PAYROLL1.PRG.

You can see that the program computed the wages correctly. However, if you look closely, you see that the program is not efficient, because regular pay and overtime pay are computed twice when the number of hours is greater than 40. For example, when the condition HOURS > 40 is true, the regular pay is first computed by

REGULARPAY = HOURS*RATE

and then replaced by

REGULARPAY = 40*RATE

To avoid repetition, you can revise the computational logic as follows:

If hours worked is less than or equal to 40,

calculate: Regular Pay = Hours x Wage Rate
Overtime Pay = 0

If hour worked is more than 40,

calculate: Regular Pay = 40 x Wage Rate
Overtime Pay = (Hours-40) x Wage Rate x 1.5

This way, only one formula is used to compute the wages, depending on the data condition. The new computational logic can be converted in a program by introducing the phrase ELSE in the IF . . . ENDIF command.

IF . . . ELSE . . . ENDIF

The ELSE phrase in the IF . . . ENDIF command adds a second
condition that directs the computer to one section for a true
condition and to another section for a false condition. When the
condition in the IF clause is false, the program to be executed is
enclosed between ELSE and ENDIF:

```
IF <condition>

   <program section for the condition being true>

ELSE

   <program section for the condition being false>

ENDIF
```

An example of IF . . . ELSE . . . ENDIF is

```
IF HOURS<=40
   REGULARPAY=HOURS*RATE
   OVERTIME=0
ELSE
   REGULARPAY=40*RATE
   OVERTIME=(HOURS-40)*R*1.5
ENDIF
```

You can use the example in the program PAYROLL2.PRG to
accomplish the same task performed by the PAYROLL1.PRG
program (see figure 10.7).

Both programs are identical, except that PAYROLL2.PRG requires
fewer steps than PAYROLL1.PRG. In the examples, the instruction
lines in the program section have been indented three characters.
Because an instruction can begin anywhere on the program line, the
indentation does not affect the processing operation. The
indentation is used only to make the program more readable, but
you may wish to adopt the format to make your programs clearer.

In the PAYROLL2.PRG program, the data is divided into two
sections: one for cases when HOURS<=40, and one for when
HOURS>40. Many times, however, you need to handle more than
two conditions. To compute personal income taxes, for example,
you need a formula for each income bracket. Computing quantity
discount is another example in which you need a set of discount
factors for different levels of quantity. To manage these applications,
you can use nested IF . . . ENDIF commands to check data ranges.

Nesting IF . . . ENDIF commands means to enclose one
IF . . . ENDIF program segment within another, such as

    IF <condition>

      . . .

      . . .

      IF <condition>

        . . .

        . . .

        IF <condition>

          . . .

          . . .

        ENDIF

        . . .

        . . .

      ENDIF

      . . .

      . . .

    ENDIF

```
*****  Program: PAYROLL2.PRG   *****
* Another payroll program for processing the WAGES.DBF
SET TALK OFF
SET ECHO OFF
* Get worker's name
?
ACCEPT "    Enter Worker's First Name .... " TO FIRSTNAME
ACCEPT "                   Last Name ..... " TO LASTNAME
USE WAGES
LOCATE FOR LAST_NAME=LASTNAME.AND.FIRST_NAME=FIRSTNAME
* Start computing wage
IF HOURS<=40
   REGULARPAY=HOURS*RATE
   OVERTIME=0
ELSE
   REGULARPAY=40*RATE
   OVERTIME=(HOURS-40)*RATE*1.5
ENDIF
?
? "    Worker's Name : "+TRIM(FIRST_NAME)+" "+TRIM(LAST_NAME)
?
? "         Regular Pay ........ "+STR(REGULARPAY,7,2)
? "         Overtime Pay ....... "+STR(OVERTIME,7,2)
? "         Total Gross Pay ..... "+STR(REGULARPAY+OVERTIME,7,2)
?
RETURN
```

Fig. 10.7. Using IF . . . ENDIF.

The following problem for computing income tax illustrates nested IF . . . ENDIF commands. Table 10.1 represents the percentage withholding tax table for a single worker from June, 1983, through January, 1985.

Table 10.1
Percentage Withholding Tax Table*
For Wages Paid after June, 1983, and before January, 1985
For a Single Worker

If weekly wage is	Amount to withhold
Under $27	$0
$27 - not over $79	12% of excess over $27
$79 - not over $183	$6.24 + 15% of excess over $79
$183 - not over $277	$21.84 + 19% of excess over $183
$277 and over	$39.70 + 25% of excess over $277

partially taken from 1984 Federal Income Tax Table

The program segment for computing the amount of withholding tax (WITHHOLD) can be written with nested IF . . . ENDIF commands as the following (assuming that the variable GROSSWAGE contains the weekly gross pay):

```
IF GROSSWAGE >27
   WITHHOLD=.12*(GROSSWAGE-27)
      IF GROSSWAGE > 79
         WITHHOLD=6.24+.15*(GROSSWAGE-79)
            IF GROSSWAGE > 183
               WITHHOLD=21.84+.19*(GROSSWAGE-183)
                  IF GROSSWAGE > 277
                     WITHHOLD=39.7+.25*(GROSSWAGE-277)
                  ENDIF
            ENDIF
      ENDIF
ENDIF
```

Figure 10.8 shows the program that uses nested IF . . . ENDIF commands to compute the weekly withholding tax for workers in WAGES.DBF.

When NESTEDIF.PRG is executed, you see the output shown in figure 10.9.

In the example, if the gross wage is greater than 277, the amount of withholding tax (WITHHOLD) is repeatedly computed and replaced.

```
*****  Program: NESTEDIF.PRG  *****
* Computing Withholding using nested IF commands
SET TALK OFF
SET ECHO OFF
* Get worker's name
?
ACCEPT "    Enter Worker's First Name .... " TO FIRSTNAME
ACCEPT "                 Last Name ..... " TO LASTNAME
USE WAGES
LOCATE FOR LAST_NAME=LASTNAME.AND.FIRST_NAME=FIRSTNAME
* Start computing wage
IF HOURS<=40
   REGULARPAY=HOURS*RATE
   OVERTIME=0
ELSE
    REGULARPAY=40*RATE
    OVERTIME=(HOURS-40)*RATE*1.5
ENDIF
GROSSWAGE=REGULARPAY+OVERTIME
* Determine withholding taxes
WITHHOLD=0
IF GROSSWAGE >27
    WITHHOLD=.12*(GROSSWAGE-27)
      IF GROSSWAGE > 79
        WITHHOLD=6.24+.15*(GROSSWAGE-79)
          IF GROSSWAGE > 183
            WITHHOLD=21.84+.19*(GROSSWAGE-183)
              IF GROSSWAGE > 277
                WITHHOLD=39.7+.25*(GROSSWAGE-277)
              ENDIF
          ENDIF
      ENDIF
ENDIF
NETWAGE=GROSSWAGE-WITHHOLD
?
? "     Worker's Name : "+TRIM(FIRST_NAME)+" "+TRIM(LAST_NAME)
?
? "        Regular Pay ........ "+STR(REGULARPAY,7,2)
? "        Overtime Pay ........ "+STR(OVERTIME,7,2)
? "        Total Gross Pay ..... "+STR(REGULARPAY+OVERTIME,7,2)
? "        Tax Withheld ........ "+STR(WITHHOLD,7,2)
? "        Net Pay ............. "+STR(NETWAGE,7,2)
RETURN
```

Fig. 10.8. Using nested IF . . . ENDIF commands.

Because the two-branch IF . . . ENDIF command is ineffective for this type of problem, you may wish to use the multiple-branch DO CASE . . . ENDCASE command.

DO CASE . . . ENDCASE

The DO CASE . . . ENDCASE command defines multiple conditions that determine the specific section of a program to be executed when a given condition is met. A CASE clause is used to define each

```
. DO NESTEDIF

    Enter Worker's First Name .... Albert
                    Last Name ..... Williams

    Worker's Name : Albert L. Williams

            Regular Pay ......... 340.00
            Overtime Pay ........  38.25
            Total Gross Pay ..... 378.25
            Tax Withheld ........  65.01
            Net Pay .............  313.24

.
```

Fig. 10.9. Output from NESTEDIF.PRG.

condition. You can use as many conditions as necessary to define the conditional branchings. The phrases DO CASE and ENDCASE enclose all the CASE clauses used, as in

```
DO CASE
   CASE <condition 1>
       <program section for condition 1 being true>
   CASE <condition 2>
       <program section for condition 2 being true>
   CASE <condition 3>
       <program section for condition 3 being true>
   . . .
   . . .
ENDCASE
```

In this segment, if the first condition in the first CASE clause is true, the program section below the clause is executed. If the condition is not true, the section is ignored. In the same way, if the second condition is true, the corresponding program section is processed. For example, the nested IF . . . ENDIF commands in NESTEDIF.PRG can be written as

```
DO CASE
   CASE GROSSWAGE<27
       WITHHOLD=0
   CASE GROSSWAGE>=27 .AND. GROSSWAGE <79
       WITHHOLD=.12*(GROSSWAGE-27)
   CASE GROSSWAGE>=79 .AND. GROSSWAGE <183
       WITHHOLD=6.24+.15*(GROSSWAGE-79)
   CASE GROSSWAGE>=183 .AND. GROSSWAGE <277
       WITHHOLD=21.84+.19*(GROSSWAGE-183)
```

```
                    CASE GROSSWAGE>=277
                         WITHHOLD=39.7+.25*(GROSSWAGE-277)
            ENDCASE
```

To understand the power of the multiple-branch commands, you can convert the nested IF . . . ENDIF commands in the NESTEDIF.PRG program to CASE conditions (see fig. 10.10).

The output from the program is shown in figure 10.11.

```
*****  Program: DOCASES.PRG   *****
* Computing Withholding using DOCASE commands
SET TALK OFF
SET ECHO OFF
* Get worker's name
?
ACCEPT "    Enter Worker's First Name .... " TO FIRSTNAME
ACCEPT "                     Last Name ..... " TO LASTNAME
USE WAGES
LOCATE FOR LAST_NAME=LASTNAME.AND.FIRST_NAME=FIRSTNAME
* Computing gross wage
DO CASE
   CASE HOURS<=40
      REGULARPAY=HOURS*RATE
      OVERTIME=0
   CASE HOURS>40
      REGULARPAY=40*RATE
      OVERTIME=(HOURS-40)*RATE*1.5
ENDCASE
GROSSWAGE=REGULARPAY+OVERTIME
* Determine amount of tax withholding
DO CASE
   CASE GROSSWAGE<27
      WITHHOLD=0
   CASE GROSSWAGE>=27 .AND. GROSSWAGE <79
      WITHHOLD=.12*(GROSSWAGE-27)
   CASE GROSSWAGE>=79 .AND. GROSSWAGE <183
      WITHHOLD=6.24+.15*(GROSSWAGE-79)
   CASE GROSSWAGE>=183 .AND. GROSSWAGE <277
      WITHHOLD=21.84+.19*(GROSSWAGE-183)
   CASE GROSSWAGE>=277
      WITHHOLD=39.7+.25*(GROSSWAGE-277)
ENDCASE
NETWAGE=GROSSWAGE-WITHHOLD
?
? "    Worker's Name : "+TRIM(FIRST_NAME)+" "+TRIM(LAST_NAME)
?
? "          Regular Pay ........ "+STR(REGULARPAY,7,2)
? "          Overtime Pay ........ "+STR(OVERTIME,7,2)
? "          Total Gross Pay ..... "+STR(REGULARPAY+OVERTIME,7,2)
? "          Tax Withheld ........ "+STR(WITHHOLD,7,2)
? "          Net Pay ............. "+STR(NETWAGE,7,2)
RETURN
```

Fig. 10.10. Replacing IF . . . ENDIF with CASE conditions.

```
.  DO DOCASES

     Enter Worker's First Name .... Albert
                     Last Name ..... Williams

     Worker's Name : Albert L. Williams

          Regular Pay ......... 340.00
          Overtime Pay ........  38.25
          Total Gross Pay ..... 378.25
          Tax Withheld ........  65.01
          Net Pay .............  313.24
.
```

Fig. 10.11. Results of DO CASE program.

In some database applications, all possible conditions cannot be anticipated. For this reason, you need to prepare the program to accommodate situations not included in CASE clauses. The OTHERWISE phrase can be used to include the situations not defined in the CASE clauses, as in

```
DO CASE
   CASE <condition 1>
      <program section for condition 1 being true>
   CASE <condition 2>
      <program section for condition 2 being true>
   CASE <condition 3>
      <program section for condition 3 being true>
   . . .

   . . .
   OTHERWISE
      <program section when all above conditions are false>.
   . . .
ENDCASE
```

For example, to modify DOCASES.PRG to make the last CASE clause (GROSSWAGE>=277) an OTHERWISE clause and rewrite the program section for determining withholding tax, you enter

```
* Determine amount of tax withholding
DO CASE
   CASE GROSSWAGE<27
      WITHHOLD=0
   CASE GROSSWAGE>=27 .AND. GROSSWAGE <79
      WITHHOLD=.12*(GROSSWAGE-27)
   CASE GROSSWAGE>=79 .AND. GROSSWAGE <183
      WITHHOLD=6.24+.15*(GROSSWAGE-79)
```

```
CASE GROSSWAGE>=183 .AND. GROSSWAGE <277
    WITHHOLD=21.84+.19*(GROSSWAGE-183)
OTHERWISE
    WITHHOLD=39.7+.25*(GROSSWAGE-277)
ENDCASE
```

Program Loops

The conditional branching commands are powerful tools for data manipulation; however, the commands can use only one record at a time. After processing one data record, the program returns to the dot prompt. If you want to process a different data record, you must execute the program again, which can be time-consuming if you have a large set of data records. To compute the weekly wage of the employees in the WAGES.DBF file, you need a program to repeat the section of wage computation for each data record. You can use program loops to solve the problem.

DO WHILE . . . ENDDO

A *program loop* is a section of a program to be repeated during the processing stage. The section to be repeated is enclosed between the DO WHILE and ENDDO phrases:

```
DO WHILE <a condition>
    . . .
    . . . <the program section to be repeated>
    . . .
ENDDO
```

The condition in DO WHILE determines whether the program section in the loop is processed. If the condition is true, the program section is executed; otherwise, the program section is skipped and the computer proceeds from the program line following ENDDO. After the ENDDO phrase is encountered, the computer returns to the DO WHILE statement. Then the computer is instructed to verify the condition before proceeding. If you are familiar with BASIC programming, you will see similarities between the DO WHILE . . . ENDDO and the FOR NEXT loop. The condition in the DO WHILE phrase can be one of the following:

A logical variable, such as

```
DO WHILE MALE
```

The contents of a logical variable, such as

DO WHILE .T.

An alphanumeric qualifier, such as

DO WHILE ANSWER<>"QUIT"

DO WHILE AREA_CODE="206"

DO WHILE AREA_CODE="206".OR.AREA_CODE="503"

DO WHILE SUBSTR(MODEL,1,3)>
"RCA".AND.SUBSTR(DTOC(DATE),7,2)="84"

A numeric qualifier, such as

DO WHILE KOUNT<=5
DO WHILE ANNUAL_PAY>20000
DO WHILE UNITS_SOLD<=3.OR.UNITS_SOLD>=10
DO WHILE UNITS_SOLD*UNITPRICE >= 10000

An end-of-file mark EOF(), such as

DO WHILE .NOT. EOF()

An Infinite Program Loop

The condition in the DO WHILE phrase determines how many times the loop is repeated. By using .T. as the condition, you create an infinite program loop:

DO WHILE .T.

. . .

. . .

ENDDO

Because the condition must always be true, the program will repeat infinitely unless you include a way to terminate the process. INFLOOPS.PRG shows an example of an infinite loop (see fig. 10.12).

```
*****   Program: INFLOOPS.PRG   *****
* An infinite program loop
SET TALK OFF
SET ECHO OFF
DO WHILE .T.
   ? "Hello !"
ENDDO
RETURN
```

Fig. 10.12. An Infinite program loop.

When the program is executed, the phrase *Hello !* is displayed continually. You can press Esc to stop the infinite loop, and the following message is displayed:

```
Called from - B:INFLOOPS.prg
Terminate command file? (Y/N)
```

By answering Y to the question, you can terminate the program and exit from the infinite loop. The output from the program is shown in figure 10.13.

```
. DO INFLOOPS
Hello !
Hello !
Hello !
Hello !
Hello !
Hello !
Hello !
Hello !
Hello !
Hello !
Hello !
Hello !
Hello !
Hello !
Hello !
Hello !
Hello !
Hello !
Called from - B:INFLOOPS.prg
Terminate command file? (Y/N) Yes
Do cancelled
.
```

Fig. 10.13. Example of an infinite loop.

A conditional branching operation can also be used to terminate an infinite loop. For example, LOOPEXIT.PRG shows how to exit from the loop, using the contents of the memory variable ANSWER, which is entered with a WAIT command (see fig. 10.14).

WAIT TO

The WAIT TO command assigns a character to a memory variable in the form

. WAIT "a prompting message" TO <an alphanumeric variable>

The WAIT command stops the program until another key is pressed. The key is entered in the memory variable specified in the WAIT TO command after a prompt, such as

```
*****    Program: LOOPEXIT.PRG    *****
* An exit from the infinite program loop
SET TALK OFF
SET ECHO OFF
DO WHILE .T.
    ?
    ACCEPT "What is your name ? " TO NAME
    ?
    ? "Good morning! "+NAME
    ?
    WAIT "Do you want to continue (Y/N) ? " TO ANSWER
    IF UPPER(ANSWER)="Y"
        RETURN
    ENDIF
ENDDO
RETURN
```

Fig. 10.14. Exiting an infinite loop with the WAIT TO command.

. WAIT "Do you want to continue (Y/N) ?" TO ANSWER

In LOOPEXIT.PRG, the variable ANSWER was used to determine whether the program loop was continued. If the answer to the question is Y, the computer returns to the dot prompt by using the IF . . . ENDIF command. Otherwise, the program loop repeats until the contents of ANSWER is Y. The results of the LOOPEXIT.PRG are shown in figure 10.15.

```
. DO LOOPEXIT

What is your name ? George

Good morning! George

Do you want to continue (Y/N) ? n

What is your name ? Jane

Good morning! Jane

Do you want to continue (Y/N) ? Y

.
```

Fig. 10.15. Results of LOOPEXIT.PRG.

A Program Loop Counter

Another program loop can be designed to repeat the loop a specified number of times, which requires a counter variable to record the number of passes the program makes. When the specified number is reached, the computer exits the program loop. A program loop counter is shown in the program KLOOPS.PRG (see fig. 10.16). The counter variable used in the program is KOUNT (the word COUNT cannot be used as a variable name).

```
*****  Program: KLOOPS.PRG  *****
* Control program loops with a counter variable
SET TALK OFF
SET ECHO OFF
* Initialize the counter, KCOUNT
* (Do not use "COUNT" as variable name, it is a reserved word)
KOUNT=1
DO WHILE KOUNT<=5
   ?"Value of the Counter is ", KOUNT
   * Increase the counter by 1
   KOUNT=KOUNT+1
ENDDO
RETURN
```

Fig. 10.16. The KLOOPS.PRG program.

The counter variable KOUNT is initially set to 1. Because the condition in the DO WHILE phrase is true (KOUNT<=5), the program loop is processed:

?"Value of the Counter is ", KOUNT

Each time the program section within the program loop is processed, the counter is increased by 1:

KOUNT=KOUNT+1

As long as the value of KOUNT is less than or equal to 5, the program loop is repeated. When the value of KOUNT exceeds 5 and the condition in DO WHILE is no longer true, the program is terminated. As you can see, the program repeats the loop only five times (see fig. 10.17).

```
. DO KLOOPS
Value of the Counter is          1
Value of the Counter is          2
Value of the Counter is          3
Value of the Counter is          4
Value of the Counter is          5
.
```

Fig. 10.17. Results of KLOOPS.PRG.

The following commands affect the number of passes made by a program loop:

```
KOUNT=1
DO WHILE KOUNT <= 5
KOUNT=KOUNT+1
```

To alter the number of passes of the program loop, you can change one or more of these commands.

EOF( )

A program loop is an efficient way to process data records in a database file. With a program loop, you instruct the computer to examine one data record at a time through the end of the file. The program can be terminated when all the data records have been processed, using the system function EOF() as the condition in the DO WHILE phrase:

```
DO WHILE .NOT. EOF()
    . . .
    . . . <the program section to be repeated>
    . . .
ENDDO
```

Like a logical variable, the EOF() function returns an .F. logical state if the end-of-file mark is not encountered in the database file. When the end-of-file mark is reached, EOF() returns a .T. logical state. With an end of file checker in a DO WHILE phrase, the program loop will be repeated only if the end-of-file mark is not found. Figure 10.18 illustrates how to use the EOF() function, using EMPLOYEE.DBF to create a phone list. The SKIP command instructs the computer to go to the next data record after one record is processed.

```
*****    Program: PHONLIST.PRG    *****
* Producing a phone list with a program loop
SET TALK OFF
SET ECHO OFF
* Select the database file
USE EMPLOYEE
?
? " Employee' Name       Telephone Number"
?
* The program loop ends when end of file is reached
DO WHILE .NOT. EOF()
  ?LAST_NAME,FIRST_NAME,AREA_CODE,PHONE_NO
  * Skip to next data record
  SKIP
ENDDO
RETURN
```

Fig. 10.18. Using the EOF( ) function.

The output produced by PHONLIST.PRG is shown in figure 10.19.

```
. DO PHONLIST

Employee's Name                    Telephone Number

Smith          James C.            206 123-4567
Zeller         Albert K.           212 457-9801
Gregory        Doris A.            503 204-8567
Nelson         Harry M.            315 576-0235
Baker          Tina B.             415 567-8967
Chapman        Kirk D.             618 625-7845
Thompson       Mary W.             213 432-6782
Duff           Charles N.          206 456-9873
Lee            Winston E.          503 365-8512
Hanson         Thomas T.           206 573-5085
.
```

Fig. 10.19. Output of PHONLIST.PRG.

The program PHONLIST.PRG examines and displays all phone numbers in the EMPLOYEE.DBF database file. To display a subset of the phone numbers, you can use the IF . . . ENDIF command. The program LIST206.PRG in figure 10.20 shows an example.

```
***** Program: LIST206.PRG *****
* Listing phone numbers with area code of 206
SET TALK OFF
SET ECHO OFF
* Select the database file
USE EMPLOYEE
?
?
GO TOP
DO WHILE .NOT. EOF()
     IF AREA_CODE="206"
        ?LAST_NAME,FIRST_NAME,AREA_CODE,PHONE_NO
     ENDIF
     SKIP
ENDDO
RETURN
```

Fig. 10.20. Using IF . . . ENDIF with EOF( ).

The output from the program is shown in figure 10.21.

```
.DO LIST206

Smith      James C.        206 123-4567
Duff       Charles N.      206 456-9873
Hanson     Thomas T.       206 573-5085
.
```

Fig. 10.21. Output from LIST206.PRG.

LIST206.PRG displays only the phone numbers with an area code of 206, but you can make the program more versatile with a memory variable. The program BYARCODE.PRG shows how to enter the area code with an ACCEPT TO command (see fig. 10.22).

```
*****   Program: BYARCODE.PRG   *****
* Listing phone numbers by a given area code
SET TALK OFF
SET ECHO OFF
USE EMPLOYEE
* Get the area code to be searched
?
ACCEPT "Enter the area code to be searched:  " TO AREACODE
?
GO TOP
DO WHILE .NOT. EOF()
   IF AREA_CODE=AREACODE
      ?LAST_NAME,FIRST_NAME,AREA_CODE,PHONE_NO
   ENDIF
   SKIP
ENDDO
?
RETURN
```

Fig. 10.22. Using LIST206 with a memory variable.

In figure 10.23, BYARCODE.PRG is executed three times, each time with a different searching area code.

```
. DO BYARCODE

Enter the area code to be searched: 206

Smith     James C.       206 123-4567
Duff      Charles N.     206 456-9873
Hanson    Thomas T.      206 573-5085

. DO BYARCODE

Enter the area code to be searched: 503

Gregory   Doris A.       503 204-8567
Lee       Winston E.     503 365-8512

. DO BYARCODE

Enter the area code to be searched: 415

Baker     Tina B.        415 567-8967

.
```

Fig. 10.23. BYARCODE with different variables.

LIST206.PRG and BYARCODE.PRG search every data record and select only those that satisfy the IF condition. The approach is acceptable, but searching each data record can use valuable time when a large set of data records is involved. If you index your database file before using the search operation, you will save a considerable amount of time.

For example, the program in figure 10.24 first sorts the data records by area code so that numbers with the same area codes are grouped together. To display a phone number with a given area code, such as 206, you need only to place the record pointer at the beginning of the group. Then the data records in that group are displayed until a different area code is encountered. The SEEK command places the record pointer at the beginning of the 206 group.

```
***** Program: SORTFONE.PRG *****
* Sort and list phone numbers with area code of 206
SET TALK OFF
SET ECHO OFF
USE EMPLOYEE
* Sort by area code
INDEX ON AREA_CODE TO SORTFONE
* Find the first "206" area code
SEEK "206"
DO WHILE AREA_CODE="206"
  ?LAST_NAME,FIRST_NAME,AREA_CODE,PHONE_NO
  * Skip to next data record
  SKIP
ENDDO
RETURN
```

Fig. 10.24. The SEEK command.

The results of SORTFONE.NDX are shown in figure 10.25.

The file SORTFONE.NDX is a target file for the indexing operation. The file will be created whenever you invoke the index command, as in

. INDEX ON AREA_CODE TO SORTFONE

If SORTFONE.NDX was created by the last command, the following warning message is displayed when the command is encountered again:

SORTFONE. NDX already exists, overwrite it? (Y/N)

When this happens, enter Y. If you want to avoid a warning message during processing, you can erase the old SORTFONE.NDX before

```
. DO SORTFONE
Smith       James C.      206 123-4567
Duff        Charles N.    206 456-9873
Hanson      Thomas T.     206 573-5085
.
```

Fig. 10.25. Results of SORTFONE.

you start the indexing operation. You can add the following command line to the program before the INDEX command line:

```
. . .
ERASE SORTFONE.NDX
INDEX ON AREA_CODE TO SORTFONE
. . .
```

However, if your program contains the ERASE SORTFONE.NDX command, the first time you execute the program, you may get another warning message:

File does not exist

The message is only a warning that the index file SORTFONE.NDX has not been created.

Skipping Part of a Program Loop

In LOOPEXIT.PRG, you can exit the loop with an IF condition:

```
DO WHILE .T.
    . . .

    . . .
    IF UPPER(ANSWER)="Y"
        RETURN
    ENDIF
ENDDO
```

In the example, when the condition in the IF command is true, the computer is directed to exit from the program loop and return to the dot prompt. At times, you need to skip part of a program loop and "jump back" to the beginning. Suppose that you want to display all the phone numbers with an area code of 206, except for the employee with the last name of Smith. You can do this with a LOOP command.

LOOP

The LOOP command directs the computer to go to the beginning of the DO WHILE . . . ENDDO structure. When the command is encountered within a program loop section, the program returns to the beginning of the DO WHILE . . . ENDDO structure and ignores the rest of the program loop commands. For example, when the following LOOP command is executed, the processing skips to the next data record and begins another pass of the program loop:

```
DO WHILE AREA_CODE="206"
    IF LAST_NAME="Smith"
        SKIP
        LOOP
    ELSE
        ?LAST_NAME,FIRST_NAME,AREA_CODE,PHONE_NO
    ENDIF
ENDDO
```

The SKIPLOOP.PRG program is shown in figure 10.26.

The output from the program is displayed in figure 10.27.

```
***** Program: SKIPLOOP.PRG *****
* Sort and list phone numbers with area code of 206
SET TALK OFF
SET ECHO OFF
USE EMPLOYEE
* Sort by area code
INDEX ON AREA_CODE TO SORTFONE
* Find the first "206" area code
SEEK "206"
DO WHILE AREA_CODE="206"
    IF LAST_NAME="Smith"
        SKIP
        LOOP
    ELSE
        ?LAST_NAME,FIRST_NAME,AREA_CODE,PHONE_NO
        SKIP
    ENDIF
ENDDO
RETURN
```

Fig. 10.26. The SKIPLOOP.PRG program.

```
.DO SKIPLOOP
SOFTFONE.ndx already exists, overwrite it? (Y/N) Yes
Duff        Charles N.    206 456-9873
Hanson      Thomas T.     206 573-5085
.
```

Fig. 10.27. The results of SKIPLOOP.

EXIT

To abort the program looping process, you can use the EXIT command. EXIT instructs the program to leave the loop and proceed from the command line following the ENDDO line. The BYELOOP.PRG program is an example of the EXIT command (see fig. 10.28).

The results of BYELOOP.PRG can be seen in figure 10.29.

The output shows that EXIT stops the loop, but not the program.

```
*****    Program: BYELOOP.PRG    *****
* An exit from the infinite program loop
SET TALK OFF
SET ECHO OFF
DO WHILE .T.
    ?
    ACCEPT "What is your name ? " TO NAME
    ?
    ? "Good morninig ! "+NAME
    ?
    WAIT "Do you want to continue (Y/N) ? " TO ANSWER
    IF UPPER(ANSWER)="Y"
        EXIT
    ENDIF
ENDDO
?
? "Goodbye, "+NAME+" !"
RETURN
```

Fig. 10.28. Using the EXIT command.

```
. DO BYELOOP

What is your name ? George

Good morninig ! George

Do you want to continue (Y/N) ? y

Goodbye, George !
.
```

Fig. 10.29. Results of BYELOOP.

Nested Loops

In the program BYARCODE.PRG, you listed phone numbers by area code and found that you could process only one record at a time.

Because the program was executed again whenever you processed a new area code, the program was inefficient. If you want to repeat the program several times, you can extend it by putting the original program segment in a loop. The original program already has a DO WHILE . . . ENDDO loop, so the extended program will have two program loops, one within another. The diagram in figure 10.30 shows this structure, which is called a nested loop design.

```
DO WHILE <condition 1>
    ...
    ...
    DO WHILE <condition 2>
        ...
        ...
        ...
    ENDDO
    ...
    ...
ENDDO
```

Fig. 10.30. Nested loop design.

To understand how nested loops work, you can modify the program by adding an outside program loop (see fig. 10.31).

```
*****    Program: NESTLOOP.PRG    *****
* An example of a nested loop
SET TALK OFF
SET ECHO OFF
USE EMPLOYEE
* This is the outer loop
DO WHILE .T.
    ?
    ?
    ACCEPT "Enter the area code to be searched (END to quit): " TO AREACODE
    IF AREACODE="END"
        EXIT
    ENDIF
    ?
    GO TOP
    * This is the inner loop
    DO WHILE .NOT. EOF()
        IF AREA_CODE=AREACODE
            ?LAST_NAME,FIRST_NAME,AREA_CODE,PHONE_NO
        ENDIF
        SKIP
    ENDDO
ENDDO
RETURN
```

Fig. 10.31. Nested loop program.

The output of the program is shown in figure 10.32.

```
.  DO NESTLOOP

Enter the area code to be searched (END to quit): 206

Smith          James C.      206 123-4567
Duff           Charles N.    206 456-9873
Hanson         Thomas T.     206 573-5985

Enter the area code to be searched (END to quit): 503

Gregory        Doris A.      503 204-8567
Lee            Winston E.    503 365-8512

Enter the area code to be searched (END to quit): END
.
```

Fig. 10.32. Output of NESTLOOP.PRG.

As you can see, the program will process area codes until the word END is entered. END was used as the terminator for the outside program loop. When END is entered in the variable AREACODE, the program exits the program loop.

The example in NESTLOOP.PRG shows the simplest form of a nested loop. For more sophisticated applications, you may need nested loops several levels deep. The maximum number of levels allowed by dBASE III are not stated in the manual, but you should be able to use four or five levels of nested loops without any problem. Five levels of nested loops would be sufficient to handle most database management applications. Figure 10.33 shows the structure of multiple-level nested loops.

Each loop must be enclosed between DO WHILE and ENDDO phrases, and an ENDDO phrase must terminate each DO WHILE phrase. If a phrase is missing, the looping process does not work correctly and produces erroneous results.

```
DO WHILE <condition 1>
   . . .
   . . .
   DO WHILE <condition 2>
      . . .
      . . .
      DO WHILE <condition 3>
         . . .
         . . .
      ENDDO
      . . .
      . . .
      DO WHILE <condition 4>
         . . .
         . . .
         DO WHILE <condition 5>
            . . .
            . . .
         ENDDO
         . . .
      ENDDO
      . . .
   ENDDO
   . . .
   . . .
   DO WHILE <condition 6>
      . . .
   ENDDO
   . . .
ENDDO
```

Fig. 10.33. Multiple-level nested loops.

Chapter Summary

This chapter has introduced two of the most powerful programming features of dBASE III. With conditional branching, you can change the normal processing path according to specified conditions. Conditional branching operations use the IF . . . ENDIF and DO CASE . . . ENDCASE procedures. With ELSE and OTHERWISE options, you can meet any data condition and direct the program any way you choose.

With program loops, you can repeat a portion of a program until an EXIT condition is met. By setting up a counter variable within a program loop, you can control the number of passes the program makes. This chapter also introduced the nested loop structure for repetitive processing that is required by many database management applications.

The next chapter explains the important role conditional branching and program loops play in program demodulation and menu design.

11

Program Demodulation

An Overview

Program demodulation involves designing your database management program around several small subprograms or procedures. Modules are generally small and easy to create. After being tested, the modules can be linked together to form a complete system. When a new application arises, you can reorganize the appropriate program modules to create another database management system.

Because this program structure uses various modules to perform data management tasks, you will learn different ways to pass information among modules. The dBASE III commands used to control the memory variables are PUBLIC and PRIVATE. This chapter also explains how to maintain several database files at the same time and join the files together with the SELECT, UPDATE, and APPEND FROM commands. With a few simple dBASE III commands, you can also design a graphics program to display diagrams.

Designing Program Modules

As you have seen, using dBASE III is not difficult. The small example programs presented in the previous chapters can be used to form the base of a more sophisticated database management system. Although a real database management program may be large and complicated, you will see the advantages in structuring the system in simple program modules.

A small program module is easy to create. After each module is designed, you can test the module for syntax and logical errors before linking the modules together as a complete system.

With program demodulation, you can easily reorganize the program modules whenever necessary. Reorganizing a system involves modifying only some of the program modules and is often a simple task. A program file cannot exceed 4,096 characters (4K bytes), so program demodulation is necessary to keep your file within memory limitations.

Figure 11.1 shows a program with three modules. Each program module is an individual procedure or program file (.PRG), such as PROGA.PRG, PROGB.PRG, and PROGC.PRG.

```
*****    Program: MAINPROG.PRG    *****
* This the main program
...
...
* Go do module A
    DO PROGA
    * Return from module A
...
...
* Go do module B
    DO PROGB
    * Return from module B
...
...
* Go do module C
    DO PROGC
    * Return from module C
...
...

RETURN
```

Fig. 11.1. A sample structure of program modules.

Each module is a program file that ends with a RETURN command to send the program back to the main program:

```
***** Program: PROGA.PRG *****
* A program module
   . . .
   . . .
   . . .
RETURN
```

When MAINPROG.PRG is executed and DO PROGA is encountered, the computer transfers control to the module PROGA. After PROGA.PRG is processed, the RETURN command in the module returns the program control to the main program. Then the computer proceeds from the command line following DO PROGA in the main program.

To understand how the computer passes control between the program and program module, you can use the program MAINPROG.PRG (see fig. 11.2). The program modules PROGA.PRG (fig. 11.3) and PROGB.PRG (fig. 11.4) are also shown.

```
*****    Program: MAINPROG.PRG    *****
* The main program
?"***   We are now in the Main Program !"
* Go to PROGA.PRG
   DO PROGA
   ?
   ?"We have returned from PROGA.PRG !"
?
* Go to PROGB.PRG
   DO PROGB
   ?
   ?"We have returned from PROGB.PRG !"
RETURN
```

Fig. 11.2. Example of program modules.

```
*****   Program: PROGA.PRG   *****
* Program Module A
SET TALK OFF
SET ECHO OFF
?
?"            We have entered PROGA.PRG !"
* Return to main program
RETURN
```

Fig. 11.3. Program module A.

```
*****    Program: PROGB.PRG    *****
* Program Module B
?
?"              We have entered PROGB.PRG !"
* Return to main program
RETURN
```

Fig. 11.4. Program module B.

When MAINPROG.PRG is executed, the program begins processing from the main program. When DO PROGA is encountered, the program switches to the PROGA.PRG module. At RETURN, the program returns to the main program immediately following the DO PROGA command line (see fig. 11.5).

```
. DO MAINPROG
***  We are now in the Main Program !

          We have entered PROGA.PRG !

We have returned from PROGA.PRG !


          We have entered PROGB.PRG !

We have returned from PROGB.PRG !
 .
```

Fig. 11.5. Program to display modules.

The structures you have seen are two-level module designs. In other words, you saw the program change from the first level (main program) to the second level (PROGA.PRG or PROGB.PRG) and then back to the main program. If necessary, you can extend the number of module levels to accommodate more sophisticated database management programs. For example, the structure in figure 11.6 shows a three-level module design.

In a multilevel module design, the first level (main program) is the highest level. The program modules are numbered sequentially from the upper to lower levels. When you enter a lower-level module from a higher-level module, the execution starts at the first program line of the lower-level module. When RETURN is encountered in a model, the control returns to the next higher-level model. Figure 11.6 shows that when RETURN is found in PROGZ.PRG, the program returns to PROGY.PRG from which PROGZ.PRG was called.

```
* Structure of main program (This is not an actual program)
...
...
DO PROGX
  <-----------   * Module PROGX.PRG
...                ...
...                ...
...                DO PROGY
...                  <------------   * Module PROGY.PRG
...                ...                ...
RETURN             ...                ...
                   ...                RETURN
                   RETURN
```

Fig. 11.6. Linking multiple program modules.

Passing Memory Variables between Program Modules

As you have seen, you can pass program control easily, using DO and RETURN. However, special instructions are required to pass memory variable data from one program module to another. With dBASE III, you can pass only higher-level module data to lower-level modules. The programs in figures 11.7 through 11.9 show how variable data elements are transferred among different program modules.

When you execute the main program in figure 11.7, you see the output shown in figure 11.10.

```
*****    Program: MAIN.PRG*****
* The main program
SET TALK OFF
SET ECHO OFF
?
INPUT "Enter Value of A ...  " TO A
INPUT "      Value of B ...  " TO B
?
? "In Main Program:"
? "A=",A
? "B=",B
* Go to ADDAB.PRG
DO SUMA&B
?
? "We have returned to MAIN.PRG from SUMA&B.prg !"
RETURN
```

Fig. 11.7. Modules with memory variable data.

```
*****    Program: SUMA&B.PRG    *****
* Program module to add A and B
?
?"             We have entered SUMA&B.PRG !"
* Do not use the reserved word SUM for the variable name!
SUMAB=A+B
? "                     A = ",A
? "                     B = ",B
? "            SUM OF A, B = ",SUMAB
* Go to PRINTA&B.prg
DO PRINTA&B
?
?"             We have returned to SUMA&B.prg from PRINTA&B.prg !"
* Return to main program
RETURN
```

Fig. 11.8. Modules with memory variable data.

```
*****   Program: PRINTA&B.PRG   *****
* Module to print results from SUMA&B.prg
?
? "                              We have entered PRINTA&B.PRG !"
? "                                     A = ",A
? "                                     B = ",B
? "                            SUM OF A, B = ",SUMAB
* Return to SUMA&B.prg
RETURN
```

Fig. 11.9. Module to print data.

```
. DO MAIN

Enter Value of A ...   123
      Value of B ...   456

In Main Program:
A=         123
B=         456

             We have entered SUMA&B.PRG !
                     A =         123
                     B =         456
            SUM OF A, B =        579

                            We have entered PRINTA&B.PRG !
                                     A =         123
                                     B =         456
                            SUM OF A, B =        579

             We have returned to SUMA&B.prg from PRINTA&B.prg !

We have returned to MAIN.PRG from SUMA&B.prg !
.
```

Fig. 11.10. Output from main program.

Variables A and B are created in the main program and then passed to the next level SUMA&B.PRG. The variable SUMAB is generated in the second level and passed to the third-level module PRINTA&B.PRG.

However, data elements created in a lower-level module cannot be automatically passed to a higher-level module. The problem is illustrated in the main program MAINPAY.PRG of figure 11.11 and in the program module CALWAGE.PRG of figure 11.12.

```
*****    Program: MAINPAY.PRG    *****
* Main program to compute weekly gross pay
SET TALK OFF
SET ECHO OFF
* Get worker's name
?
ACCEPT "    Enter Worker's First Name .... " TO FIRSTNAME
ACCEPT "                    Last Name ..... " TO LASTNAME
USE WAGES
LOCATE FOR LAST_NAME=LASTNAME .AND. FIRST_NAME=FIRSTNAME
* Call out CALWAGE.prg for computing wage
DO CALWAGE
* Display results returned from CALWAGE.prg
?
? "    Worker's Name : "+TRIM(FIRST_NAME)+" "+TRIM(LAST_NAME)
?
? "        Hours Worked ........ "+STR(HOURS,7,0)
? "        Hourly Wage Rate .... "+STR(RATE,7,2)
? "        Regular Pay ......... "+STR(REGULARPAY,7,2)
? "        Overtime Pay ........ "+STR(OVERTIME,7,2)
? "        Total Gross Pay ..... "+STR(REGULARPAY+OVERTIME,7,2)
?
RETURN
```

Fig. 11.11. The MAINPAY.PRG program.

```
*****    Program: CALWAGE.PRG    *****
* Module calculate GROSSWAGE with given HOURS, PAYRATE
IF HOURS<=40
  REGULARPAY=HOURS*RATE
  OVERTIME=0
ELSE
  REGULARPAY=40*RATE
  OVERTIME=(HOURS-40)*RATE*1.5
ENDIF
RETURN
```

Fig. 11.12. Program module CALWAGE.PRG.

The output from the main program MAINPAY.PRG is shown in figure 11.13.

```
.  DO MAINPAY

     Enter Worker's First Name ....  Albert
                     Last Name .....  Williams

     Worker's Name : Albert L. Williams

               Hours Worked ........    43
               Hourly Wage Rate ....   8.50
Variable not found
                                                        ?
? "           Regular Pay ........ "+STR(REGULARPAY,7,2)
Called from - B:MAINPAY.prg
Terminate command file? (Y/N)
```

Fig. 11.13. Output from MAINPAY.PRG.

The variable REGULARPAY is not recognized by the main program, and an error message is displayed:

Variable not found

REGULARPAY is recognized only by CALWAGE.PRG (where the variable was created). To ensure that higher-level modules can share data created in lover-level modules, you can declare the variables PUBLIC.

PUBLIC

With the PUBLIC command, you can decide which memory variables can be accessed from every program module at any level. The memory variables must be entered in the PUBLIC command, such as

PUBLIC <memory variable list>

For example, to solve the problem in figure 11.13, you can add the following command line in front of PUBLIC.PRG to pass the variables back and forth between the main program and the lower-level module:

PUBLIC REGULARPAY,OVERTIME

When you run the program PUBLIC.PRG, you see the results shown in figure 11.15. The contents of the public variables REGULARPAY and OVERTIME have been successfully returned to the main program.

```
*****    PROGRAM: PUBLIC.PRG    *****
* Main program to compute weekly gross pay
SET TALK OFF
SET ECHO OFF
* Declare all public variables
PUBLIC REGULARPAY,OVERTIME
* Get worker's name
?
ACCEPT "    Enter Worker's First Name .... " TO FIRSTNAME
ACCEPT "                    Last Name ..... " TO LASTNAME
USE WAGES
LOCATE FOR LAST_NAME=LASTNAME.AND.FIRST_NAME=FIRSTNAME
* Call out CALWAGE.prg for computing wage
DO CALWAGE
* Display results returned from CALWAGE.prg
?
? "    Worker's Name : "+TRIM(FIRST_NAME)+" "+TRIM(LAST_NAME)
?
? "            Hours Worked ........ "+STR(HOURS,7,0)
? "            Hourly Wage Rate .... "+STR(RATE,7,2)
? "            Regular Pay ......... "+STR(REGULARPAY,7,2)
? "            Overtime Pay ........ "+STR(OVERTIME,7,2)
? "            Total Gross Pay ..... "+STR(REGULARPAY+OVERTIME,7,2)
?
RETURN
```

Fig. 11.14. Using PUBLIC variables.

```
. DO PUBLIC

    Enter Worker's First Name .... Albert
                    Last Name ..... Williams

    Worker's Name : Albert L. Williams

            Hours Worked ........      43
            Hourly Wage Rate ....    8.50
            Regular Pay ......... 340.00
            Overtime Pay ........   38.25
            Total Gross Pay ..... 378.25


.
```

Fig. 11.15. Results of PUBLIC.PRG.

PUBLIC memory variables can be created at any level and can be used throughout the whole program structure. Memory variables can also be designated as PRIVATE so that the variables are recognized only within the creating module.

PRIVATE

With the PRIVATE command, you can use memory variables with the same names as variables in other levels. However, when you leave a program module that uses a PRIVATE variable, the variable is emptied, and a higher-level module fills the contents of the variable. A PRIVATE command can be written as

    PRIVATE ALL
    PRIVATE <memory variable list>
    PRIVATE ALL LIKE <memory variable description>
    PRIVATE ALL EXCEPT <memory variable description>

Examples of PRIVATE are

    PRIVATE ALL
    PRIVATE REGULARPAY,OVERTIME
    PRIVATE ALL LIKE *NET
    PRIVATE ALL EXCEPT NET?????

In a PRIVATE command, you can use an asterisk (*) or a question mark (?) to mask the skeleton for describing the private variables. (To review masking a memory variable, see Chapter 6.)

Private variables are illustrated in the programs FIRST.PRG (fig. 11.16) and SUBPROG.PRG (fig. 11.17).

The results of these programs are shown in figure 11.18.

The variables (A and STRING) created by the FIRST.PRG program are declared PRIVATE by the SUBPROG.PRG module. The variables are then used as new variables in the program module SUBPROG.PRG, and different data elements are assigned to each. However, when you leave the program module and return to the

```
*****    Program: FIRST.PRG    *****
A=123
STRING="A Test String"
?
?" Before entering SUBPROG.prg: "
?"          A = ",A
?"       STRING = ",STRING
DO SUBPROG
?
?" After returning from SUBPROG.prg"
?"          A = ",A
?"       STRING = ",STRING
RETURN
```

Fig. 11.16. The FIRST.PRG program.

```
*****     Program: SUBPROG.PRG    *****
* Hide those variables created by FIRST.PRG
PRIVATE A,STRING
?
?"               We have entered SUBPROG.PRG !"
A=999
STRING="We have changed!"
?"                          A = ",A
?"                     STRING = ",STRING
RETURN
```

Fig. 11.17. The SUBPROG.PRG program.

```
. DO FIRST

  Before entering SUBPROG.prg:
          A =           123
     STRING =  A Test String

             We have entered SUBPROG.PRG !
                       A =           999
                  STRING =  We have changed!

  After returning from SUBPROG.prg
          A =           123
     STRING =  A Test String
.
```

Fig. 11.18. Results of FIRST and SUBPROG.PRG.

main program, the variables lose their PRIVATE status and resume the previous data elements.

You can change the status of a memory variable at any time. If you wish to change a public variable to a private variable, or a private variable to a public variable, you need only to modify the commands.

Passing Data Records between Program Modules

Unlike memory variables, a data record is considered public and can be shared by every module in the program structure. You can USE a database file in a program module and retain the data record position throughout the program structure. In the program MAINGET.PRG (fig. 11.19), the module GETFILE.PRG accesses the database file

```
*****    Program: MAINGET.PRG    *****
* The main program to get records
SET TALK OFF
SET ECHO OFF
* Go to get a file from GETFILE.prg module
DO GETFILE
* Display the record returned from GETRECRD.prg
?
? "Data record retrieved from GETFILE.Prg and GETRECRD.prg"
?
DISPLAY
* Look at the next data record
SKIP
?
? "Returned from GETFILE.prg!"
?
DISPLAY
RETURN
```

Fig. 11.19. Main program to use modules.

EMPLOYEE.DBF. From the program module GETFILE.PRG (fig. 11.20), you can call another module, GETRECRD.PRG, to position the record pointer at the fifth data record. The program module GETRECRD.PRG is shown in figure 11.21.

```
*****    Program: GETFILE.PRG    *****
* Open a database file
USE EMPLOYEE
RECORDNO=5
* Go to get No.5 data record
DO GETRECRD
* Return to main program
RETURN
```

Fig. 11.20. Program module GETFILE.PRG.

```
*****    Program: GETRECRD.PRG    *****
* Set the record pointer at record no. RECORDNO set by GETFILE.prg
GOTO RECORDNO
RETURN
```

Fig. 11.21. The module GETRECRD.PRG.

The output of these program modules is shown in figure 11.22.

When you return to the main program after using the modules GETFILE.PRG and GETRECRD.PRG, the record pointer is still positioned at data record 5. The fields of the data record can be accessed by any module or the main program.

```
. DO MAINGET

Data record retrieved via GETFILE.Prg and GETRECRD.prg

Record#   FIRST_NAME   LAST_NAME   AREA_CODE  PHONE_NO  MALE  BIRTH_DATE  ANNUAL_PAY
      5   Kirk D.      Chapman     618        625-7845  .T.   08/04/61      20737.50

Returned from GETFILE.prg!

Record#   FIRST_NAME   LAST_NAME   AREA_CODE  PHONE_NO  MALE  BIRTH_DATE  ANNUAL_PAY
      6   Mary W.      Thompson    213        432-6782  .F.   06/18/55      25725.00
.
```

Fig. 11.22. Output of MAINGET.PRG.

A Graphics Program Module

dBASE III's programming tools can also be used to generate graphics output. To develop a program module to produce a bar chart, you need to set up a database file containing the necessary data elements. Figure 11.23 shows the structure of the database file BARCHART.DBF.

```
. USE BARCHART
. DISPLAY STRUCTURE
Structure for database : B:BARCHART.dbf
Number of data records :      5
Date of last update    : 03/25/85
Field  Field name   Type         Width     Dec
    1  CLASSCOUNT   Numeric        2
    2  CLASSLABEL   Character     20
** Total **                       23

. LIST ALL
Record#   CLASSCOUNT  CLASSLABEL
      1          30   GROUP A
      2          25   GROUP B
      3          55   GROUP C
      4          45   GROUP D
      5          20   GROUP E
.
```

Fig. 11.23. Using a graphics program module.

The database file stores five data records, each of which contains the class frequency (CLASSCOUNT) and a class description

(CLASSLABEL). A bar chart of the class frequencies might look like the diagram shown in figure 11.24.

```
I
IXXXXXXXXXXXXXXXXXXXXXXXXXXXXXX
IXXXXXXXXXXXXXXXXXXXXXXXXXXXXXX        GROUP A (30)
IXXXXXXXXXXXXXXXXXXXXXXXXXXXXXX
I
IXXXXXXXXXXXXXXXXXXXXXXXXX
IXXXXXXXXXXXXXXXXXXXXXXXXX        GROUP B (25)
IXXXXXXXXXXXXXXXXXXXXXXXXX
I
IXXXXXXXXXXXXXXXXXXXXXXXXXXXXXXXXXXXXXXXXXXXXXXXXXXXXXXX
IXXXXXXXXXXXXXXXXXXXXXXXXXXXXXXXXXXXXXXXXXXXXXXXXXXXXXXX        GROUP C (55)
IXXXXXXXXXXXXXXXXXXXXXXXXXXXXXXXXXXXXXXXXXXXXXXXXXXXXXXX
I
IXXXXXXXXXXXXXXXXXXXXXXXXXXXXXXXXXXXXXXXXXXXXXX
IXXXXXXXXXXXXXXXXXXXXXXXXXXXXXXXXXXXXXXXXXXXXXX        GROUP D (45)
IXXXXXXXXXXXXXXXXXXXXXXXXXXXXXXXXXXXXXXXXXXXXXX
I
IXXXXXXXXXXXXXXXXXXXX
IXXXXXXXXXXXXXXXXXXXX        GROUP E (20)
IXXXXXXXXXXXXXXXXXXXX

                     THIS IS A SAMPLE BAR CHART
```

Fig. 11.24. A sample bar chart.

In the diagram, each wide bar represents a frequency class. The width of a horizontal bar is determined by the class frequency and is shown as a graphics symbol (X). The module PRINTBAR.PRG can display a horizontal bar (a set of graphics symbols) with the width of a given number of characters (NCHARS) (see fig. 11.25).

```
*****    Program: PRINTBAR.PRG    *****
* Module to print a bar with NCHARS characters long
KOUNT=1
* Use a given ASCII character for a graphic symbol
GRAFSYMBOL="X"
* Set the first character of BAR to the graphic symbol
BAR=GRAFSYMBOL
* Build the bar with graphic symbols
DO WHILE KOUNT<=(NCHARS-1)
BAR=BAR+GRAFSYMBOL
KOUNT=KOUNT+1
ENDDO
* Display the bar
?SPACE(3)+"I"
?SPACE(3)+"I"+BAR
?SPACE(3)+"I"+BAR+SPACE(3)+TRIM(ALABEL)+"  ("+STR(KOUNT,2,0)+")"
?SPACE(3)+"I"+BAR
RETURN
```

Fig. 11.25. Module for bar chart with NCHARS variable.

PRINTBAR.PRG generates a bar graph by joining a given number of graphics symbols together to form a bar, such as

XXXXXXXXXXXXXXXXXXXXXXXXXXXXXX

The width (or length) of the horizontal bar is determined by the class frequency. The loop structure DO WHILE . . . ENDDO is used to build the bar with a variable (NCHARS) number of graphics symbols. After the bar is created, you can display the bar three times to form a wider diagram, such as

XXXXXXXXXXXXXXXXXXXXXXXXXXXXXX
XXXXXXXXXXXXXXXXXXXXXXXXXXXXXX
XXXXXXXXXXXXXXXXXXXXXXXXXXXXXX

You can add a class description or label, such as GROUP A(30):

XXXXXXXXXXXXXXXXXXXXXXXXXXXXXX
XXXXXXXXXXXXXXXXXXXXXXXXXXXXXX   GROUP A (30)
XXXXXXXXXXXXXXXXXXXXXXXXXXXXXX

Each time you use the module PRINTBAR.PRG with a class frequency (NCHARS) and a label (ALABEL), a wide horizontal bar is displayed. You can set up a loop in the program BARCHART.PRG to retrieve the data records from BARCHART.DBF and use the PRINTBAR.PRG module to produce a horizontal bar (see fig. 11.26).

```
*****    Program: BARCHART.PRG    *****
* A program to show a bar chart by using data from BARCHART.DBF
SET TALK OFF
SET ECHO OFF
CLEAR
USE BARCHART.DBF
DO WHILE .NOT. EOF()
* Get class count and class description
NCHARS=CLASSCOUNT
ALABEL=CLASSLABEL
DO PRINTBAR
SKIP
ENDDO
?
?"                      THIS IS A SAMPLE BAR CHART"
RETURN
```

Fig. 11.26. Using BARCHART.DBF to display a bar chart.

To print the bar chart, add the SET PRINT ON command before BARCHART.PRG. After printing, you can deactivate the printer by inserting the SET PRINT OFF command before the RETURN line.

In figure 11.24, X was used as the graphics symbol to form the horizontal bar. You can use other letters to produce different horizontal bars (see fig. 11.27).

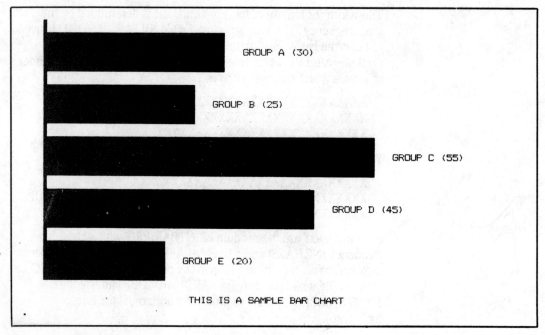

GROUP A (30)

GROUP B (25)

GROUP C (55)

GROUP D (45)

GROUP E (20)

THIS IS A SAMPLE BAR CHART

Fig. 11.27. A sample bar chart.

The bar chart was produced by an ASCII graphics character on an IBM PC. Some additional ASCII graphics characters used by the IBM PC are shown in figure 11.28. For a detailed description of the ASCII characters, see Appendix A.

To produce the bar chart shown in figure 11.27, use ASCII character 219 in place of X and ASCII character 222 for I (vertical axis). Figure 11.29 shows the FANCYBAR.PRG program module.

The main program DOFANCY.PRG that calls the FANCYBAR.PRG module is shown in figure 11.30.

If you use ASCII character 222 as both the graphics symbol and the vertical axis, you produce a different bar design. (see fig. 11.31).

If you enter the graphics programs, you can reproduce the results on your IBM monochrome or generic graphics monitor. However, to print these bar charts, your printer must be equipped with special graphics capability. (If you are unsure whether your printer has this capability, check your printer manual.) Figures 11.29 and 11.30 were generated on an Epson printer with the use of custom screen print software.

```
. TYPE GRAFCHAR.PRG
*****    Program: GRAFCHAR.PRG    *****
* Display some ASCII graphic characters
SET TALK OFF
SET ECHO OFF
?
?
?"    Some Useful ASCII Graphic Characters Supported by an IBM PC"
CHARNO=219
?
?
DO WHILE CHARNO<=223
?"           ASCII Character No.  "+STR(CHARNO,3,0)+":  "+CHR(CHARNO)
?
CHARNO=CHARNO+1
ENDDO
RETURN

.


                              CHRI=220

                     I=O


. DO GRAFCHAR


    Some Useful ASCII Graphic Characters Supported by an IBM PC


          ASCII Character No. 219: █

          ASCII Character No. 220: ▄

          ASCII Character No. 221: ▌

          ASCII Character No. 222: ▐

          ASCII Character No. 223: ▀

.
```

Fig. 11.28. ASCII graphics characters.

```
*****     Program: FANCYBAR.PRG    *****
* Module to print a bar with NCHARS characters long
KOUNT=1
* Use a given ASCII character for a graphic symbol
GRAFSYMBOL=CHR(219)
* Set the first character of BAR to the graphic symbol
BAR=GRAFSYMBOL
* Build the bar with graphic symbols
DO WHILE KOUNT<=(NCHARS-1)
BAR=BAR+GRAFSYMBOL
KOUNT=KOUNT+1
ENDDO
* Display the bar
?SPACE(3)+CHR(222)
?SPACE(3)+CHR(222)+BAR
?SPACE(3)+CHR(222)+BAR+SPACE(3)+TRIM(ALABEL)+" ("+STR(KOUNT,2,0)+")"
?SPACE(3)+CHR(222)+BAR
RETURN
```

Fig. 11.29. The FANCYBAR.PRG program module.

```
*****     Program: DOFANCY.PRG    *****
* A program to show a bar chart by using data from BARCHART.DBF
SET TALK OFF
SET ECHO OFF
CLEAR
USE BARCHART.DBF
DO WHILE .NOT. EOF()
* Get class count and class description
NCHARS=CLASSCOUNT
ALABEL=CLASSLABEL
DO FANCYBAR
SKIP
ENDDO
?
?"                    THIS IS A SAMPLE BAR CHART"
RETURN
```

Fig. 11.30. The main program DOFANCY.PRG.

Accessing Multiple Database Files

Up to this point, you have used only one database file at a time, and the record pointer has been positioned at the current active record. You have been able to access the current data record at any time, in any program module, and at any level.

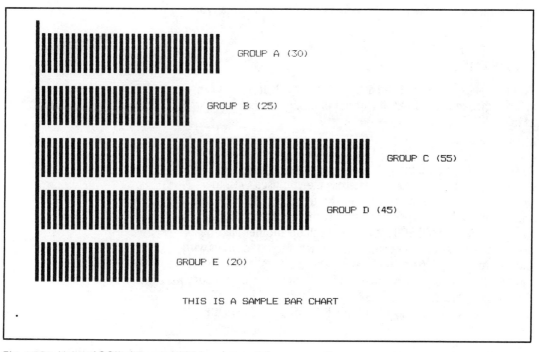

Fig. 11.31. Using ASCII character 222 in a bar graph.

However, if you open another database file with the USE command, the current active database file is replaced, and the data record pointer is repositioned. As a result, you cannot return to a data record of the original database file. This can be a serious problem if you need to access more than one database file at the same time. To solve this problem, use the SELECT command.

SELECT

You can use the SELECT command to choose a database file and store it in an active work area. In dBASE III, you can use up to ten different work areas. The format of the SELECT command is

. SELECT <work area>

The work area can be designated by a number (1 through 10), or a letter (A through J), such as

. SELECT 1
. SELECT A

For instance, to put EMPLOYEE.DBF in the first work area, you enter

. SELECT 1
. USE EMPLOYEE

When a database file has been assigned to a work area, you can activate the file with SELECT without entering the database name, as in

. SELECT 1

Although you can use ten different work areas, only one database file is active at a time. The last database file you used with the SELECT command is the active file, and the other files remain in the background work area. You can switch another file to the foreground, using SELECT. When you call up another file, the previous database file marks the current data record location with the record pointer. When the previous file is brought back to the foreground, the data record marked is still the active data record for that database file. In figure 11.32, the program GETFILES.PRG alternates between the EMPLOYEE.DBF and QTYSOLD.DBF databases.

```
*****   Program: GETFILES.PRG   *****
* Accessing different database files in the same program
SET TALK OFF
SET ECHO OFF
* Put EMPLOYEE.dbf in work area 1
SELECT 1
USE EMPLOYEE
GOTO 5
DISPLAY
* Put QTYSOLD.dbf in work area 2
SELECT 2
USE QTYSOLD
DISPLAY
* Switch back to EMPLOYEE.dbf
SELECT 1
* Go to the next data record
SKIP
DISPLAY
RETURN
```

Fig. 11.32. Accessing different database files.

The output from the program is shown in figure 11.33. As you can see, the record pointers remained intact.

```
. DO GETFILES
Record#  FIRST_NAME     LAST_NAME   AREA_CODE PHONE_NO MALE BIRTH_DATE ANNUAL_PAY
     5   Kirk D.        Chapman       618      625-7845 .T.  08/04/61    20737.50
Record#  DATE       MODEL        UNITS_SOLD
     1   12/07/84 RCA-XA100            2
Record#  FIRST_NAME     LAST_NAME   AREA_CODE PHONE_NO MALE BIRTH_DATE ANNUAL_PAY
     6   Mary W.        Thompson      213      432-6782 .F.  06/18/55    25725.00
.
```

Fig. 11.33. Output of GETFILES.PRG.

You can also use the database file name as an alias:

. SELECT 1 ALIAS
. USE EMPLOYEE

. . .

. . .
. SELECT 2
. USE . . .

. . .

. . .
. SELECT EMPLOYEE

By adding ALIAS to the SELECT 1 phrase, you name the work area EMPLOYEE. Whenever you want to switch that database file to the foreground, you can enter SELECT EMPLOYEE instead of SELECT 1.

You cannot use the database file name for the work area designation without the ALIAS command. If you try to access a file by the file name, and if the file has been assigned to a SELECT number, the error message **ALIAS name already in use** appears (see fig. 11.34). When this happens, you can solve the problem by using the CLOSE DATABASE command.

```
. SELECT 1
. USE EMPLOYEE
. SELECT 2
. USE QTYSOLD
. USE EMPLOYEE
ALIAS name already in use
               ?
USE EMPLOYEE
Do you want some help? (Y/N) No
.
```

Fig. 11.34. Error message with SELECT.

An Example of Multiple Database File Processing

To see how SELECT can be used to process multiple database files, you can use an example of inventory evaluation. The database files with the necessary data are shown in figures 11.35 through 11.38. The database STOCKS.DBF stores the inventory items. Each data record contains the description of an inventory item and the quantities on-hand and on-order. The costs of the inventory items are stored in the database file COSTS.DBF.

```
Structure for database : B:STOCKS.DBF
Number of data records :      11
Date of last update    : 03/20/85
Field   Field name   Type        Width    Dec
    1    STOCK_NO     Character      12
    2    MODEL_NO     Character      10
    3    MFG          Character       9
    4    OPTIONS      Character      25
    5    ON_HAND      Numeric         3
    6    ON_ORDER     Numeric         3
** Total **                         63
```

Fig. 11.35. Structure of database file STOCKS.DBF.

```
Record# STOCK_NO     MODEL_NO   MFG       OPTIONS               ON_HAND ON_ORDER
    1   ST-01-19P-01 RCA-XA100  RCA       Standard                  5       2
    2   ST-01-25C-02 RCA-XA200  RCA       Stereo, Wireless Remote  10       5
    3   ST-02-19P-01 ZENITH-19P ZENITH    Standard, Portable        7       3
    4   ST-02-21C-02 ZENITH-21C ZENITH    Standard, Wire Remote     3       2
    5   ST-02-25C-03 ZENITH-25C ZENITH    Stereo, Wireless Romote   5       5
    6   ST-03-17P-01 SONY1700P  SONY      Standard                  4       4
    7   ST-03-26C-02 SONY2600XT SONY      Stereo, Wireless Remote   5       5
    8   ST-03-19P-01 PANAV019PT PANASONIC Monitor, Wireless Remote  3       2
    9   ST-03-25C-02 PANAV25CTX PANASONIC Monitor, Wireless Remote  4       5
   10   ST-04-19P-01 SANYO-19-P SANYO     Standard                  3       2
   11   ST-04-21C-02 SANYO-21-C SANYO     Table Model, Wire Remote  5       4
```

Fig. 11.36. Necessary data for inventory evaluation.

```
Structure for database : B:COSTS.dbf
Number of data records :      11
Date of last update    : 03/20/85
Field   Field name   Type        Width    Dec
    1    STOCK_NO     Character      12
    2    MODEL_NO     Character      10
    3    LIST_PRICE   Numeric         7       2
    4    OUR_COST     Numeric         7       2
    5    DLR_COST     Numeric         7       2
** Total **                         44
```

Fig. 11.37. Structure of database COSTS.DBF.

```
Record#   STOCK_NO      MODEL_NO     LIST_PRICE  OUR_COST  DLR_COST
      1   ST-01-19P-01  RCA-XA100        349.95    229.50    259.95
      2   ST-01-25C-02  RCA-XA200        595.00    389.00    459.00
      3   ST-02-19P-01  ZENITH-19P       385.00    255.00    325.00
      4   ST-02-21C-02  ZENITH-21C       449.95    339.00    389.50
      5   ST-02-25C-03  ZENITH-25C       759.95    589.00    669.50
      6   ST-03-17P-01  SONY1700P        450.95    330.00    380.50
      7   ST-03-26C-02  SONY2600XT      1390.95    850.00   1095.00
      8   ST-03-19P-01  PANAVO19PT       579.95    395.00    425.00
      9   ST-03-25C-02  PANAV25CTX      1095.95    795.00    885.00
     10   ST-04-19P-01  SANYO-19-P       369.00    249.00    319.00
     11   ST-04-21C-02  SANYO-21-C       525.95    365.50    425.50
```

Fig. 11.38. Inventory of COSTS.DBF.

The program in figure 11.39 computes the value of each inventory item. To compute the inventory value, use the program loop DO WHILE . . . ENDDO to access each of the items in STOCKS.DBF. Then locate the corresponding costs and stock numbers of the items in COSTS.DBF. You can use the program to switch between the two database files.

```
*****   Program : VALUES.PRG   *****
* A program to compute value of each stock item
SET TALK OFF
SET ECHO OFF
?
?"                    Value of Stock Items"
?
?" Stock No.       Model     Quantity    Unit Cost    Total Value"
* Put database files to work areas
SELECT 1
USE STOCKS
SELECT 2
USE COSTS
* Get stock items sequentially from STOCKS.dbf
DO WHILE .NOT. EOF()
SELECT 1
STOCKNO=STOCK_NO
* Get its cost from COSTS.dbf
SELECT 2
LOCATE FOR STOCK_NO=STOCKNO
* Store cost in memory variable
COST=OUR_COST
* Return toSTOCKS.dbf
SELECT 1
VALUE=COST*ON_HAND
? STOCK_NO+"  "+MODEL_NO+"   "+STR(ON_HAND,5,0)+STR(COST,14,2)+STR(VALUE,13,2)
* Process next stock item
SKIP
ENDDO
```

Fig. 11.39. A program to compute the value of each item.

The output of VALUES.PRG is shown in figure 11.40.

The VALUES.PRG stores the stock number (STOCK_NO) from the records in STOCKS.DBF in a memory variable named STOCKNO. Then the contents of the memory variable are used as a search key to find the cost in COSTS.DBF, as in

. LOCATE FOR STOCK_NO=STOCKNO

```
. DO VALUES

                 Value of Stock Items

   Stock No.        Model    Quantity   Unit Cost   Total Value
  ST-01-19P-01   RCA-XA100        5       229.50       1147.50
  ST-01-25C-02   RCA-XA200       10       389.00       3890.00
  ST-02-19P-01   ZENITH-19P       7       255.00       1785.00
  ST-02-21C-02   ZENITH-21C       3       339.00       1017.00
  ST-02-25C-03   ZENITH-25C       5       589.00       2945.00
  ST-03-17P-01   SONY1700P        4       330.00       1320.00
  ST-03-26C-02   SONY2600XT       5       895.00       4475.00
  ST-03-19P-01   PANAVO19PT       3       395.00       1185.00
  ST-03-25C-02   PANAV25CTX       4       795.00       3180.00
  ST-04-19P-01   SANYO-19-P       3       249.00        747.00
  ST-04-21C-02   SANYO-21-C       5       365.50       1827.50
  .
```

Fig. 11.40. The output of VALUES.PRG.

Joining Database Files

With the UPDATE command, you can change the data records in the active file, using data from another database file.

UPDATE

UPDATE uses data from a source file to change records in the active database file. To UPDATE a file, you match the records in two databases on a specified key field. The format of the command is

. UPDATE ON <key field> FROM <source file> REPLACE <existing field> WITH <expression>

When you use UPDATE, you can update only the active file, and the source file must be in a background work area. Make sure that both the source file and the file to be updated have been sorted or indexed. If you have not sorted the files, you must add the word RANDOM to the end of the command.

Suppose that the database file NEWCOSTS.DBF contains new cost information on the stock items. The contents of the database file are shown in figure 11.41.

```
. USE NEWCOSTS
. DISPLAY STRUCTURE
Structure for database : B:NEWCOSTS.dbf
Number of data records :        3
Date of last update     : 03/26/85
Field   Field name   Type        Width      Dec
    1   STOCK_NO     Character     12
    2   MODEL_NO     Character     10
    3   OUR_COST     Numeric        7         2
** Total **                       30

. LIST
Record#   STOCK_NO       MODEL_NO     OUR_COST
      1   ST-03-26C-02  SONY2600XT     850.00
      2   ST-01-25C-02  RCA-XA200      369.00
      3   ST-02-21C-02  ZENITH-25C     559.00
.
```

Fig. 11.41. The database file NEWCOSTS.DBF.

The structure of NEWCOSTS.DBF was defined by copying the structure from the file COSTS.DBF:

. USE COSTS
. COPY STRUCTURE TO NEWCOSTS.DBF

The unnecessary data fields were deleted after the structure was copied to the new file. The data records in NEWCOSTS.DBF contain the revised costs for the stock items. Instead of returning to COSTS.DBF to update each of the new cost items, you can use an UPDATE command. The program used for the updating operation is shown in figure 11.42.

```
*****   Program: UPDACOST.prg   *****
* Use data in NEWCOSTS.dbf to update COSTS.dbf
SET TALK OFF
SET ECHO OFF
SELECT B
USE NEWCOSTS
INDEX ON STOCK_NO TO SORT1
SELECT A
USE COSTS
INDEX ON STOCK_NO TO SORT2
UPDATE ON STOCK_NO FROM NEWCOSTS REPLACE OUR_COST WITH B->OUR_COST
RETURN
```

Fig. 11.42. Using the UPDATE command.

The UPDATE command used in the UPDACOST.PRG is

. UPDATE ON STOCK_NO FROM NEWCOSTS REPLACE
OUR_COST WITH B->OUR_COST

The symbol B-> designates the work area where the data field is found. After UPDACOST.PRG is executed, the costs of the items in COSTS.DBF have been updated. For example, the cost of ST-03-26C-02 is now $850.00 instead of the original $895.00 (see fig. 11.43).

```
. DO UPDACOST
. USE COSTS
. LIST
Record#   STOCK_NO    MODEL_NO     LIST_PRICE  OUR_COST  DLR_COST
      1   ST-01-19P-01 RCA-XA100       349.95    229.50    259.95
      2   ST-01-25C-02 RCA-XA200       595.00    369.00    459.00
      3   ST-02-19P-01 ZENITH-19P      385.00    255.00    325.00
      4   ST-02-21C-02 ZENITH-21C      449.95    559.00    389.50
      5   ST-02-25C-03 ZENITH-25C      759.95    589.00    669.50
      6   ST-03-17P-01 SONY1700P       450.95    330.00    380.50
      7   ST-03-26C-02 SONY2600XT     1390.95    850.00   1095.00
      8   ST-03-19P-01 PANAVO19PT      579.95    395.00    425.00
      9   ST-03-25C-02 PANAV25CTX     1095.95    795.00    885.00
     10   ST-04-19P-01 SANYO-19-P      369.00    249.00    319.00
     11   ST-04-21C-02 SANYO-21-C      525.95    365.50    425.50
.
```

Fig. 11.43. Results of UPDACOST.PRG.

You can also use UPDATE to add the contents of the records in a source file to the corresponding records in the master file. For example, RESTOCK.PRG updates the items in the master file STOCKS.DBF, using the data records in the source file RECEIVED.DBF (see fig. 11.44).

```
*****    Program: RESTOCK.PRG    *****
* Use data in NEWITEMS.dbf to update STOCKS.dbf
SET TALK OFF
SET ECHO OFF
SELECT B
USE RECEIVED
INDEX ON STOCK_NO TO SORT1
SELECT A
USE STOCKS
INDEX ON STOCK_NO TO SORT2
UPDATE ON STOCK_NO FROM RECEIVED REPLACE ON_HAND WITH ON_HAND+B->ON_HAND
RETURN
```

Fig. 11.44. Using new data to update STOCKS.DBF.

In figure 11.45, you see the contents of the master file STOCKS.DBF before the updating operation is performed.

```
. USE STOCKS
. LIST STOCK_NO,MODEL_NO,ON_HAND,ON_ORDER
Record#    STOCK_NO        MODEL_NO        ON_HAND ON_ORDER
        1  ST-01-19P-01    RCA-XA100             5        2
        2  ST-01-25C-02    RCA-XA200            10        5
        3  ST-02-19P-01    ZENITH-19P            7        3
        4  ST-02-21C-02    ZENITH-21C            3        2
        5  ST-02-25C-03    ZENITH-25C            5        5
        6  ST-03-17P-01    SONY1700P             4        4
        7  ST-03-26C-02    SONY2600XT            5        5
        8  ST-03-19P-01    PANAVO19PT            3        2
        9  ST-03-25C-02    PANAV25CTX            4        5
       10  ST-04-19P-01    SANYO-19-P            3        2
       11  ST-04-21C-02    SANYO-21-C            5        4
.
```

Fig. 11.45. STOCKS.DBF before the sorting operation.

The structure and the contents of the source file RECEIVED.DBF are displayed in figure 11.46.

```
. USE RECEIVED
. DISPLAY STRUCTURE
Structure for database : e:RECEIVED.dbf
Number of data records :      3
Date of last update    : 07/30/85
Field  Field name   Type       Width    Dec
    1  STOCK_NO     Character      12
    2  MODEL_NO     Character      10
    3  ON_HAND      Numeric         3
** Total **                       26

. LIST
Record#    STOCK_NO        MODEL_NO        ON_HAND
        1  ST-03-26C-02    SONY2600XT            2
        2  ST-01-25C-02    RCA-XA200             1
        3  ST-02-21C-02    ZENITH-21C            2
.
```

Fig. 11.46. Structure and contents of RECEIVED.DBF.

After you execute RESTOCK.PRG, you can see that the on-hand quantities are updated (see fig. 11.47).

APPEND FROM

You can also join files, using the APPEND FROM command. With APPEND FROM, you can take data records from the source file and

```
. DO RESTOCK
SORT1.ndx already exists, overwrite it? (Y/N) Yes
SORT2.ndx already exists, overwrite it? (Y/N) Yes
. USE STOCKS
. LIST STOCK_NO,MODEL_NO,ON_HAND,ON_ORDER
Record#  STOCK_NO       MODEL_NO    ON_HAND ON_ORDER
       1 ST-01-19P-01 RCA-XA100         5        2
       2 ST-01-25C-02 RCA-XA200        11        5
       3 ST-02-19P-01 ZENITH-19P        7        3
       4 ST-02-21C-02 ZENITH-21C        5        2
       5 ST-02-25C-03 ZENITH-25C        5        5
       6 ST-03-17P-01 SONY1700P         4        4
       7 ST-03-26C-02 SONY2600XT        7        5
       8 ST-03-19P-01 PANAVO19PT        3        2
       9 ST-03-25C-02 PANAV25CTX        4        5
      10 ST-04-19P-01 SANYO-19-P        3        2
      11 ST-04-21C-02 SANYO-21-C        5        4
.
```

Fig. 11.47. Results of RESTOCK.DBF.

append the files to the active database file, with or without a qualifier. The form of the command is

. APPEND FROM <name of source file>
<a qualifier, if needed>

The source file may or may not have the same data structure as the active database file. The APPEND FROM command appends only the data fields common to both files. If you want to append NEWITEMS.DBF to STOCKS.DBF, you can enter

. USE STOCKS
. APPEND FROM NEWITEMS

To append only selective records (those with model number RCA-200XA), you can add a qualifier to APPEND FROM, such as

. APPEND FROM NEWITEMS FOR MODEL_NO="RCA-200XA"

A program to append the records of NEWITEMS.DBF to the STOCKS.DBF database is shown in figure 11.48.

```
*****   Program: ADDITEMS.prg   *****
* Append data records of NEWITEMS.dbf to STOCKS.dbf
SET TALK OFF
SET ECHO OFF
USE STOCKS
APPEND FROM NEWITEMS
RETURN
```

Fig. 11.48. Program to append records to STOCKS.DBF.

The structure and contents of the source file NEWITEMS.DBF are
displayed in figure 11.49.

```
Structure for database  :  B:NEWITEMS.dbf
Number of data records  :      2
Date of last update     :  03/26/85
Field   Field name   Type       Width    Dec
   1    STOCK_NO     Character     12
   2    MODEL_NO     Character     10
   3    MFG          Character      9
   4    OPTIONS      Character     25
   5    ON_HAND      Numeric        3
   6    ON_ORDER     Numeric        3
** Total **                       63


Record# STOCK_NO    MODEL_NO  MFG      OPTIONS                 ON_HAND ON_ORDER
      1 ST-05-19P-01 PHILCO-19X PHILCO  Standard                   5       0
      2 ST-05-25C-01 GE-2500-ST GE      Stereo, Wireless Remote    3       1
```

Fig. 11.49. Structure and contents of NEWITEMS.DBF.

After the appending operation, you see the contents of
STOCKS.DBF as shown in figure 11.50.

```
Record# STOCK_NO    MODEL_NO   MFG       OPTIONS                    ON_HAND ON_ORDER
      1 ST-01-19P-01 RCA-XA200  RCA       Standard                      5       2
      2 ST-01-25C-02 RCA-XA200  RCA       Stereo, Wireless Remote      11       5
      3 ST-02-19P-01 ZENITH-19P ZENITH    Standard, Portable            7       3
      4 ST-02-21C-02 ZENITH-21C ZENITH    Standard, Wire Remote         5       2
      5 ST-02-25C-03 ZENITH-25C ZENITH    Stereo, Wireless Romote       5       5
      6 ST-03-17P-01 SONY1700P  SONY      Standard                      4       4
      7 ST-03-26C-02 SONY2600XT SONY      Stereo, Wireless Remote       7       5
      8 ST-03-19P-01 PANAV019PT PANASONIC Monitor, Wireless Remote      3       2
      9 ST-03-25C-02 PANAV25CTX PANASONIC Monitor, Wireless Remote      4       5
     10 ST-04-19P-01 SANYO-19-P SANYO     Standard                      3       2
     11 ST-04-21C-02 SANYO-21-C SANYO     Table Model, Wire Remote      5       4
     12 ST-05-19P-01 PHILCO-19X PHILCO    Standard                      5       0
     13 ST-05-25C-01 GE-2500-ST GE        Stereo, Wireless Remote       3       1
```

Fig. 11.50. Results of the appending operation.

Using the Macro Function

Up to this point, you have used a fixed field name in the conditional
qualifier of a LOCATE command, such as FOR STOCK_NO=. You
have also specified a fixed database file name in a USE command,
such as USE EMPLOYEE or USE QTYSOLD. A program with fixed
field names and database file names can be used only to process
those fields and files. If you want the program to process a different

database file, you must edit the database file name in the USE command.

With a more flexible program, you could process different data items by simply entering the names. The macro function of dBASE III was created for that purpose. By placing the & symbol before a memory variable name, you can use the contents of the variable as a data field or database file name. For example, if you store the string EMPLOYEE in a memory variable FILENAME in the form

. STORE "EMPLOYEE" TO FILENAME

or

FILENAME="EMPLOYEE"

You can then activate the database file by entering

. USE &FILENAME

By changing the contents of the variable FILENAME, you can activate different database files without changing the USE command in the program. The program GETDATA.PRG shows how to find the data record containing a given key data item (KEYITEM) in a key field (KEYFIELD) of a key database file (KEYFILE) (see fig. 11.51).

The results of the program are shown in figure 11.52.

```
*****    Program: GETDATA.prg    *****
* Search a key data item in a key field of a key file
SET TALK OFF
SET ECHO OFF
?
ACCEPT "        Enter Name of Database File .... " TO KEYFILE
ACCEPT "                      Data Field ....... " TO KEYFIELD
ACCEPT "                      The Search Key ... " TO KEYITEM
* Activate the keyfile
USE &KEYFILE
* Locate the key item
LOCATE FOR &KEYFIELD=KEYITEM
* Display the data record found
?
? "The Data Record Found:"
DISPLAY
?
RETURN
```

Fig. 11.51. The GETDATA.PRG program.

```
. DO GETDATA

        Enter Name of Database File .... EMPLOYEE
                      Data Field ....... LAST_NAME
                      The Search Key ... Nelson

The Data Record Found:
Record#  FIRST_NAME   LAST_NAME  AREA_CODE PHONE_NO MALE BIRTH_DATE ANNUAL_PAY
      3  Harry M.     Nelson      315       576-0235 .T.  02/15/58    30450.00
. DO GETDATA

        Enter Name of Database File .... COSTS
                      Data Field ....... STOCK_NO
                      The Search Key ... ST-03-26C-02

The Data Record Found:
Record#  STOCK_NO     MODEL_NO   LIST_PRICE OUR_COST DLR_COST
      7  ST-03-26C-02 SONY2600XT    1390.95   850.00  1095.00

.
```

Fig. 11.52. Results of GETDATA.PRG.

Chapter Summary

This chapter has introduced program modules. From the examples, you have seen different types of program structures. Some program structures involved two-level modules, and others used a multiple-level design. A program module can be accessed from any other module in the program. You can switch from one program module to another, using the DO command. As you move to different modules, the program control is passed from one module to another. When you enter a program module, the processing begins at the very first command line of the module. When you return to the main program, the processing returns to the line following the DO command.

The contents of the variables cannot be passed to another module without special instructions. In dBASE III, memory variables created in a higher-level module can be passed to a lower-level module, but the reverse is not true. PUBLIC variables can be shared within a whole program, whereas PRIVATE variables can be used only in a particular program module.

With program modules, you can design powerful programs to perform sophisticated data management functions, such as joining and updating files. The next chapter explains linking the modules with a menu to form an integrated database management system.

12

An Integrated Database Management System

An Overview

The introduction to this book stated that dBASE III's programming capability is one of its most powerful features. No other database software has programming tools that match those of dBASE III. If you use this programming feature in the batch processing mode, you can create well-designed, menu-driven programs that make database management functions simple enough for nonprogrammers to use effectively.

In Chapters 8 through 10, you saw how a program can be written to perform a specific database management task. In Chapter 11 the concept of program demodulation was introduced. You can design a complex database management system around several small, simple, functional program modules. This chapter shows you how to integrate these program modules with a menu-driven structure.

The chapter presents for an illustration a database management system that uses a multiple-level, menu-driven program. The program consists of commonly used program modules for performing such functions as billing, controlling inventory, and maintaining customers' accounts. These modules are deliberately kept simple so that they can be easily understood.

Note that this database management program by no means represents a complete, practical system. Instead, the program is only a simple example to show how a database program can be designed to perform various data management functions. Nevertheless, even though the example itself is not adequate for handling complex data of a large corporation, the program does provide valuable insights on how to design a sophisticated database management system.

An Integrated Database Management Program

You will recall that program demodulation divides a complex database management system into simple program modules. Each module performs a specific task. Using program demodulation, you can design a large database management system by creating several small program modules. After you design and test them, you can link them as a complete program by using a set of menus.

A simple database management system for Super Stereo and Television Distributors, Inc., a television wholesaler, is shown as an example. The company currently performs the following five basic data management functions:

Maintaining business accounts for each retailer

Billing customers for purchases made during a specified period

Maintaining stock information, including descriptions and costs

Monitoring and controlling inventory level

Maintaining personnel files

Main Menu Design

You can define the five basic functions as data management tasks in a main menu design. When you invoke the main program MAINMENU.PRG, using the dot command

. DO MAINMENU

the menu shown in figure 12.1 is displayed. The program that produces the main menu is shown in figure 12.2.

```
**********************************
***          MAIN MENU        ***
**********************************


    Task Code              Task

      [A]          ACCOUNT Maintenance

      [B]          Prepare BILLING

      [C]          COST Maintenance

      [I]          INVENTORY Control

      [P]          PERSONNEL File Maintenance

      [Q]          Quit


 Enter your choice (type in task code)
```

Fig. 12.1. Results of MAINMENU.PRG.

You can select a task from the main menu by entering the task code A, B, C, etc., after the prompt:

Enter your choice (type in task code)

When you select A, B, C, I, or P, the computer passes program control to one of the corresponding modules: ACCTMENU.PRG, BILLING.PRG, COSTMENU.PRG, INVNMENU.PRG, or EMPLMENU.PRG. When you select Q, the program returns to the dot prompt. The logical flow of program control within the database management system is shown in figure 12.3.

The Account Maintenance Submenu: ACCTMENU.PRG

Each program module represents a data management function that consists of a number of subtasks. They are defined with a second-level submenu, such as ACCTMENU.PRG. The program module ACCTMENU.PRG defines the tasks required to maintain the accounts. The tasks include the following:

```
*****  Program: MAINMENU.PRG   *****
* The Main Program, Display Main Menu
SET TALK OFF
SET ECHO OFF
STORE " " TO CHOICE
DO WHILE .T.
   CLEAR
   ?"                       ********************************"
   ?"                       ***          MAIN MENU       ***"
   ?"                       ********************************"
   ?
   ?
   ?"                       Task Code          Task"
   ?
   ?"                          [A]        ACCOUNT Maintenance"
   ?
   ?"                          [B]        Prepare BILLING"
   ?
   ?"                          [C]        COST Maintenance"
   ?
   ?"                          [I]        INVENTORY Control"
   ?
   ?"                          [P]        PERSONNEL File Maintenance"
   ?
   ?"                          [Q]        Quit"
   ?
   ?
   WAIT "                     Enter your choice (type in task code) " TO CHOICE
   DO CASE
      CASE UPPER(CHOICE)="A"
           DO ACCTMENU
      CASE UPPER(CHOICE)="B"
           DO BILLING
      CASE UPPER(CHOICE)="C"
           DO COSTMENU
      CASE UPPER(CHOICE)="I"
           DO INVNMENU
      CASE UPPER(CHOICE)="P"
           DO EMPLMENU
    CASE UPPER(CHOICE)="Q"
           RETURN
      OTHERWISE
         LOOP
   ENDCASE
ENDDO
```

Fig. 12.2. The MAINMENU.PRG program.

Adding a new retailer's account

Deleting an existing account when necessary

Examining or modifying the contents of an existing account

Preparing and printing a mailing list of all existing accounts

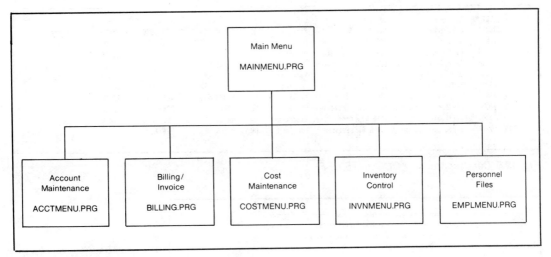

Fig. 12.3. A main menu design.

The database file ACCOUNTS.DBF contains information on the existing accounts. The structure of the file can be seen in figure 12.4.

```
. USE ACCOUNTS
. DISPLAY STRUCTURE
Structure for database : B:ACCOUNTS.dbf
Number of data records :      10
Date of last update    : 04/10/85
Field  Field name  Type        Width   Dec
    1  ACCT_NO     Character       5
    2  ACCT_NAME   Character      20
    3  ADDRESS     Character      20
    4  CITY        Character      12
    5  STATE       Character       2
    6  ZIP         Character       5
    7  AREA_CODE   Character       3
    8  PHONE_NO    Character       8
    9  MAX_CREDIT  Numeric         8
** Total **                       84
```

Fig. 12.4. Structure of ACCOUNTS.DBF.

ACCOUNTS.DBF contains data records for ten retailers. These records are shown in figure 12.5.

The submenu for selecting the account maintenance tasks is shown in figure 12.6. The program module ACCTMENU.PRG is presented in figure 12.7.

```
Record#  ACCT_NO  ACCT_NAME        ADDRESS             CITY       STATE  ZIP    AREA_CODE  PHONE_NO   MAX_CREDIT
      1  10001    SUPER SOUNDS     123 Main Street     Portland   OR     97201  503        224-6890   25000
      2  10002    ABC T.V. STORE   3459 Fifth Avenue   Portland   OR     97203  503        246-5687   20000
      3  10003    ACE SUPERVISION  2345 Columbia St.   Vacouver   WA     98664  206        892-4569   12000
      4  10004    DYNAVISION T.V. SHOP 13560 S.W. Division Portland OR   97201  503        287-8754   22000
      5  10005    Tower Stereo & TV 7865 Highway 99    Vancouver  WA     98665  206        574-7892   10000
      6  10006    REDDING SUPER TV 1245 Lakeview Drive Redding    CA     94313  432        877-6543   20000
      7  10007    National TV & Stereo 4567 Oak Street Portland   OR     97204  503        289-6832   25000
      8  10008    Superior TV & Sound 5789 S.W. Broadway Portland OR     97202  503        224-6541   5000
      9  10009    Electronic Mart  2568 Evergreen Blvd. Vancouver WA     98662  503        256-4578   15000
     10  10010    Stereo Super Store 12008 S. Division Portland   OR     97206  503        224-7275   20000
```

Fig. 12.5. Data records in ACCOUNTS.DBF.

```
======================================
===    ACCOUNT MAINTENANCE SUBMENU    ===
======================================


Task Code            Task

   [A]     ADD a new account

   [D]     DELETE an existing account

   [E]     EXAMINE/EDIT an account

   [M]     Print MAILING LIST

   [Q]     QUIT, return to mainmenu


Enter your choice (type in task code)
```

Fig. 12.6. Account maintenance submenu.

When you select task code A, D, E, or M, the computer passes
control to one of the program modules: ADDACCT.PRG,
DELTACCT.PRG, EDITACCT.PRG, or MAILLIST.PRG. If you
select Q, the computer passes control back to the main program
MAINMENU.PRG. The logical links between ACCTMENU.PRG and
the submodules are shown in figure 12.8.

ADDACCT.PRG

The program module ADDACCT.PRG is called from
ACCTMENU.PRG. You can use the module to append a new data
record to the database file ACCOUNTS.DBF. ADDACCT.PRG is
shown in figure 12.9.

```
*****  Program: ACCTMENU.PRG   *****
* Display Account Maintenance Submenu
SET TALK OFF
SET ECHO OFF
STORE " " TO CHOICE
DO WHILE .T.
   CLEAR
   ?
   ?
   ?"                  ======================================"
   ?"                  ===   ACCOUNT MAINTENANCE SUBMENU   ==="
   ?"                  ======================================"
   ?
   ?
   ?"                  Task Code            Task"
   ?
   ?"                     [A]     ADD a new account"
   ?
   ?"                     [D]     DELETE an existing account"
   ?
   ?"                     [E]     EXAMINE/EDIT an account"
   ?
   ?"                     [M]     Print MAILING LIST"
   ?
   ?"                     [Q]     QUIT, return to mainmenu"
   ?
   ?
   WAIT "                Enter your choice (type in task code) " TO CHOICE
   DO CASE
      CASE UPPER(CHOICE)="A"
         DO ADDACCT
      CASE UPPER(CHOICE)="D"
         DO DELTACCT
      CASE UPPER(CHOICE)="E"
         DO EDITACCT
      CASE UPPER(CHOICE)="M"
         DO MAILLIST
      CASE UPPER(CHOICE)="Q"
         RETURN
   ENDCASE
ENDDO
RETURN
```

Fig. 12.7. Program module ACCTMENU.PRG.

This program uses the custom format file ACCOUNT.FMT to label the record fields (see fig. 12.10).

When you invoke ADDACCT.PRG, you see the custom form used to append a record (see fig. 12.11). When you have entered the contents of the data fields, press Ctrl-End to append the data to the database file and exit the program module.

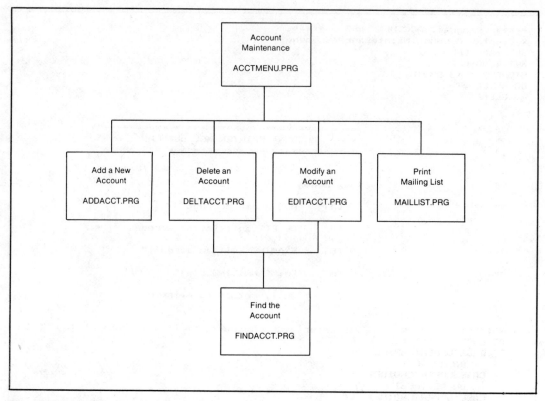

Fig. 12.8. Account maintenance submenu.

```
*****    Program: ADDACCT.PRG    *****
* Add a new account to ACCOUNTS.DBF
SET TALK OFF
SET ECHO OFF
USE ACCOUNTS
* Use custom format ACCOUNT.FMT
SET FORMAT TO ACCOUNT.FMT
APPEND BLANK
READ
RETURN
```

Fig. 12.9. The ADDACCT.PRG program.

```
*****  A Format File: ACCOUNT.FMT   *****
* Format file for editing or appending an account
@3,10 SAY "      Account Number: " GET ACCT_NO
@5,10 SAY "        Account Name: " GET ACCT_NAME
@7,10 SAY "             Address: " GET ADDRESS
@9,10 SAY "                City: " GET CITY
@11,10 SAY "               State: " GET STATE
@13,10 SAY "            ZIP Code: " GET ZIP
@15,10 SAY "           Area Code: " GET AREA_CODE
@17,10 SAY "        Phone Number: " GET PHONE_NO
@19,10 SAY "        Credit Limit: " GET MAX_CREDIT
```

Fig. 12.10. Format file ACCOUNT.FRM.

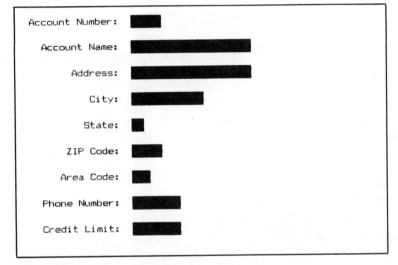

Fig. 12.11. Custom form in ADDACCT.PRG.

DELTACCT.PRG

The DELTACCT.PRG program module removes a data record from the database file ACCOUNTS.DBF. DELTACCT.PRG is shown in figure 12.12.

Before you can delete an account from ACCOUNTS.DBF, you must locate the account with the program module FINDACCT.PRG. The logical memory variable ACCTFOUND stores the results of the FINDACCT.PRG program module. If the account has been found, .T. is stored in ACCTFOUND. Otherwise, .F. is assigned to the variable.

```
*****    Program: DELTACCT.PRG    *****
* Delete an existing account
SET TALK OFF
SET ECHO OFF
* Find the account by its account number
DO FINDACCT
IF .NOT. ACCTFOUND
   * No such account found
   RETURN
ELSE
* Delete the account found
DELETE
PACK
@10,1 SAY "                    The account has been deleted !"
RETURN
ENDIF
RETURN
```

Fig. 12.12. The DELTACCT.PRG program.

FINDACCT.PRG

FINDACCT.PRG locates an account by the account number
(ACCT_NO). A listing of FINDACCT.PRG is shown in figure 12.13.

```
*****    Program: FINDACCT.PRG    *****
* Find an accoung by its account number
PUBLIC ACCTFOUND
SET TALK OFF
SET ECHO OFF
ACCTFOUND=.T.
CLEAR
?
?
?
?
ACCEPT "                Enter account number : " TO ACCTNO
* Find the account
USE ACCOUNTS
LOCATE FOR ACCT_NO=ACCTNO
IF EOF()
   * No such account
   ACCTFOUND=.F.
   RETURN
ENDIF
RETURN
```

Fig. 12.13. The FINDACCT.PRG program.

When you enter FINDACCT.PRG, you will see

Enter Account No.

When you enter the account number to be deleted, the number is assigned to the memory variable ACCTNO. Then the content of ACCT_NO is used to locate the data record with that account number in the ACCT_NO data field. If the account number is not found before the end of the file, the content of the variable ACCTFOUND is .F. Otherwise, the content of the variable is .T.

EDITACCT.PRG

The EDITACCT.PRG program module finds the account to be edited by calling the program module FINDACCT.PRG. When the account is found, the format file ACCOUNT.FMT is used to display the data fields for modification. For example, after you enter 10005 in response to the FINDACCT.PRG prompt, the contents of the account are displayed with the custom labels specified in the ACCOUNT.FMT file (see fig. 12.15). The program module EDITACCT.PRG is shown in figure 12.14.

```
*****    Program: EDITACCT.PRG    *****
* Edit an existing account
SET TALK OFF
SET ECHO OFF
* Find the account by its account number
DO FINDACCT
IF .NOT. ACCTFOUND
    * No such account found, Return to account submenu
    RETURN
ENDIF
* Use custom format ACCOUNT.FMT
SET FORMAT TO ACCOUNT.FMT
READ
RETURN
```

Fig. 12.14. The EDITACCT.PRG program.

If you do not need to modify the account, press Esc to return to the ACCTMENU.PRG program module. To modify the account, use the editing keystrokes described in earlier chapters. When you finish editing, press Ctrl-End to return to the ACCTMENU.PRG program module.

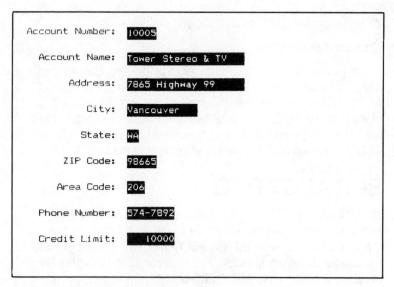

Fig. 12.15. The EDITACCT.PRG entry form.

MAILLIST.PRG

The MAILLIST.PRG program module prints a mailing list of all addresses in ACCOUNTS.DBF. The mailing list can be constructed and ordered by one of the three search keys shown in the screen display of figure 12.16.

```
        Choose one of the following search keys:


            [A]    By ACCOUNT NUMBER

            [S]    By STATE

            [Z]    By Zip Code

            [Q]    Quit, return to mainmenu




    Enter your choice (type in the search key)
```

Fig. 12.16. Search keys in MAILLIST.PRG.

After you choose a search key, MAILLIST.PRG requests the range of accounts to be included in the mailing list. For example, if you select option A, the screen display shown in figure 12.17 appears.

```
Enter:   Beginning account number ... 10003

         Ending account number ...... 10006




       Beginning account number must belong to an existing account!



Turn on and align the printer, strike any key to begin printing!
```

Fig. 12.17. Searching by account number.

After you enter the account numbers, you see a prompt to turn on the printer. When you press a key, a mailing list of the specified accounts is printed (see fig. 12.18).

```
ACE SUPERVISION
2345 Columbia St.
Vacouver,  WA  98664


DYNAVISION T.V. SHOP
13560 S.W. Division
Portland,  OR  97201


Tower Stereo & TV
7865 Highway 99
Vancouver,  WA  98665


REDDING SUPER TV
1245 Lakeview Drive
Redding,  CA  94313
```

Fig. 12.18. Results of MAILLIST.PRG.

The logic for producing a mailing list involves indexing the database file ACCOUNT.DBF according to the search key (by account number, by state, or by ZIP code). Once the database file is in order, the indexed file supplies the names and address of the accounts between the beginning key code (stored in the memory variable BCODE) and the ending key code (stored in ECODE).

Depending on the search key you choose, the key codes may contain account numbers, state codes, or ZIP codes. The beginning key code (BCODE) is used to position the record pointer at the first account in the selected range. The beginning code must be an existing key code, or no accounts will be located. A listing of MAILLIST.PRG is shown in figure 12.19.

```
*****   Program: MAILLIST.PRG   *****
* Print mailing list of accounts in ACCOUNTS.DBF
SET ECHO OFF
SET TALK OFF
CLEAR
@3,1SAY " "
?"                Choose one of the following search keys:"
?
?
?"                    [A]   By ACCOUNT NUMBER"
?
?"                    [S]   By STATE"
?
?"                    [Z]   By Zip Code"
?
?"                    [Q]   Quit, return to mainmenu"
@20,1SAY " "
WAIT "            Enter your choice (type in the search key) " TO CHOICE
DO CASE
   CASE UPPER(CHOICE)="A"
     CLEAR
     @15,10 SAY "Beginning account number must belong to an existing account!"
     @3,10SAY " "
     ACCEPT "            Enter:  Beginning account number ... " TO BCODE
     ?
     ACCEPT "                    Ending account number ...... " TO ECODE
     @20,1SAY " "
     WAIT " Turn on and align the printer, strike any key to begin printing!"
     USE ACCOUNTS
     INDEX ON ACCT_NO TO KEYCODE
     SEEK BCODE
     SET PRINT ON
     DO WHILE ACCT_NO>=BCODE.AND.ACCT_NO<=ECODE
        ?SPACE(5)+ACCT_NAME
        ?SPACE(5)+ADDRESS
        ?SPACE(5)+TRIM(CITY)+",  "+STATE+"  "+ZIP
        ?
        ?
        SKIP
     ENDDO
   CASE UPPER(CHOICE)="Z"
     CLEAR
     @15,10 SAY "Beginning zip code must be an existing zip code !"
```

(Continued on next page)

```
    @3,10SAY " "
    ACCEPT "              Enter:  Beginning zip code ....... " TO BCODE
    ?
    ACCEPT "                     Ending zip code .. ....... " TO ECODE
    @20,1SAY " "
    WAIT " Turn on and align the printer, strike any key to begin printing!"
    USE ACCOUNTS
    INDEX ON ZIP TO KEYCODE
    SEEK BCODE
    SET PRINT ON
    DO WHILE ZIP>=BCODE .AND. ZIP<=ECODE
        ?SPACE(5)+ACCT_NAME
        ?SPACE(5)+ADDRESS
        ?SPACE(5)+TRIM(CITY)+",   "+STATE+" "+ZIP
        ?
        ?
        SKIP
    ENDDO
  CASE UPPER(CHOICE)="S"
    CLEAR
    @15,10 SAY "Beginning state code must belong to an existing account!"
    @3,10SAY " "
    ACCEPT "              Enter:  Beginning state code ....... " TO BCODE
    ?
    ACCEPT "                     Ending state code ......... " TO ECODE
    @20,1SAY " "
    WAIT " Turn on and align the printer, strike any key to begin printing!"
    INDEX ON STATE TO KEYCODE
    SEEK BCODE
    SET PRINT ON
    DO WHILE STATE>=BCODE .AND. STATE<=ECODE
        ?SPACE(5)+ACCT_NAME
        ?SPACE(5)+ADDRESS
        ?SPACE(5)+TRIM(CITY)+",   "+STATE+"   "+ZIP
        ?
        ?
        SKIP
    ENDDO
  CASE UPPER(CHOICE)="Q"
    RETURN
ENDCASE
SET PRINT OFF
* Clean up working file, KEYCODE.NDX
CLOSE INDEX
ERASE KEYCODE.NDX
RETURN
```

Fig. 12.19. A listing of MAILLIST.PRG.

The Billing Submenu: BILLING.PRG

The second major data management function is billing, which includes preparing and printing invoices for sales made within a specific period. Billing programs can be complex, depending on the type of business involved. The billing example in this section has been kept simple so that you can easily understand the programming logic.

Two program modules are involved in the billing operation: BILLING.PRG and PRINTINV.PRG. BILLING.PRG gathers the information about the invoice items, and PRINTINV.PRG displays and prints the invoice. The logical link between these two program modules is shown in figure 12.20.

The BILLING.PRG program can be described as a series of five steps.

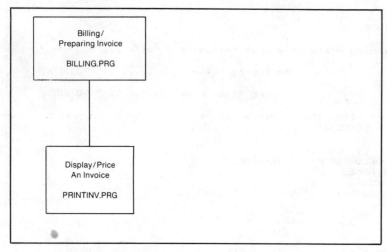

Fig. 12.20. Billing submenu.

Step 1

The program asks you to enter the following information:

  Invoice number

  Invoice date (automatically set with the current date)

  Account number

The form requesting the information is shown in figure 12.21.

Step 2

The account number you enter is checked against the ACCOUNT.DBF database file to determine the validity of the

```
Invoice Number :
   Invoice Date :  04/10/85
 Account Number :
```

Fig. 12.21. Form requesting information.

number. If the account is valid, the customer's name and address are displayed (see fig. 12.22). The items are saved in a temporary database file INVOICE.DBF and in memory variables that can later be passed on to the next program module, PRINTINV.PRG.

```
Invoice Number :  10001          Account Name : Tower Stereo & TV
   Invoice Date :  04/10/85           Address : 7865 Highway 99
 Account Number :  10005                        Vancouver  WA  98665


                       Quantity   Quantity   Quantity
   Stock No.   Model No.  Ordered   Shipped   Back Ordered   Unit Price
```

Fig. 12.22. Valid account number entered.

Step 3

The program then requests information on the items sold. For each item, the requested information includes the following:

Stock number

Quantity ordered

Quantity shipped

Quantity back-ordered (automatically computed as quantity ordered minus quantity shipped)

Figure 12.23 is an example of the screen display.

Step 4

After you enter the stock number, quantity ordered, quantity shipped, and quantity back-ordered, the program verifies the stock number with records in COSTS.DBF. If the stock number is valid, the model number and the unit price are displayed (see fig. 12.24).

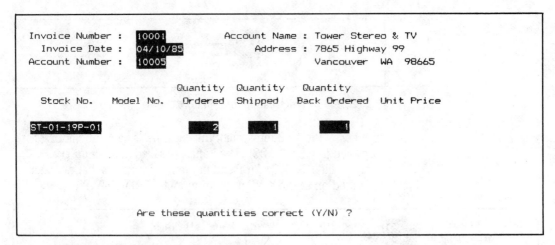

Fig. 12.23. Screen display of requested information.

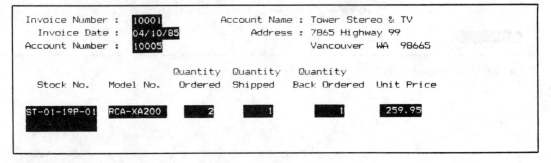

Fig. 12.24. Display with valid stock number.

The items are then saved in the temporary file SALE.DBF and in the memory variables that will be passed to another module. When the item is saved, the program requests information on the next item.

After you have entered all the items sold, press RETURN at the stock number field (see fig. 12.25). This keystroke causes PRINTINV.PRG to be activated and displays the invoice on the screen.

Step 5

When you select PRINTINV.PRG, the program retrieves the information from the memory variables that contain the account number, invoice number, invoice date, account address, etc. Information including stock numbers, order quantities, unit prices,

Fig. 12.25. Screen with all information entered.

etc., is obtained from the temporary database file SALE.DBF. These items are then organized and displayed as an invoice (see fig. 12.26). You can then print the invoice by selecting P in response to the prompt at the bottom of the screen.

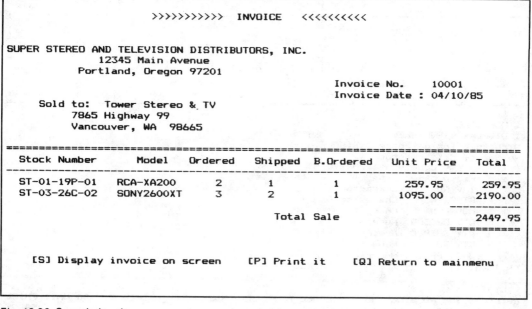

Fig. 12.26. Sample invoice.

After you print the invoice, the program updates the inventory of stock items in the STOCKS.DBF database file by subtracting the quantities shipped (QTY_SHIPED) stored in the SALE.DBF file. The program then appends to the permanent database file

INVOICES.DBF the invoice information, which is temporarily stored in INVOICE.DBF. The structure of the database files INVOICE.DBF and INVOICES.DBF is the same. Figure 12.27 shows the structure and content of INVOICE.DBF after the processing of Invoice No. 10001.

```
. USE INVOICE
. DISPLAY STRUCTURE
Structure for database : B:INVOICE.dbf
Number of data records :     1
Date of last update    : 04/10/85
Field  Field name  Type         Width   Dec
    1   INV_NO      Character       5
    2   INV_DATE    Date            8
    3   ACCT_NO     Character       5
** Total **                        19

. LIST
Record#   INV_NO INV_DATE ACCT_NO
     1    10001  04/10/85 10005
.
```

Fig. 12.27. Structure of INVOICE.DBF.

The structure and content of SALE.DBF after the processing of Invoice No. 10001 are shown in figure 12.28.

```
. USE SALE
. DISPLAY STRUCTURE
Structure for database : B:SALE.dbf
Number of data records :     3
Date of last update    : 04/10/85
Field  Field name  Type         Width   Dec
    1   INV_NO      Character       5
    2   STOCK_NO    Character      12
    3   MODEL_NO    Character      10
    4   QTY_ORDERD  Numeric         5
    5   QTY_SHIPED  Numeric         5
    6   QTY_BO      Numeric         5
    7   UNIT_PRICE  Numeric         7     2
** Total **                        50

. LIST
Record#   INV_NO STOCK_NO     MODEL_NO    QTY_ORDERD QTY_SHIPED QTY_BO UNIT_PRICE
     1    10001  ST-01-19P-01 RCA-XA200           2          1      1     259.95
     2    10001  ST-03-26C-02 SONY2600XT          3          2      1    1095.00
     3
.
```

Fig. 12.28. Structure of SALE.DBF.

STOCKS.DBF contains all items currently on hand or on order. The structure and content of STOCKS.DBF after printing Invoice No. 10001 are shown in figure 12.29.

```
Structure for database : B:STOCKS.dbf
Number of data records :      11
Date of last update    : 03/10/85
Field   Field name   Type        Width     Dec
    1   STOCK_NO     Character      12
    2   MODEL_NO     Character      10
    3   MFG          Character       9
    4   OPTIONS      Character      25
    5   ON_HAND      Numeric         3
    6   ON_ORDER     Numeric         3
** Total **                         63


Record# STOCK_NO    MODEL_NO   MFG      OPTIONS                   ON_HAND ON_ORDER
     1  ST-01-19P-01 RCA-XA100  RCA      Standard                     5       2
     2  ST-01-25C-02 RCA-XA200  RCA      Stereo, Wireless Remote     11       5
     3  ST-02-19P-01 ZENITH-19P ZENITH   Standard, Portable           7       3
     4  ST-02-21C-02 ZENITH-21C ZENITH   Standard, Wire Remote        5       2
     5  ST-02-25C-03 ZENITH-25C ZENITH   Stereo, Wireless Romote      5       5
     6  ST-03-17P-01 SONY1700P  SONY     Standard                     4       4
     7  ST-03-26C-02 SONY2600XT SONY     Stereo, Wireless Remote      7       5
     8  ST-03-19P-01 PANAV019PT PANASONIC Monitor, Wireless Remote    3       2
     9  ST-03-25C-02 PANAV25CTX PANASONIC Monitor, Wireless Remote    4       5
    10  ST-04-19P-01 SANYO-19-P SANYO    Standard                     3       2
    11  ST-04-21C-02 SANYO-21-C SANYO    Table Model, Wire Remote     5       4
```

Fig. 12.29. Structure of STOCKS.DBF.

The structure and content of COSTS.DBF are shown in figure 12.30. This file contains cost information on the stock items.

The program module BILLING.PRG is listed in figure 12.31.

PRINTINV.PRG

BILLING.PRG calls the program module PRINTINV.PRG, which displays and prints the invoice. The ? and ?? output commands are used to display the invoice. You can use the commands with the @ . . . SAY PICTURE commands to generate a different output format. A list of PRINTINV.PRG is shown in figure 12.32.

```
Structure for database : B:COSTS.dbf
Number of data records :        11
Date of last update     : 03/10/85
Field  Field name   Type        Width      Dec
    1   STOCK_NO     Character      12
    2   MODEL_NO     Character      10
    3   LIST_PRICE   Numeric         7        2
    4   OUR_COST     Numeric         7        2
    5   DLR_COST     Numeric         7        2
** Total **                        44


Record#   STOCK_NO       MODEL_NO    LIST_PRICE OUR_COST DLR_COST
      1   ST-01-19P-01   RCA-XA100      349.95   229.50   259.95
      2   ST-01-25C-02   RCA-XA200      595.00   369.00   459.00
      3   ST-02-19P-01   ZENITH-19P     385.00   255.00   325.00
      4   ST-02-21C-02   ZENITH-21C     449.95   559.00   389.50
      5   ST-02-25C-03   ZENITH-25C     759.95   589.00   669.50
      6   ST-03-17P-01   SONY1700P      450.95   330.00   380.50
      7   ST-03-26C-02   SONY2600XT    1390.95   850.00  1095.00
      8   ST-03-19P-01   PANAVO19PT     579.95   395.00   425.00
      9   ST-03-25C-02   PANAV25CTX    1095.95   795.00   885.00
     10   ST-04-19P-01   SANYO-19-P     369.00   249.00   319.00
     11   ST-04-21C-02   SANYO-21-C     525.95   365.50   425.50
```

Fig. 12.30. Structure of COST.DBF.

```
*****    Program: BILLING.PRG    *****
* A Billing Program
SET TALK OFF
SET ECHO OFF
PUBLIC INVNO,INVDATE,ACCTNO,ACCTNAME,MADDRESS,CITYSTZIP
* Enter Invoice Number, Date, Account Number via keyboard
CLEAR
DO WHILE .T.
   * Clean up working file, INVOICE.DBF
   USE INVOICE
   DELETE ALL
   PACK
   APPEND BLANK
   * Set invoice date to today's date
   REPLACE INV_DATE WITH DATE()
   @3,1 SAY "  Invoice Number : " GET INV_NO
   @4,1 SAY "    Invoice Date : " GET INV_DATE
   @5,1 SAY "  Account Number : " GET ACCT_NO
   READ
   INVNO=INV_NO
   INVDATE=INV_DATE
   ACCTNO=ACCT_NO
   * Get account name, address, etc. from ACCOUNTS.DBF
   USE ACCOUNTS
   LOCATE FOR ACCT_NO=ACCTNO
   IF EOF()
      CLEAR
      ?"  Invalid Account Number, Reenter !"
      LOOP
```

(Continued on next page)

```
        ELSE
            @1,1 SAY "                                                "
            EXIT
        ENDIF
    ENDDO
@3,35 SAY " Account Name : " +ACCT_NAME
@4,35 SAY "         Address : " +ADDRESS
@5,51 SAY TRIM(CITY)+"  "+STATE+"   "+ZIP
ACCTNAME=ACCT_NAME
MADDRESS=ADDRESS
CITYSTZIP=TRIM(CITY)+", "+STATE+"   "+ZIP
* Enter sale information
@7,5 SAY "                      Quantity  Quantity   Quantity"
@8,5 SAY "Stock No.   Model No.  Ordered  Shipped  Back Ordered  Unit Price"
SELECT 1
USE SALE
SELECT 2
USE COSTS
SELECT 1
DELETE ALL
PACK
ITEMNO=1
APPEND BLANK
DO WHILE .T.
    @9+ITEMNO,1 SAY " " GET STOCK_NO
    READ
    IF STOCK_NO=" "
        EXIT
    ENDIF
    STOCKNO=STOCK_NO
    @9+ITEMNO,28 SAY " " GET QTY_ORDERD
    @9+ITEMNO,38 SAY " " GET QTY_SHIPED
    READ
    REPLACE QTY_BO WITH QTY_ORDERD-QTY_SHIPED
    @9+ITEMNO,50 SAY " " GET QTY_BO
    READ
    @21,1 SAY " "
    WAIT "                      Are these quantities correct (Y/N) ? " TO ANSWER
    IF UPPER(ANSWER)="Y"
        * Erase the prompt
        @22,15 SAY "                                                  "
        * Get model no and unit price from COSTS.DBF
        SELECT 2
        LOCATE FOR STOCK_NO=STOCKNO
        IF EOF()
            * No such stock item
            SELECT 1
            LOOP
        ENDIF
        * The stock item has been found
        @9+ITEMNO,15 SAY " " GET MODEL_NO
        @9+ITEMNO,61 SAY " " GET DLR_COST
        CLEAR GET
        MODELNO=MODEL_NO
        UNITPRICE=DLR_COST
        SELECT 1
        * Save model no and unit price to SALE.DBF
        REPLACE INV_NO WITH INVNO
        REPLACE MODEL_NO WITH MODELNO
        REPLACE UNIT_PRICE WITH UNITPRICE
```

(Continued on next page)

```
        * Go to get next stock item sold
        ITEMNO=ITEMNO+1
        APPEND BLANK
        LOOP
    ELSE
        LOOP
    ENDIF
ENDDO
CLOSE DATABASE
DO PRINTINV
RETURN
```

Fig. 12.31. Listing of BILLING.PRG.

```
*****    Program: PRINTINV.PRG    *****
* Display and Print Invoice
* Clear totals
ANSWER="S"
DO WHILE .T.
   ITEMTOTAL=0
   GRANDTOTAL=0
   CLEAR
   ?"                        >>>>>>>>>>>  INVOICE    <<<<<<<<<<"
   ?
   ?
   ?"SUPER STEREO AND TELEVISION DISTRIBUTORS, INC."
   ?"            12345 Main Avenue"
   ?"          Portland, Oregon 97201"
   ? SPACE(50)+"Invoice No.    "+INVNO
   ? SPACE(50)+"Invoice Date : "+DTOC(INVDATE)
   ? SPACE(5)+"Sold to:    "+ACCTNAME
   ? SPACE(10)+MADDRESS
   ? SPACE(10)+CITYSTZIP
   ?
   ?"================================================================="
   ??"==============="
   ?"  Stock Number      Model   Ordered    Shipped  B.Ordered    Unit Price "
   ??"  Total"
   ?"-----------------------------------------------------------------"
   ??"---------------"
   * Display stock items sold in SALE.DBF
   SELECT A
   USE SALE
   DO WHILE INV_NO<>" " .AND. .NOT. EOF()
       ITEMTOTAL=UNIT_PRICE*QTY_SHIPED
       GRANDTOTAL=GRANDTOTAL+ITEMTOTAL
       ? "  "+STOCK_NO+"   "+MODEL_NO+ "    "+STR(QTY_ORDERD,3,0)+"        "
       ??STR(QTY_SHIPED,3,0)+"        "+STR(QTY_BO,3,0)+"       "
       ??STR(UNIT_PRICE,10,2)+STR(ITEMTOTAL,12,2)
       SKIP
   ENDDO
   ?SPACE(68)+"------------"
   ?SPACE(40)+" Total Sale "+SPACE(15)+STR(GRANDTOTAL,12,2)
   ?SPACE(68)+"==========="
   ?
   ?
```

(Continued on next page)

```
    IF  UPPER(ANSWER)="P"
        * Invoice has been printed, update inventory level
        SELECT A
        INDEX ON STOCK_NO TO SORT1
        SELECT B
        USE STOCKS
        INDEX ON STOCK_NO TO SORT2
        UPDATE ON STOCK_NO FROM SALE REPLACE ON_HAND WITH ON_HAND-A->QTY_SHIPED
        ERASE SORT1.NDX
        ERASE SORT2.NDX
        * Save records in INVOICE.dbf to permanent file INVOICES.dbf
        USE INVOICES
        APPEND FROM INVOICE
        RETURN
    ENDIF
    ?"     [S] Display invoice on screen     [P] Print it    "
    ??" [Q] Return to mainmenu "
    WAIT " " TO ANSWER
    DO CASE
        CASE UPPER(ANSWER)="S"
            LOOP
        CASE UPPER(ANSWER)="P"
            SET PRINT ON
            LOOP
        CASE UPPER(ANSWER)="Q"
            RETURN
    ENDCASE
ENDDO
RETURN
```

Fig. 12.32. Listing of PRINTINV.PRG.

Cost Maintenance Submenu: COSTMENU.PRG

The program module COSTMENU.PRG selects the tasks necessary to maintain the price and cost information for each item in stock. The functions include the following:

Adding a new cost item to COSTS.DBF

Deleting a cost item

Examining and editing the contents of a cost item

When you select COSTMENU.PRG, the functions appear as tasks in the cost maintenance submenu (see fig. 12.33). A listing of COSTMENU.PRG is shown in figure 12.34.

The modules ADDACCT.PRG, DELTACCT.PRG, and EDITACCT.PRG are used to perform the cost maintenance function.

```
========================================
===      COST MAINTENANCE SUBMENU      ===
========================================


Task Code          Task

   [A]      ADD a new cost item

   [D]      DELETE an existing cost item

   [E]      EXAMINE/EDIT an cost item

   [Q]      QUIT, return to mainmenu


Enter your choice (type in task code)
```

Fig. 12.33. COSTMENU.PRG submenu.

```
****  Program: COSTMENU.PRG    *****
  Display COST Maintenance Submenu
SET TALK OFF
SET ECHO OFF
STORE " " TO CHOICE
DO WHILE .T.
   CLEAR
   ?
   ?
   ?"                    ========================================"
   ?"                    ===      COST MAINTENANCE SUBMENU      ==="
   ?"                    ========================================"
   ?
   ?
   ?"               Task Code          Task"
   ?
   ?"                  [A]      ADD a new cost item"
   ?
   ?"                  [D]      DELETE an existing cost item"
   ?
   ?"                  [E]      EXAMINE/EDIT an cost item"
   ?
   ?"                  [Q]      QUIT, return to mainmenu"
   ?
   ?
   WAIT "               Enter your choice (type in task code) " TO CHOICE
   DO CASE
      CASE UPPER(CHOICE)="A"
         DO ADDCOST
      CASE UPPER(CHOICE)="D"
         DO DELTCOST
      CASE UPPER(CHOICE)="E"
         DO EDITCOST
      CASE UPPER(CHOICE)="Q"
         RETURN
   ENDCASE
ENDDO
RETURN
```

Fig. 12.34. Listing of COSTMENU.PRG.

Before a cost item is edited or deleted, it is searched by stock number and located with FINDITEM.PRG. Figure 12.35 shows how the modules are linked.

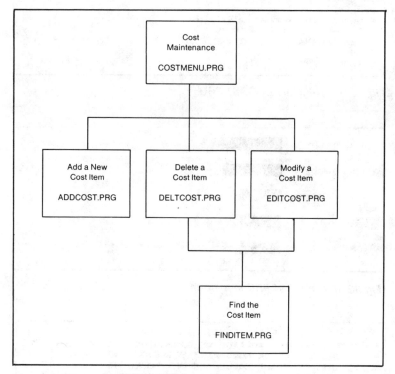

Fig. 12.35. Program module links.

ADDCOST.PRG

COSTMENU.PRG calls the program module ADDCOST.PRG, which appends a new data record to COSTS.DBF. A listing of the program is given in figure 12.36.

ADDCOST.PRG displays an entry form to append the new record, using the custom field labels in the COST.FMT format file. The entry form is shown in figure 12.37. COST.FMT is listed in figure 12.38.

DELTCOST.PRG

DELTCOST.PRG calls the FINDITEM.PRG program module, which finds a cost item by stock number. Similar to ACCTFOUND, the

```
*****    Program: ADDCOST.PRG    *****
* Add a new cost item to COSTS.DBF
SET TALK OFF
SET ECHO OFF
USE COSTS
* Use custom format COST.FMT
SET FORMAT TO COST.FMT
APPEND BLANK
READ
RETURN
```

Fig. 12.36. Listing of ADDCOST.PRG.

Stock Number:

Model Number:

List Price:

Our Cost:

Dealer Cost:

Fig. 12.37. ADDCOST.PRG entry form.

```
*****  A Format File: COST.FMT    *****
* Format file for editing or appending a cost item
@3,10 SAY "    Stock Number: " GET STOCK_NO
@5,10 SAY "    Model Number: " GET MODEL_NO
@7,10 SAY "      List Price: " GET LIST_PRICE
@9,10 SAY "        Our Cost: " GET OUR_COST
@11,10 SAY "     Dealer Cost: " GET DLR_COST
```

Fig. 12.38. Listing of COST.FRM.

logical variable ITEMFOUND indicates whether the item is found.
DELTCOST.PRG is listed in figure 12.39.

FINDITEM.PRG

Similar to FINDACCT.PRG, the program module FINDITEM.PRG
locates a data record in COSTS.DBF by the contents of the data field
STOCK_NO. When the record is found, the content of
ITEMFOUND is .T. FINDITEM.PRG is listed in figure 12.40.

```
*****    Program: DELTCOST.PRG    *****
* Delete an existing cost item
SET TALK OFF
SET ECHO OFF
* Find the stock item by its stock number
USE COSTS
DO FINDITEM
IF .NOT. ITEMFOUND
   * No such stock item found
   RETURN
ELSE
* Delete the cost item found
DELETE
PACK
@10,1 SAY "              The cost item has been deleted !"
RETURN
ENDIF
RETURN
```

Fig. 12.39. Listing of DELCOST.PRG.

```
*****    Program: FINDITEM.PRG    *****
* Find a stock item by its stock number
PUBLIC ITEMFOUND
SET TALK OFF
SET ECHO OFF
ITEMFOUND=.T.
CLEAR
?
?
?
?
ACCEPT "              Enter stock number: " TO STOCKNO
* Find the account
LOCATE FOR STOCK_NO=STOCKNO
IF EOF()
   * No such account
   ITEMFOUND=.F.
   RETURN
ENDIF
RETURN
```

Fig. 12.40. Listing of FINDITEM.PRG.

EDITCOST.PRG

EDITCOST.PRG calls FINDITEM.PRG to find the record to be edited. The stock number is used as the search key, and the data record is then displayed, using COST.FMT. If you do not wish to edit the record, press Esc to return to COSTMENU.PRG. After you have modified the record, press Ctrl-End to exit the program module. EDITCOST.PRG is shown in figure 12.41.

```
*****   Program: EDITCOST.PRG   *****
* Edit an existing cost item
SET TALK OFF
SET ECHO OFF
* Find the cost item by its stock number
USE COSTS
DO FINDITEM
IF .NOT. ITEMFOUND
   * No such stock item found
   RETURN
ENDIF
* Use custom format COST.FMT
SET FORMAT TO COST.FMT
READ
RETURN
```

Fig. 12.41. Listing of EDITCOST.PRG.

Inventory Control Submenu: INVNMENU.PRG

The program module INVNMENU.PRG defines the tasks needed to maintain inventory control. These tasks include the following control functions:

Adding a new stock item to the inventory database file STOCKS.DBF

Deleting a stock item in the inventory database file

Examining and editing the contents of a data record

Adjusting the inventory level of a stock item

Evaluating the total inventory value for each stock item on hand

The submenu used to perform these inventory control functions is shown in figure 12.42. The program module INVNMENU.PRG is listed in figure 12.43.

When you select A, D, E, J, or V, the program calls one of the corresponding program modules: ADDITEM.PRG, DELTITEM.PRG, EDITITEM.PRG, ADJSTOCK.PRG, and VALUES.PRG. FINDITEM.PRG is used to locate the stock item. Figure 12.44 shows how the modules are linked.

```
========================================
===     INVENTORY CONTROL SUBMENU     ===
========================================


Task Code           Task

   [A]      ADD a new stock item

   [D]      Delete an existing item

   [E]      EXAMINE/EDIT a stock item

   [J]      ADJUSTING inventory level

   [V]      Evaluation of inventory

   [Q]      QUIT, return to mainmenu


Enter your choice (type in task code)
```

Fig. 12.42. Inventory control submenu.

ADDITEM.PRG

ADDITEM.PRG appends a new data record to the database file STOCKS.DBF, using the custom file STOCK.FMT. A listing of the program is given in figure 12.45.

When ADDITEM.PRG is called from INVNMENU.PRG, an entry form is displayed (see fig. 12.46). The STOCK.FMT format file that produces the entry form is shown in figure 12.47.

DELTITEM.PRG

After DELTITEM.PRG locates the stock item by stock number, the module deletes the record from STOCKS.DBF. DELTITEM.PRG calls FINDITEM.PRG to locate the stock item. As in the other submenus, ITEMFOUND is the memory variable that indicates whether the item is found. The DELTITEM.PRG program module is listed in figure 12.48.

EDITITEM.PRG

You can use EDITITEM.PRG to edit or modify the contents of a data record in the STOCKS.DBF database file. FINDITEM locates the

```
*****  Program: INVNMENU.PRG   *****
* Display Inventory Control Submenu
SET TALK OFF
SET ECHO OFF
STORE " " TO CHOICE
DO WHILE .T.
   CLEAR
   ?
   ?
   ?"                      ====================================="
   ?"                      ===     INVENTORY CONTROL SUBMENU    ==="
   ?"                      ====================================="
   ?
   ?
   ?"                 Task Code            Task"
   ?
   ?"                    [A]      ADD a new stock item"
   ?
   ?"                    [D]      Delete an existing item"
   ?
   ?"                    [E]      EXAMINE/EDIT a stock item"
   ?
   ?"                    [J]      ADJUSTING inventory level"
   ?
   ?"                    [V]      Evaluation of inventory"
   ?
   ?"                    [Q]      QUIT, return to mainmenu"
   ?
   ?
   WAIT "                 Enter your choice (type in task code) " TO CHOICE
   DO CASE
      CASE UPPER(CHOICE)="A"
         DO ADDITEM
      CASE UPPER(CHOICE)="D"
         DO DELTITEM
      CASE UPPER(CHOICE)="E"
         DO EDITITEM
      CASE UPPER(CHOICE)="J"
         DO ADJSTOCK
      CASE UPPER(CHOICE)="V"
         DO VALUES
      CASE UPPER(CHOICE)="Q"
         RETURN
   ENDCASE
ENDDO
RETURN
```

Fig. 12.43. Listing of INVNMENU.PRG.

stock item to be edited, and the custom format file STOCK.FMT is
used to label the data fields in the data record. EDITITEM.PRG is
listed in figure 12.49.

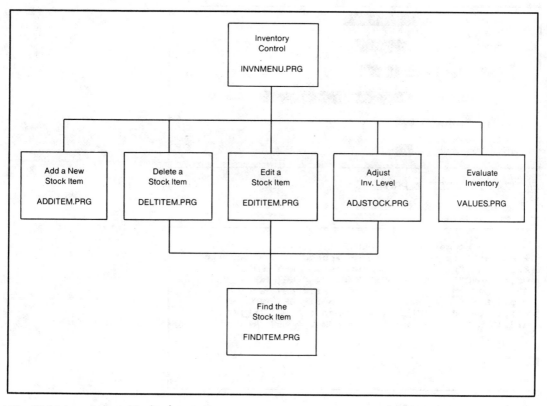

Fig. 12.44. Inventory control submenu.

```
*****    Program: ADDITEM.PRG    *****
* Add a new stock item to STOCKS.DBF
SET TALK OFF
SET ECHO OFF
USE STOCKS
* Use custom format STOCK.FMT
SET FORMAT TO STOCK.FMT
APPEND BLANK
READ
RETURN
```

Fig. 12.45. Listing of ADDITEM.PRG.

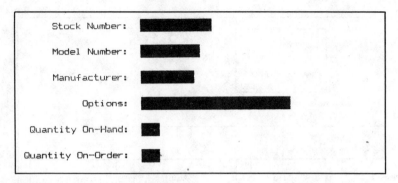

Fig. 12.46. The ADDITEM.PRG entry form.

```
*****   A Format File: STOCK.FMT    *****
* Format file for editing or appending a stock item
@3,10 SAY "        Stock Number: " GET STOCK_NO
@5,10 SAY "        Model Number: " GET MODEL_NO
@7,10 SAY "        Manufacturer: " GET MFG
@9,10 SAY "             Options: " GET OPTIONS
@11,10 SAY "    Quantity On-Hand: " GET ON_HAND
@13,10 SAY "   Quantity On-Order: " GET ON_ORDER
```

Fig. 12.47. Listing of STOCK.FMT.

```
*****     Program: DELTITEM.PRG    *****
* Delete an existing stock item
SET TALK OFF
SET ECHO OFF
* Find the stock item by its stock number
USE STOCKS
DO FINDITEM
IF .NOT. ITEMFOUND
   * No such stock item found
   RETURN
ELSE
* Delete the stock item found
DELETE
PACK
@10,1 SAY "                The stock item has been deleted !"
RETURN
ENDIF
RETURN
```

Fig. 12.48. Listing of DELTITEM.PRG.

```
*****   Program: EDITITEM.PRG   *****
* Edit an existing stock item
SET TALK OFF
SET ECHO OFF
* Find the stock item by its stock number
USE STOCKS
DO FINDITEM
IF .NOT. ITEMFOUND
   * No such stock item found
   RETURN
ENDIF
* Use custom format STOCK.FMT
SET FORMAT TO STOCK.FMT
READ
RETURN
```

Fig. 12.49. Listing of EDITITEM.PRG.

ADJSTOCK.PRG

The inventory level, represented by the on-hand quantity and on-order quantity in STOCKS.DBF, must be adjusted in one of the following situations:

When the inventory level is reduced because of sales

When the on-order quantity is received

When adjustments must be made to avoid a discrepancy between the database file and the warehouse record

Inventory adjustments as a result of sales were discussed earlier in this chapter (see BILLING.PRG, p. 285). After an invoice is printed with PRINTINV.PRG, the on-hand quantity of the item is adjusted to reflect the quantity shipped. You can use the program module ADJSTOCK.PRG to adjust the current inventory level (on-hand quantity and on-order quantity) for the other two situations. After FINDITEM.PRG locates the stock item, ADJSTOCK.PRG displays the current inventory level (see fig. 12.50).

Below the inventory information, you see the request for adjustments. You can enter them from the keyboard, using negative or positive values.

For example, if two units of item number ST-03-25C-02 have arrived, you can enter the adjustments as shown in figure 12.50 (that is, add two units to quantity on-hand and subtract two units from on-order quantity). As you can see from the prompt at the

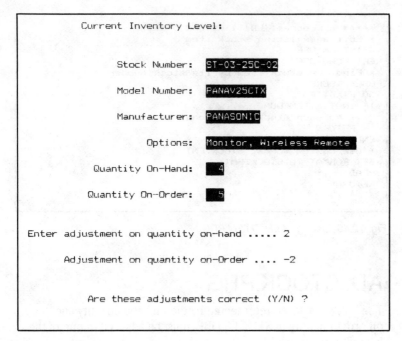

Fig. 12.50. ADJSTOCK.PRG entry form.

bottom of the screen, if you enter adjustments incorrectly, you can reenter them. After the adjustments are complete, the program changes the data fields accordingly and displays the inventory level (see fig. 12.51).

ADJSTOCK.PRG is listed in figure 12.52.

VALUES.PRG

INVNMENU.PRG calls the VALUES.PRG program module to compute and display the total value of each item in stock. The inventory value of a stock item is calculated by multiplying its on-hand quantity (STOCKS.DBF) by the cost (OUR_COST) in the COSTS.DBF database file. Figure 12.53 shows a sample inventory evaluation report produced with VALUES.PRG. A listing of VALUES.PRG is shown in figure 12.54.

```
           Inventory Level After Adjustments:


                   Stock Number:  ST-03-250-02

                   Model Number:  PANAV25CTX

                   Manufacturer:  PANASONIC

                        Options:  Monitor, Wireless Remote

               Quantity On-Hand:     6

              Quantity On-Order:     3




        [A] Adjust inventory again   [Q] Return to mainmenu
```

Fig. 12.51. ADJSTOCK.PRG entry form after adjustments.

```
*****    Program: ADJSTOCK.PRG    *****
* Adjusting level of inventory of an existing stock item
SET TALK OFF
SET ECHO OFF
* Get the stock item
USE STOCKS
DO FINDITEM
IF .NOT. ITEMFOUND
   * No such stock item found
   RETURN
ENDIF
* Display current inventory level
DO WHILE .T.
   CLEAR
   ?
   ?"           Current Inventory Level:"
   ?
   @5,10 SAY "         Stock Number: " GET STOCK_NO
   @7,10 SAY "         Model Number: " GET MODEL_NO
   @9,10 SAY "         Manufacturer: " GET MFG
   @11,10 SAY "              Options: " GET OPTIONS
   @13,10 SAY "     Quantity On-Hand: " GET ON_HAND
   @15,10 SAY "    Quantity On-Order: " GET ON_ORDER
   CLEAR GET
   DO WHILE .T.
      @17,1 SAY " "
      INPUT "    Enter adjustment on quantity on-hand ..... " TO ADJONHAND
      @19,1 SAY " "
```

(Continued on next page)

```
        INPUT "              Adjustment on quantity on-Order .... " TO ADJONORDER
        @22,1 SAY " "
        WAIT "              Are these adjustments correct (Y/N) ?" TO ANSWER
        IF UPPER(ANSWER)="Y"
           EXIT
        ELSE
           LOOP
        ENDIF
     ENDDO
     * Adjust the inventory level
     REPLACE ON_HAND WITH ON_HAND+ADJONHAND
     REPLACE ON_ORDER WITH ON_ORDER+ADJONORDER
     * Display inventory level after adjustements
     CLEAR
     ?
     ?"          Inventory Level After Adjustments:"
     @5,10 SAY "         Stock Number: " GET STOCK_NO
     @7,10 SAY "         Model Number: " GET MODEL_NO
     @9,10 SAY "         Manufacturer: " GET MFG
     @11,10 SAY "              Options: " GET OPTIONS
     @13,10 SAY "     Quantity On-Hand: " GET ON_HAND
     @15,10 SAY "    Quantity On-Order: " GET ON_ORDER
     CLEAR GET
     DO WHILE .T.
        @22,10 SAY " "
        WAIT "    [A] Adjust inventory again  [Q] Return to mainmenu " TO CHOICE
        DO CASE
           CASE UPPER(CHOICE)="Q"
              RETURN
           CASE UPPER(CHOICE)="A"
              EXIT
           OTHERWISE
              LOOP
        ENDCASE
     ENDDO
  ENDDO
ENDDO
RETURN
```

Fig. 12.52. Listing of ADJSTOCK.PRG.

Personnel File Maintenance Submenu: EMPLMENU.PRG

The EMPLMENU.PRG program module maintains the personnel files of the employees. The data management tasks include the following:

Adding a new employee's record to EMPLOYEE.DBF

Deleting an employee's record

Examining or modifying the contents of a record

Sorting records by different data fields and producing an employee roster

```
                    Value of Stock Items


    Stock No.       Model      Quantity   Unit Cost   Total Value
  -----------   ------------   --------   ---------   -----------
  ST-01-19P-01   RCA-XA100        5        229.50       1147.50
  ST-01-25C-02   RCA-XA200       11        369.00       4059.00
  ST-02-19P-01   ZENITH-19P       7        255.00       1785.00
  ST-02-21C-02   ZENITH-21C       5        559.00       2795.00
  ST-02-25C-03   ZENITH-25C       5        589.00       2945.00
  ST-03-17P-01   SONY1700P        4        330.00       1320.00
  ST-03-26C-02   SONY2600XT       7        850.00       5950.00
  ST-03-19P-01   PANAVO19PT       3        395.00       1185.00
  ST-03-25C-02   PANAV25CTX       6        795.00       4770.00
  ST-04-19P-01   SANYO-19-P       3        249.00        747.00
  ST-04-21C-02   SANYO-21-C       5        365.50       1827.50
                                ---                   ---------
            Total                61                    28531.00
                                ===                   =========


    [P] Print reports          [Q] Return to mainmenu
```

Fig. 12.53. Sample inventory report with VALUES.PRG.

The structure and content of EMPLOYEE.DBF are shown in figure 12.55. The submenu used to select the personnel file maintenance tasks is shown in figure 12.56. The program that produces the submenu, EMPLMENU.PRG, is listed in figure 12.57.

When you select A, D, E, or S, the computer passes control to the corresponding module: ADDEMPL.PRG, DELTEMPL.PRG, EDITEMPL.PRG, and SORTEMPL.PRG, respectively. If you choose Q, the program returns to the main program MAINMENU.PRG. Figure 12.58 shows the link between the modules.

ADDEMPL.PRG

ADDEMPL.PRG appends a new data record to the database file EMPLMENU.PRG, using the custom file EMPLOYEE.FMT. The format file is shown in figure 12.59, and a listing of ADDEMPL.PRG is shown in figure 12.60.

DELTEMPL.PRG

As in other modules, FINDEMPL.PRG is used to locate the record before DELTEMPL.PRG deletes the record. Figure 12.61 shows the DELTEMPL.PRG program module. A listing of FINDEMPL.PRG is shown in figure 12.62.

```
*****    Program : VALUES.PRG    *****
* A program to compute value of each stock item
SET TALK OFF
SET ECHO OFF
DO WHILE .T.
CLEAR
?
?SPACE(32)+"Value of Stock Items"
?
?
?SPACE(10)+" Stock No.       Model      Quantity    Unit Cost    Total Value"
?SPACE(10)+"-----------   ------------   --------   ----------   ------------"
* Put database files to work areas
SELECT 1
USE STOCKS
SELECT 2
USE COSTS
* Clear counter and accumulator
TOTALUNITS=0
TOTALVALUE=0
* Get stock items sequentially from STOCKS.dbf
DO WHILE .NOT. EOF()
SELECT 1
STOCKNO=STOCK_NO
* Get its cost from COSTS.dbf
SELECT 2
LOCATE FOR STOCK_NO=STOCKNO
* Store cost in memory variable
COST=OUR_COST
* Return toSTOCKS.dbf
SELECT 1
VALUE=COST*ON_HAND
?SPACE(10)+ STOCK_NO+"   "+MODEL_NO+"   "+STR(ON_HAND,5,0)+STR(COST,14,2)
??STR(VALUE,13,2)
* Increase counter and accumulator
TOTALUNITS=TOTALUNITS+ON_HAND
TOTALVALUE=TOTALVALUE+VALUE
* Process next stock item
SKIP
ENDDO
?SPACE(38)+"---"+SPACE(19)+"--------"
?SPACE(21)+"Total"+SPACE(10)+STR(TOTALUNITS,5,0)+SPACE(14)
??STR(TOTALVALUE,13,2)
?SPACE(38)+"==="+SPACE(19)+"========"
?
?
SET PRINT OFF
?"          [P] Print reports                 [Q] Return to mainmenu"
WAIT " " TO CHOICE
DO CASE
   CASE UPPER(CHOICE)="P"
      SET PRINT ON
      LOOP
   CASE UPPER(CHOICE)="Q"
      RETURN
   OTHERWISE
      LOOP
ENDCASE
ENDDO
RETURN
```

Fig. 12.54. Listing of VALUES.PRG.

```
Structure for database : B:EMPLOYEE.dbf
Number of data records :        9
Date of last update     : 03/15/85
Field   Field name    Type         Width     Dec
    1   FIRST_NAME    Character       12
    2   LAST_NAME     Character       10
    3   AREA_CODE     Character        3
    4   PHONE_NO      Character        8
    5   MALE          Logical          1
    6   BIRTH_DATE    Date             8
    7   ANNUAL_PAY    Numeric          8       2
** Total **                           51
```

Record#	FIRST_NAME	LAST_NAME	AREA_CODE	PHONE_NO	MALE	BIRTH_DATE	ANNUAL_PAY
1	James C.	Smith	216	123-4567	.T.	07/04/60	23100.00
2	Albert K.	Zeller	212	457-9801	.T.	10/10/59	29347.50
3	Harry M.	Nelson	315	576-0235	.T.	02/15/58	30450.00
4	Tina B.	Baker	415	567-7777	.F.	10/12/56	27195.00
5	Kirk D.	Chapman	618	625-7845	.T.	08/04/61	20737.50
6	Mary W.	Thompson	213	432-6782	.F.	06/18/55	25725.00
7	Charles N.	Duff	216	456-9873	.T.	07/22/64	14175.00
8	Winston E.	Lee	513	365-8512	.T.	05/14/39	36645.00
9	Thomas T.	Hanson	216	573-5085	.T.	12/24/45	30397.50

Fig. 12.55. The EMPLOYEE.DBF file.

```
========================================
===     PERSONNEL FILE   SUBMENU    ===
========================================


Task Code                Task

   [A]      ADD a new employee record

   [D]      Delete an existing employee record

   [E]      EXAMINE/EDIT an employee record

   [S]      SORT employee records

   [Q]      QUIT, return to mainmenu


Enter your choice (type in task code)
```

Fig. 12.56. The EMPLMENU.PRG submenu.

The memory variable EMPLFOUND is used to indicate whether the employee record is found.

```
*****  Program: EMPLMENU.PRG   *****
* Display personnel file sub-menu
SET TALK OFF
SET ECHO OFF
STORE " " TO CHOICE
DO WHILE .T.
   CLEAR
   ?
   ?
   ?"                       =====================================" 
   ?"                       ===      PERSONNEL FILE   SUBMENU   ===" 
   ?"                       =====================================" 
   ?
   ?
   ?"                  Task Code             Task" 
   ?
   ?"                    [A]     ADD a new employee record" 
   ?
   ?"                    [D]     Delete an existing employee record" 
   ?
   ?"                    [E]     EXAMINE/EDIT an employee record" 
   ?
   ?"                    [S]     SORT employee records" 
   ?
   ?"                    [Q]     QUIT, return to mainmenu" 
   ?
   ?
   WAIT "                 Enter your choice (type in task code) " TO CHOICE
   DO CASE
      CASE UPPER(CHOICE)="A"
         DO ADDEMPL
      CASE UPPER(CHOICE)="D"
         DO DELTEMPL
      CASE UPPER(CHOICE)="E"
         DO EDITEMPL
      CASE UPPER(CHOICE)="S"
         DO SORTEMPL
      CASE UPPER(CHOICE)="Q"
         RETURN
   ENDCASE
ENDDO
RETURN
```

Fig. 12.57. Listing of EMPLMENU.PRG.

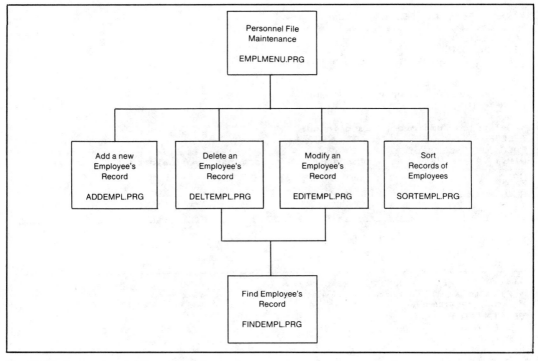

Fig. 12.58. Account maintenance submenu.

```
*****   A Format File: EMPLOYEE.FMT   *****
* Format file for editing or appending the record of an employee
@3,10 SAY " Employee's First Name : " GET FIRST_NAME
@5,10 SAY "            Last Name : " GET LAST_NAME
@7,10 SAY "            Area Code : " GET AREA_CODE
@9,10 SAY "    Home Phone Number : " GET PHONE_NO
@11,10 SAY "        Male? (T/F) : " GET MALE
@13,10 SAY "           Birth Date : " GET BIRTH_DATE
@15,10 SAY "        Annual Salary : " GET ANNUAL_PAY PICTURE "$###,###"
```

Fig. 12.59. Listing of EMPLOYEE.FMT.

```
*****    Program: ADDEMPL.PRG   *****
* Add a new employee record to EMPLOYEE.dbf
SET TALK OFF
SET ECHO OFF
USE EMPLOYEE
* Use custom format EMPLOYEE.FMT
SET FORMAT TO EMPLOYEE.FMT
APPEND BLANK
READ
RETURN
```

Fig. 12.60. Listing of ADDEMPL.PRG.

```
*****    Program: DELTEMPL.PRG    *****
* Delete an existing employee record
SET TALK OFF
SET ECHO OFF
* Find the employee by first & last name
DO FINDEMPL
IF .NOT. EMPLFOUND
   * No such employee record found
   RETURN
ELSE
* Delete the employee record found
DELETE
PACK
@10,1 SAY "              The employee record has been deleted !"
RETURN
ENDIF
RETURN
```

Fig. 12.61. Listing of DELTEMPL.PRG.

```
*****    Program: FINDEMPL.PRG    *****
* Find an employee record by first name and last name
PUBLIC EMPLFOUND
SET TALK OFF
SET ECHO OFF
EMPLFOUND=.T.
CLEAR
?
?
?
?
ACCEPT "          Enter employee's first name : " TO FIRSTNAME
?
ACCEPT "                         Last name : " TO LASTNAME
* Find the employee record
USE EMPLOYEE
LOCATE FOR UPPER(FIRST_NAME)=UPPER(FIRSTNAME).AND.;
   UPPER(LAST_NAME)=UPPER(LASTNAME)
IF EOF()
   * No such employee record
   ACCTFOUND=.F.
   RETURN
ENDIF
RETURN
```

Fig. 12.62. Listing of FINDEMPL.PRG.

EDITEMPL.PRG

EDITEMPL.PRG uses FINDEMPL.PRG to locate and display an employee's record so that you can edit the record with the format file EMPLOYEE.FMT. If you do not need to edit the record, press

Esc, and the program returns to the submenu EMPLMENU.PRG. After you enter changes, press Ctrl-End to return to the submenu.

EDITEMPL.PRG is shown in figure 12.63.

```
*****    Program: EDITEMPL.PRG    *****
* Edit an existing employee record
SET TALK OFF
SET ECHO OFF
* Find the employee record by first name and last name
DO FINDEMPL
IF .NOT. EMPLFOUND
   * No such employee record found
   RETURN
ENDIF
* Use custom format EMPLOYEE.FMT
SET FORMAT TO EMPLOYEE.FMT
READ
RETURN
```

Fig. 12.63. Listing of EDITEMPL.PRG.

SORTEMPL.PRG

SORTEMPL.PRG can sort the database file EMPLOYEE.DBF on any of the sorting keys shown in figure 12.64.

```
       Choose one of the following sorting keys:


            [B]    By employee BIRTH DATE

            [F]    By employee FIRST NAME

            [L]    By employee LAST NAME

            [P]    By employee home PHONE NUMBER

            [S]    By employee annual SALARY

            [Q]    Quit, return to mainmenu



 Enter your choice (type in the sorting key)
```

Fig. 12.64. Sorting keys for SORTEMPL.PRG.

After the sort is complete, the data records of the sorted file are displayed on the screen. For example, if you select B

(BIRTH_DATE), the data records in EMPLOYEE.DBF are ordered by birth dates and displayed (see fig. 12.65).

```
Sorted Employee Records:


Name of Employee          Phone Number        Birth Date    Annual Salary

Winston E. Lee            (513) 365-8512        05/14/39        36645
Thomas T. Hanson         (216) 573-5085        12/24/45        30398
Mary W. Thompson         (213) 432-6782        06/18/55        25725
Tina B. Baker            (415) 567-7777        10/12/56        27195
Harry M. Nelson          (315) 576-0235        02/15/58        30450
Albert K. Zeller         (212) 457-9801        10/10/59        29348
James C. Smith           (216) 123-4567        07/04/60        23100
Kirk D. Chapman          (618) 625-7845        08/04/61        20738
Charles N. Duff          (216) 456-9873        07/22/64        14175



        [P] Print sorted records on printer;   [Q] Quit
```

Fig. 12.65. EMPLOYEE.DBF sorted by BIRTH_DATE.

The program module SORTEMPL.PRG represents the last link in the integrated data management system (see fig. 12.66). A diagram that shows all the components of the integrated data management system is shown in Figure 12.67.

Chapter Summary

This final chapter has presented an integrated database management system. As you know, this simple example included only five major data management functions. The program modules presented in this chapter are not necessarily the most efficient means to accomplish data management tasks. The modules were designed to show you how to construct and execute a menu-driven data management system. Programming is an art rather than a science, so you should apply your talent to design a system more suitable to your needs. The best of luck in enjoying the powerful tools of dBASE III.

```
*****    Program: SORTEMPL.PRG    *****
* Sort employee records by a given key field
SET TALK OFF
SET ECHO OFF
* Display selection of sorting keys
DO WHILE .T.
   CLEAR
   @3,1 SAY " "
   ?"                   Choose one of the following sorting keys:"
    ?
   ?
   ?"                   [B]    By employee BIRTH DATE"
   ?
   ?"                   [F]    By employee FIRST NAME"
   ?
   ?"                   [L]    By employee LAST NAME"
   ?
   ?"                   [P]    By employee home PHONE NUMBER"
   ?
   ?"                   [S]    By employee annual SALARY"
   ?
   ?"                   [Q]    Quit, return to mainmenu"
   @20,1SAY " "
   WAIT "          Enter your choice (type in the sorting key) " TO CHOICE
   USE EMPLOYEE
   DO CASE
      CASE UPPER(CHOICE)="B"
         INDEX ON BIRTH_DATE TO SORTED
      CASE UPPER(CHOICE)="F"
         INDEX ON FIRST_NAME TO SORTED
      CASE UPPER(CHOICE)="L"
         INDEX ON LAST_NAME TO SORTED
      CASE UPPER(CHOICE)="P"
         INDEX ON AREA_CODE+PHONE_NO TO SORTED
      CASE UPPER(CHOICE)="S"
         INDEX ON ANNUAL_PAY TO SORTED
      CASE UPPER(CHOICE)="Q"
         RETURN
      OTHERWISE
         LOOP
   ENDCASE
   EXIT
ENDDO
* Display sorted employee record
DO WHILE .T.
   CLEAR
   ? "    Sorted Employee Records: "
   ?
   ?
   ?"   Name of Employee              Phone Number     Birth Date;
   Annual Salary"
   ?
   GO TOP
   DO WHILE .NOT. EOF()
      * Insert blank space to align employee name
      BLANKS=25-LEN(TRIM(FIRST_NAME)+" "+LAST_NAME)
      ?"   "+TRIM(FIRST_NAME)+" "+LAST_NAME+SPACE(BLANKS)+" ("+AREA_CODE+;
         ") "+PHONE_NO+"       "+DTOC(BIRTH_DATE)+"        "+STR(ANNUAL_PAY,7,0)
      SKIP
```

(Continued on next page)

```
    ENDDO
    SET PRINT OFF
    ?
    ?
    ?
    WAIT "                [P] Print sorted records on printer;   [Q] Quit " TO CHOICE
    DO CASE
        CASE UPPER(CHOICE)="P"
            SET PRINT ON
        CASE UPPER(CHOICE)="Q"
            EXIT
        OTHERWISE
            LOOP
    ENDCASE
ENDDO
* Clean up working index file
CLOSE INDEX
ERASE SORTED.NDX
RETURN
```

Fig. 12.66. Listing of SORTEMPL.PRG.

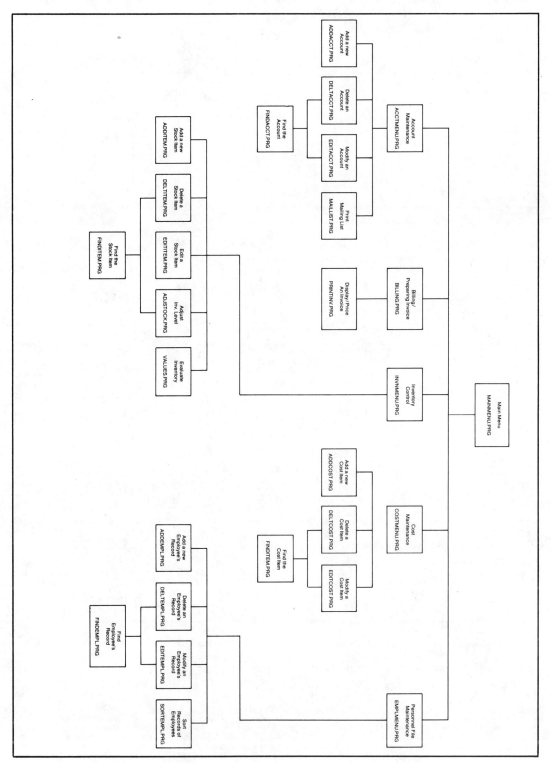

Fig. 12.67. Flowchart of complete database management system.

A
ASCII Character Set

The table lists the ASCII codes in decimal and their characters. You can display a character by using PRINT CHR$(n), where *n* is the ASCII value. You can enter each character by pressing and holding down the Alt key while you press also (on the numeric keypad) the digits of the ASCII value. Note that standard interpretations of ASCII codes 0 to 31 are presented in the Control Character column.

ASCII Value	Character	Control Character	ASCII Value	Character
000	(null)	NUL	032	(space)
001	☺	SOH	033	!
002	☻	STX	034	''
003	♥	ETX	035	#
004	♦	EOT	036	$
005	♣	ENQ	037	%
006	♠	ACK	038	&
007	(beep)	BEL	039	'
008	■	BS	040	(
009	(tab)	HT	041	)
010	(line feed)	LF	042	*
011	(home)	VT	043	+
012	(form feed)	FF	044	,

ASCII Value	Character		ASCII Value	Character
013	(carriage return)	CR	045	-
014	♫	SO	046	.
015	☼	SI	047	/
016	►	DLE	048	0
017	◄	DC1	049	1
018	↕	DC2	050	2
019	!!	DC3	051	3
020	¶	DC4	052	4
021	§	NAK	053	5
022	▬	SYN	054	6
023	↨	ETB	055	7
024	↑	CAN	056	8
025	↓	EM	057	9
026	→	SUB	058	:
027	←	ESC	059	;
028	(cursor right)	FS	060	<
029	(cursor left)	GS	061	=
030	(cursor up)	RS	062	>
031	(cursor down)	US	063	?
064	@		096	`
065	A		097	a
066	B		098	b
067	C		099	c
068	D		100	d
069	E		101	e
070	F		102	f
071	G		103	g
072	H		104	h
073	I		105	i
074	J		106	j
075	K		107	k
076	L		108	l
077	M		109	m
078	N		110	n
079	O		111	o
080	P		112	p
081	Q		113	q
082	R		114	r

ASCII Value	Character	ASCII Value	Character
083	S	115	s
084	T	116	t
085	U	117	u
086	V	118	v
087	W	119	w
088	X	120	x
089	Y	121	y
090	Z	122	z
091	[	123	¦
092	\	124	¦
093	]	125	}
094	∧	126	~
095	—	127	△
128	Ç	160	á
129	ü	161	í
130	é	162	ó
131	â	163	ú
132	ä	164	ñ
133	à	165	Ñ
134	å	166	ª
135	ç	167	º
136	ê	168	¿
137	ë	169	⌐
138	è	170	¬
139	ï	171	½
140	î	172	¼
141	ì	173	¡
142	Ä	174	«
143	Å	175	»
144	É	176	░
145	æ	177	▒
146	Æ	178	▓
147	ô	179	│
148	ö	180	┤
149	ò	181	╡
150	û	182	╢
151	ù	183	╖
152	ÿ	184	╕

ASCII Value	Character	ASCII Value	Character
153	Ö	185	╡
154	Ü	186	║
155	¢	187	╗
156	£	188	╝
157	¥	189	╜
158	Pt	190	╛
159	ƒ	191	┐
192	└	224	α
193	┴	225	β
194	┬	226	Γ
195	├	227	π
196	─	228	Σ
197	┼	229	σ
198	╞	230	μ
199	╟	231	τ
200	╚	232	Φ
201	╔	233	Θ
202	╩	234	Ω
203	╦	235	δ
204	╠	236	∞
205	═	237	Ø
206	╬	238	∈
207	╧	239	∩
208	╨	240	≡
209	╤	241	±
210	╥	242	≥
211	╙	243	≤
212	╘	244	⌠
213	╒	245	⌡
214	╓	246	÷
215	╫	247	≈
216	╪	248	°
217	┘	249	•
218	┌	250	·
219	█	251	√
220	▄	252	ⁿ
221	▌	253	^{2}
222	▐	254	■
223	▀	255	(blank 'FF')

B
Differences between dBASE II and dBASE III

I. Operating Differences

	dBASE II	*dBASE III*
Microprocessors	8080/8085/Z80 8088/8086	8088/8086
Disk Operating System	CP/M-80, CP/M-86, Z-DOS, MS-DOS, IBM PC DOS	IBM PC DOS

II. Capacity Differences

	dBASE II	*dBASE III*
Open data files allowed	2	10
Records per data file	65,535	1 billion
Characters per record	1,000	4,000
Data fields per record	32	128
Memory variables allowed	64	256
Digits allowed	10	15.9

III. File Type Differences

The dBASE III files that are not available in dBASE II are

> Label (.lbl) files
> Memory (.dbt) files

IV. Built-In Function Differences

A. The dBASE III functions that are not available in dBASE II are

ASC()   BOF()   CDOW() CMONTH() COL()   CTOC()
DAY()   DOW()   DTOC() EXP()   LOG()   LOWER()
MONTH() PCOL() PROW() ROUND()   ROW()   SPACE()
SQRT()   TIME() TYPE() YEAR()

B. Differences in Function Names:

	dBASE II	*dBASE III*
Converting to uppercase	!()	UPPER()
Number of active record	#	RECNO()
Substring	$()	SUBSTR()
Searching for Substring	@()	AT()
End-of-file mark	EOF	EOF()

V. Processing Command Differences

A. The dBASE III commands that are not available in dBASE II are

ASSIST	AVERAGE	CLOSE
COPY FILE TO	CREATE LABEL	EXIT
LABEL FORM	MODIFY LABEL	PARAMETERS
PRIVATE	PROCEDURE	PUBLIC
SEEK	SET DECIMALS	SET DELIMITER
SET DEVICE TO	SET FILTER TO	SET FIXED ON/OFF
SET FUNCTION TO	SET HELP ON/OFF	SET MENUS ON/OFF
SET PROCEDURE TO	SET RELATION TO	SET SAFETY ON/OFF
SET UNIQUE ON/OFF		

B. Differences in Command Names

	dBASE II	*dBASE III*
Clear the screen	ERASE	CLEAR
Delete a file	DELETE FILE	ERASE
Deletes all records	DELETE ALL, PACK	ZAP
Display file directory	DISPLAY FILES	DIR
Execute DOS file	QUIT TO	RUN
Exit to DOS	QUIT TO	QUIT
Return to the highest program module	None	RETURN TO MASTER

VI. Other Major Differences

A. Variable Names

dBASE II accepts a colon (:) as part of a data field or variable, such as LAST:NAME. In dBASE III, the underscore (_) is used in place of the colon, as in LAST_NAME.

B. Contents of Logical Variable

In dBASE II, T or F is assigned to a logical variable, whereas dBASE III stores .T. or .F. in the variable.

C. Displaying Output to the Printer

In dBASE III, you can display output to the printer by adding TO PRINT to the end of DISPLAY, DISPLAY MEMORY, DISPLAY STATUS, DISPLAY STRUCTURE, LIST, or TYPE.

D. Defining Data Format

dBASE II uses the USING clause to define a data format, whereas dBASE III uses the PICTURE clause.

C

Summary of Function and Control Keys

I. Default Settings for the Function Keys

Key	Command*
F1	HELP
F2	ASSIST
F3	LIST
F4	DIR
F5	DISPLAY STRUCTURE
F6	DISPLAY STATUS
F7	DISPLAY MEMORY

F8	DISPLAY
F9	APPEND
F10	EDIT

*Different commands can be assigned to these keys with the SET FUNCTION commands.

II. Control Keystrokes for Screen Editing

Keystroke	Function
Return (↵)	Moves the cursor to the next data field or line
	In APPEND: exits and saves the contents of a file from the first character of a blank data record
	In EDIT: exits and saves the file contents from the last field of the last data record
	In text editor: inserts a new line in insert mode
Up arrow (↑)	Moves the cursor up one line or one data field
Down arrow (↓)	Moves the cursor down one line one data field
Left arrow (←)	Moves the cursor left one space
Right arrow (→)	Moves the cursor right one space
Ctrl-left arrow (^←)	In BROWSE: pans one data field to the left
	In MODIFY REPORT: scrolls down the file structure display
	In MODIFY COMMAND: moves the cursor to the beginning of the line
Ctrl-right arrow (^→)	In BROWSE: pans one data field to the right

	In MODIFY REPORT: scrolls up the file structure display
	In MODIFY COMMAND: moves the cursor to the end of the line
Backspace (←)	Erases the character left of the cursor
Delete (Del)	Erases the character above the cursor
End	Moves the cursor right one word
Home	Moves the cursor left one word
Insert (Ins)	Toggles the INSERT mode on and off
Page Up (PgUp)	Moves back to previous data record
Page Down (PgDn)	Moves to next data record
Ctrl-End (^End)	Exits and saves modified data items
Escape (Esc)	Exits without saving modified data items
Ctrl-KW (^KW)	In text editor: writes the file to another file
Ctrl-KR (^KR)	In text editor: reads another file to the current text at the cursor position
Ctrl-N (^N)	Inserts a new line or data field in MODIFY STRUCTURE
Ctrl-T (^T)	Erases one word right of the cursor
Ctrl-U (^U)	In BROWSE or EDIT: marks a record to be deleted
	In MODIFY REPORT or MODIFY STRUCTURE: deletes a data field
Ctrl-Y (^Y)	Erases the entire line at the cursor

III. Keystrokes for Control Processing

Keystroke	*Function*
Ctrl-P (^P)	Toggles printer on and off
Ctrl-S (^S)	Starts and stops the screen scroll
Ctrl-X (^X)	Erases the command line in the interactive processing mode

D
Summary of
dBASE III Commands

The commands used in interactive processing and batch processing modes are summarized in this appendix. Although most of these commands have been discussed in this book, you may find a few commands that have not been introduced. In many cases, several different commands can be used to perform the same task. This book has introduced the easiest commands used to yield the best results. Feel free to explore any unfamiliar commands, using the information in this appendix.

I. Definition of Terms

<file name>

A string of up to 8 characters, including the underscore with a file identifier (for example, .dbf, .dbt, .fmt, .frm, .lbl, .mem, .ndx, .prg, and .txt). An sample file name is EMPLOYEE.DBF.

\<data field name\>

A string of up to 8 characters, including the underscore, such as

LAST_NAME

\<data field list\>

A series of data field names separated by commas, such as

LAST_NAME, FIRST_NAME, AREA_CODE, PHONE_NO

\<variable name\>

A string of up to ten characters, including underscores, such as

TOTALPRICE

\<variable list\>

A series of variable names separated by commas, such as

HOURS, PAYRATE, GROSSWAGE, TOTALSALE

\<an expression\>

An alphanumeric or numeric expression.

\<alphanumeric expression\>

A collection of alphanumeric data joined with plus signs, such as

"Employee's Name: "+TRIM(LAST_NAME)+
FIRST_NAME+MIDDLENAME

\<numeric expression\>

A collection of numeric data joined with arithmetic operators
(+, -, *, /, ^), such as

40*PAYRATE+(HOURS-40)*PAYRATE*1.5

\<expression list\>

A series of expressions separated by commas, such as

\<expression 1\>, \<expression 2\>, \<expression 3\>, . . .

<qualifier>

A clause that begins with FOR, followed by one or more conditions.

FOR AREA_CODE="206"
FOR ANNUAL_PAY>=25000
FOR LAST_NAME="Smith" .AND. FIRST_NAME="James C."

II. Listing of dBASE III Commands by Function

To Create, Modify, and Manipulate Files

APPEND FROM
CLOSE ALTERNATE
CLOSE DATABASES
CLOSE FORMAT
CLOSE INDEX
CLOSE PROCEDURE
COPY TO
COPY FILE
COPY STRUCTURE TO
CREATE
CREATE LABEL
CREATE REPORT
INDEX ON
JOIN
MODIFY COMMAND
MODIFY LABEL
MODIFY STRUCTURE
MODIFY REPORT
REINDEX
RENAME
SAVE TO
SELECT
SORT
TOTAL
USE

To Add Data Records to a Database File

APPEND
BROWSE
INSERT

To Edit Data in a Database File

BROWSE
CHANGE
DELETE
EDIT
PACK
READ
RECALL
REPLACE
UPDATE

To Display Data

@ . . . SAY
?
??
AVERAGE
BROWSE
COUNT
DISPLAY
LIST
REPORT
SUM
TEXT

To Control the Record Pointer

CONTINUE
FIND
GO BOTTOM
GOTO
GO TOP
LOCATE
SEEK
SKIP

To Use Memory Variables

ACCEPT
AVERAGE
CLEAR ALL
CLEAR MEMORY
COUNT
DISPLAY MEMORY
INPUT
READ
RELEASE
RESTORE FROM
SAVE TO
STORE
SUM
WAIT

To Program

ACCEPT TO
CANCEL
CASE
DO
DO WHILE . . . ENDDO
DO CASE . . . ENDCASE
EXIT
IF . . . ENDIF
IF . . . ELSE . . . ENDIF
INPUT
LOOP
MODIFY COMMAND
PARAMETERS
PRIVATE
PROCEDURE
PUBLIC
QUIT
RETURN
WAIT TO

To Control Media Display*

CLEAR
EJECT

SET COLOR TO
SET CONFIRM on/OFF
SET CONSOLE ON/off
SET INTENSITY ON/off
SET PRINT ON/off
SET DEVICE TO PRINT
SET DEVICE TO SCREEN
SET MARGIN TO

*Uppercase indicates default settings.

To Specify Control Parameters*

SET ALTERNATE TO
SET ALTERNATE on/OFF
SET BELL ON/off
SET CARRY on/OFF
SET DECIMALS TO
SET DEFAULT TO
SET DELETED on/OFF
SET DELIMITER on/OFF
SET ECHO on/OFF
SET ESCAPE ON/off
SET EXACT on/OFF
SET FILTER TO
SET FIXED on/OFF
SET FORMAT TO
SET FUNCTION TO
SET HEADING ON/off
SET HELP ON/off
SET INDEX TO
SET MENUS ON/off
SET PATH TO
SET PROCEDURE TO
SET RELATION TO
INTO
SET SAFETY ON/off
SET TALK ON/off
SET UNIQUE on/OFF

*Uppercase indicates default settings.

III. Summary of Commands

?

Displays the contents of an alphanumeric or numeric expression on a new display line, such as

    ? "Employee's name . . . "+FIRST_NAME+LAST_NAME
    ? HOURS*PAYRATE
    ? "Gross Pay . . . "+STR(GROSSPAY,7,2)

??

Displays output on the same display line, such as

    ?? "Invoice number: "+INVNO

@<row,column> GET

Displays user-formatted data at the screen location of <row,column>, such as

    @5,10 GET LAST_NAME
    @8,10 GET SC_NO PICTURE "###-##-####"

@<row,column> SAY

Displays user-formatted data to screen or printer at the location of <row,column>, such as

    @5,10 SAY LAST_NAME
    @5,10 SAY "Last name . . . " LAST_NAME
    @10,5 SAY "Annual salary:" ANNUAL_PAY PICTURE
    "$##,###.##"

@<row,column> SAY . . . GET

Displays user-formatted data on screen at the location of <row,column> for appending or editing a data field, such as

    @5,10 SAY "Last name : " GET LAST_NAME

ACCEPT

Assigns an alphanumeric string to a memory variable, with or without a prompt.

> ACCEPT "Enter your last name . . . " TO LASTNAME
> ACCEPT TO LASTNAME

APPEND

Adds a data record to the end of the active database file. The data fields are the field labels on the entry form.

> USE EMPLOYEE
> APPEND

APPEND BLANK

Same as APPEND but does not use a label to display the field on the entry form.

> USE EMPLOYEE
> APPEND BLANK

APPEND FROM

Adds data records from one database file (FILE1.DBF) to another database file (FILE2.DBF), with or without a qualifier.

> USE FILE2
> APPEND FROM FILE1

> USE FILE2
> APPEND FROM FILE1 FOR ACCT_NO<="10123"

ASSIST

Activates the ASSIST menu, which displays summary of commands and other help messages.

AVERAGE

Computes the average of a numeric expression and assigns the value to a memory variable, with or without a condition.

AVERAGE ANNUAL_PAY TO AVERAGEPAY
AVERAGE QTY_SOLD TO AVERAGESALE FOR
MODEL_NO="XYZ"
AVERAGE HOURS*PAYRATE TO AVERAGEPAY FOR
.NOT. MALE

BROWSE

Displays up to 17 records from the active database file to review or modify.

USE EMPLOYEE
GO TOP
BROWSE

CANCEL

Terminates the processing of a program file and returns the program to the dot prompt.

IF EOF()
    CANCEL
ENDIF

CHANGE

Displays the data records in an active database file sequentially, with or without a qualifier.

USE EMPLOYEE
CHANGE

USE EMPLOYEE
CHANGE FOR AREA_CODE="206"

CHANGE FIELDS

Displays selected data fields sequentially, with or without a qualifier.

USE EMPLOYEE
CHANGE FIELDS ANNUAL_PAY

USE EMPLOYEE
CHANGE FIELDS AREA_CODE,PHONE_NO FOR
AREA_CODE="206"

CLEAR

Clears the screen.

CLEAR ALL

Closes all open database files (including .DBF, .NDX, .FMT, and .DBT files) and releases all memory variables.

CLEAR GETS

Causes the subsequent READ command to be ignored for the @ . . . SAY . . . GET commands issued before the command, such as

```
@5,10 SAY "Account number : " GET ACCT_NO
CLEAR GETS
@7,10 Say "Account name : " GET ACCT_NAME
READ
```

CLEAR MEMORY

Releases or erases all memory variables.

CLOSE

Closes various types of files, such as

```
CLOSE ALTERNATIVE
CLOSE DATABASES
CLOSE FORMAT
CLOSE INDEX
CLOSE PROCEDURE
```

CONTINUE

Resumes the search started with the LOCATE command.

```
USE EMPLOYEE
LOCATE FOR AREA_CODE="206"
DISPLAY
CONTINUE
DISPLAY
```

COPY TO

Copies the contents of a source database file to a destination file, with or without a qualifier.

    USE SALE
    COPY TO NEWSALE.DBF
    COPY TO OLDSALE.DBF FOR ACCT_NO<="100123"

COPY TO

Copies selected fields of a source database file to a new file, with or without a qualifier.

    USE EMPLOYEE
    COPY TO ROSTER.DBF FIELDS FIRST_NAME, LAST_NAME
    COPY TO SALARY.DBF FIELDS LAST_NAME, ANNUAL_PAY
    FOR MALE

COPY FILE

Duplicates an existing dBASE III file of any type.

    COPY FILE MAINPROG.PRG TO MAIN.PRG
    COPY FILE COST.FMT TO NEWCOST.FMT
    COPY FILE ROSTER.FRM TO NAMELIST.FRM

COPY STRUCTURE

Copies the data structure to another database file.

    USE COST
    COPY STRUCTURE TO NEWCOST.DBF

COUNT

Counts the number of records in the active database file and assigns the number to a memory variable.

    USE EMPLOYEE
    COUNT TO NRECORDS
    COUNT FOR ANNUAL_PAY>="50000" .AND. MALE TO
    RICHMEN

CREATE

Sets up a new file structure and adds data records, if desired.

CREATE EMPLOYEE

CREATE LABEL ·

Displays a design form to set up a label file (.LBL).

CREATE LABEL MAILLIST

CREATE REPORT

Displays a design form to set up a report form file (.FRM).

CREATE REPORT WEEKLY

DELETE

Marks the records in the active database file with a deletion symbol (*).

USE EMPLOYEE
DELETE
DELETE RECORD 5
DELETE NEXT 3
DELETE FOR AREA_CODE="503"

DIR

Displays the file directory, such as

DIR	(displays .DBF files)
DIR *.*	(displays all files)
DIR *.PRG	(displays program files)
DIR *.NDX	(displays index files)
DIR X*.DBF	(displays .DBF file names beginning with X)
DIR ??X???.PRG	(displays .PRG file names containing six letters with X as the third character)
DIR ???.*	(displays all file names three characters long)

DISPLAY

Shows the contents of the data records.

```
USE EMPLOYEE
DISPLAY
DISPLAY RECORD 3
DISPLAY NEXT 2
DISPLAY LAST_NAME,FIRST_NAME
DISPLAY AREA_CODE,PHONE_NO FOR AREA_CODE="206"
```

DISPLAY MEMORY

Shows the contents of active memory variables.

DISPLAY STATUS

Shows the current processing situation, including the names of active files, the work area number, etc.

DISPLAY STRUCTURE

Shows the data structure of active database file.

```
USE EMPLOYEE
DISPLAY STRUCTURE
```

DO

Executes a program file.

```
DO MAINPROG
```

DO CASE . . . ENDCASE

A multiple-avenue branching command, such as

```
DO CASE
   CASE ANSWER="Y"

     . . .
   CASE ANSWER="N"

     . . .
   OTHERWISE
     RETURN
ENDCASE
```

DO WHILE . . . ENDDO

A program loop command, such as

    DO WHILE .NOT. EOF()
      . . .
      . . .
    ENDDO

EDIT

Displays a data record for editing, such as

    USE EMPLOYEE
    GOTO 5
    EDIT

    USE EMPLOYEE
    EDIT RECORD 5

EJECT

Advances the printer paper to the top of the next page.

ERASE

Removes a file from the directory. The file to be erased must be closed.

    ERASE SALE.DBF
    ERASE SAMPLE.PRG

EXIT

Exits from a program loop, such as DO WHILE . . . ENDDO.

    DO WHILE .T.
      . . .
      . . .
      IF EOF()
        EXIT
      ENDIF
      . . .
    ENDDO

FIND

Searches for the first data record in an indexed file with a specified search key, such as

    USE EMPLOYEE
    INDEX ON AREA_CODE TO AREAS
    FIND "206"
    DISPLAY

GOTO

Positions the record pointer at a specified record.

    USE EMPLOYEE
    GOTO 4

HELP

Calls up the help screens. Can be used with a key word to specify the subject, such as

    HELP
    HELP CREATE
    HELP STR

IF

A conditional branching command, such as

    WAIT "Enter your choice ([Q] to quit) " TO CHOICE
    IF CHOICE="Q"
        RETURN
    ELSE
        . . .
        . . .
    ENDIF

INDEX

Creates a key file in which all records are ordered according to the key field specified. The records can be arranged alphabetically, chronologically, or numerically.

    INDEX ON AREA_CODE TO AREACODE
    INDEX ON AREA_CODE+PHONE_NO TO PHONES

INPUT

Assigns a data element to a memory variable, using information entered from the keyboard.

    INPUT PAYRATE
    INPUT "Enter units sold :" TO UNITSSOLD

INSERT

Adds a new record to the database file at the current record location.

    USE EMPLOYEE
    GOTO 4
    INSERT
    GOTO 6
    INSERT BEFORE
    GOTO 5
    INSERT BLANK

JOIN

Creates a new database file by merging specified data records from two open database files.

    SELECT A
    USE NEWSTOCKS
    SELECT B
    USE STOCKS
    JOIN WITH NEWSTOCKS TO ALLSTOCK FOR
    STOCK_NO=A->STOCK_NO

    JOIN WITH NEWSTOCKS TO ALLSTOCK FOR
    STOCK_NO=A->STOCK_NO;
    FIELDS MODEL_NO, ON_HAND, ON_ORDER

LABEL FORM

Displays data records with labels specified in a label file.

    USE EMPLOYEE
    LABEL FORM ROSTER
    LABEL FORM ROSTER TO PRINT
    LABEL FORM ROSTER TO AFILE.TXT
    LABEL FORM ROSTER FOR AREA_CODE="206" .AND. MALE

LIST

Shows the contents of selected data records in the active database file.

    USE EMPLOYEE
    LIST
    LIST RECORD 5
    LIST LAST_NAME,FIRST_NAME
    LIST LAST_NAME,FIRST_NAME FOR AREA_CODE="206"
    .OR. MALE

LIST MEMORY

Shows name, type, and size of each active memory variable.

LIST STATUS

Lists current processing situation, including the names of active files, work area number, etc.

    LIST STATUS
    LIST STATUS TO PRINT

LIST STRUCTURE

Displays the data structure of the active database file, such as

    USE EMPLOYEE
    LIST STRUCTURE
    LIST STRUCTURE TO PRINT

LOCATE

Sequentially searches data records of the active database file for a record that satisfies a specified condition, such as

    USE EMPLOYEE
    LOCATE FOR LAST_NAME="Smith"
    LOCATE FOR UPPER(FIRST_NAME)="JAMES"
    LOCATE FOR FIRST_NAME="J" .AND. LAST_NAME="S"

LOOP

Jumps to the beginning of a program loop
(DO WHILE . . . ENDDO) from the middle of the loop.

```
DO WHILE .T.
   . . .
   . . .
   IF . . .
      LOOP
   ENDIF
   . . .
ENDDO
```

MODIFY COMMAND

Invokes the text editor to create or edit a program file (.PRG), a
format file (.FMT), or a text file (.TXT). The program file is the
default file.

```
MODIFY COMMAND MAINPROG
MODIFY COMMAND BILLING.PRG
MODIFY COMMAND EMPLOYEE.FMT
MODIFY COMMAND TEXTFILE.TXT
```

MODIFY LABEL

Creates or edits a label file (.LBL) for the active database file.

```
USE EMPLOYEE
MODIFY LABEL MAILLIST
```

MODIFY REPORT

Create or edits a report file (.FRM) for the active database file.

```
USE QTYSOLD
MODIFY REPORT WEEKLY
```

MODIFY STRUCTURE

Displays the data structure of the active database file for modification.

```
USE EMPLOYEE
MODIFY STRUCTURE
```

NOTE

Marks the beginning of a remark line in a program.

```
SET TALK OFF*
SET ECHO OFF
NOTE Enter hours worked and payrate from the keyboard
INPUT "Enter hours worked . . . " TO HOURS
INPUT " hourly rate . . . " TO PAYRATE

. . .

. . .
```

*This is a simplified payroll program.

PACK

Removes the data records marked for deletion by the DELETE command.

```
USE EMPLOYEE
DELETE RECORD 5
PACK
```

PARAMETERS

Assigns local variable names to data items that are to be passed from a calling program module.

```
***** Program: MULTIPLY.PRG *****
* A program to multiply variable A by variable B
PARAMETER A,B,C
C=A*B
RETURN
```

The preceding program is called from the main program:

```
* The main program
HOURS=38
PAYRATE=8.5
DO MULTIPLY WITH HOURS,PAYRATE,GROSSPAY
?"Gross Wage =",GROSSPAY
RETURN
```

PRIVATE

Declares private variables in a program module, for example

   PRIVATE, VARIABLEA, VARIABLEB, VARIABLEC

PROCEDURE

Identifies the beginning of each procedure in a procedure file.

PUBLIC

Declares public variables to be shared by all program modules.

   PUBLIC VARIABLEA, VARIABLEB, VARIABLEC

QUIT

Closes all open files, terminates dBASE III processing, and exits
to DOS.

READ

Activates all the @ . . . SAY . . . GET commands issued since the
last CLEAR GET was issued.

```
USE EMPLOYEE
@5,10 SAY "Last name : " GET LAST_NAME
@6,10 SAY "First name : " GET FIRST_NAME
READ
```

RECALL

Recovers all data records marked for deletion.

```
RECALL
RECALL ALL
RECALL RECORD 5
```

REINDEX

Rebuilds all active index files (.NDX).

```
USE EMPLOYEE
SET INDEX TO AREACODE
REINDEX
```

RELEASE

Deletes all or selected memory variables, such as

    RELEASE ALL
    RELEASE ALL LIKE NET*
    RELEASE ALL EXCEPT ???COST

RENAME

Changes the name of a disk file, such as

    RENAME FILE XYZ.DBF TO ABC.DBF
    RENAME MAINPROG.PRG TO MAIN.PRG
    RENAME MAILIST.LBL TO MAILLIST.LBL

REPLACE

Changes the contents of specified data fields in an
active database file.

    USE EMPLOYEE
    REPLACE ALL ANNUAL_PAY WITH ANNUAL_PAY*1.05
    REPLACE FIRST_NAME WITH "James K." FOR
    FIRST_NAME="James C."
    REPLACE ALL AREA_CODE WITH "216" FOR
    AREA_CODE="206"

REPORT FORM

Displays information from the active database file with the custom
form specified in the report form file (.RPM), such as

    USE QTYSOLD   (to screen)
    REPORT FORM WEEKLY
    REPORT FORM WEEKLY TO PRINT   (to printer)
    REPORT FORM WEEKLY TO TEXTFILE.TXT(to text file)

RESTORE FROM

Retrieves memory variables from a memory file (.MEM).

    RESTORE FROM MEMLIST.MEM
    RESTORE FROM MEMLIST ADDITIVE

RETURN

Terminates a program and returns to dot prompt or to the calling program module.

RUN

Executes an .EXE or .COM DOS disk file from within dBASE III.

    RUN B:XYZ   (where XYZ.EXE or XYZ.COM is an
                                  executable disk file in IBM DOS directory)

SAVE TO

Stores all or selected memory variables to a memory file (.MEM).

    SAVE TO ALLVARS
    SAVE TO VARLIST ALL EXCEPT NET*
    SAVE TO VARLIST ALL LIKE COST????

SEEK

Searches for the first data record in an indexed database file by a specified key expression.

    USE EMPLOYEE
    INDEX ON AREA_CODE TO AREACODE
    SEEK "206"

SELECT

Places a database file into a specified work area.

    SELECT 1
    USE EMPLOYEE
    SELECT A
    USE COSTS

SET

Sets control parameters for processing. In most cases, adequate processing can be achieved with the default settings (indicated by uppercase letters).

SET ALTERNATE ON/off

Creates a text file, designed by the SET ALTERNATE TO command, to record the processing activities.

SET BELL ON/off

Turns on/off the warning bell.

SET COLOR TO

Selects the colors used on a color monitor.

SET CONFIRM on/OFF

Controls the cursor movement from one variable to the next when the first variable is filled.

SET CONSOLE ON/off

Turns the video display on/off.

SET DEBUG off/ON

Traces the command errors during processing. When the toggle is ON, messages from SET ECHO ON are routed to the printer.

SET DECIMALS TO

Sets the number of decimal places for values, such as

> SET DECIMALS TO 4

SET DEFAULT TO

Designates the default disk drive, such as

> SET DEFAULT TO B:

SET DELETED on/OFF

Determines whether to ignore data records marked for deletion.

SET DELIMITER on/OFF

Marks field widths with delimiter defined, using the SET DELIMITER TO command.

SET DEVICE TO SCREEN/printer

Selects display medium.

SET ECHO on/OFF

Displays instructions during execution.

SET ESCAPE ON/off

Aborts execution with the Esc key.

SET EXACT on/OFF

Determines how two alphanumeric strings are compared.

SET FIXED on/OFF

Sets all numeric output to a fixed number of decimal places defined by SET DECIMALS TO

SET FORMAT

Selects custom format defined in a format file (.FMT).

SET FUNCTION

Redefines a function key for a specific command, such as

    SET FUNCTION 10 TO "QUIT"

SET HEADING ON/off

Uses field names as column titles to display data records with the DISPLAY, LIST, SUM, and AVERAGE commands.

SET HELP ON/off

Determines whether Help screen is displayed.

SET INDEX

Opens the specified index files.

SET INTENSITY ON/off

Displays data fields in reverse video with EDIT and APPEND commands.

SET MARGIN

Adjusts the left margin for all printed output, such as

SET MARGIN TO 10

SET MENUS ON/off

Displays a cursor-movement key menu.

SET PRINT off/ON

Directs output generated with @ . . . SAY commands to the printer and the screen.

SET PROCEDURE

Opens a specified procedure file.

SET SAFETY ON/off

Displays a warning message when overwriting an existing file.

SET STEP on/OFF

Stops the processing after the execution of each command.

SET TALK ON/off

Displays interactive messages during processing.

SET UNIQUE on/OFF

Prepares an ordered list with the INDEX command.

SKIP

Moves the record pointer forward or backward through the records in the database file, such as

USE EMPLOYEE
GOTO 3
DISPLAY
SKIP 3
DISPLAY
SKIP -1
DISPLAY

SORT

Rearranges data records on one or more key fields in ascending or descending order. The default setting is ascending order.

```
USE EMPLOYEE
SORT ON AREA_CODE TO AREACODE
SORT ON ANNUAL_PAY/D TO RANKED
SORT ON AREA_CODE, LAST_NAME TO PHONLIST FOR
AREA_CODE="206"
```

STORE

Assigns a data element to a memory variable

```
STORE 1 TO COUNTER
STORE "James" TO FIRSTNAME
```

SUM

Totals the value of a numeric expression and stores the total in a memory variable, such as

```
USE EMPLOYEE
STORE ANNUAL_PAY TO TOTALPAY
STORE ANNUAL_PAY*0.1 TO DEDUCTIONS
```

TEXT

Displays a block of text to the screen or printer in a program.

```
***** Program: BULLETIN.PRG *****
SET PRINT ON
TEXT
This is a sample message to be displayed on the printer
when this program is executed.
ENDTEXT
```

TOTAL

Sums the numeric values of the active database file on a key field and stores the results to another file.

```
USE STOCKS
TOTAL ON MODEL_NO TO BYMODEL
TOTAL ON STOCK_NO TO BYSTOCNO FOR
ON_HAND>="2"
```

TYPE

Displays the contents of a disk file to the screen or printer.

```
TYPE MAINPROG.PRG
TYPE EMPLOYEE.FMT TO PRINT
```

UPDATE

Uses records in one database file to update records in another file, such as

```
SELECT A

USE RECEIVED

SELECT B

USE STOCKS

UPDATE ON STOCK_NO FROM RECEIVED REPLACE
ON_HAND WITH;
ON_HAND+A->ON_HAND
```

USE

Opens an existing database file.

```
USE EMPLOYEE
```

WAIT

Pauses the processing until a key is pressed, such as

    WAIT
    WAIT TO CHOICE
    WAIT "Enter your answer (Y/N)? " TO ANSWER

ZAP

Removes all data records from the database file without deleting the data structure, such as

    USE EMPLOYEE
    ZAP

E
Built-In Functions

I. Listing of Built-In Functions

To process the time and date:

    CDOW()
    CMONTH()
    DATE()
    DAY()
    DOW()
    MONTH()
    YEAR()

To convert data field/memory variables:

    CTOD()
    DTOC()
    STR()
    VAL()

To convert alphanumeric strings:

    ASC()
    CHR()
    LOWER()
    UPPER()

To manipulate alphanumeric strings:

    AT()
    LEN()
    SPACE()
    SUBSTR()
    TRIM()

To perform mathematical operations:

    EXP()
    INT()
    LOG()
    ROUND()
    SQRT()

To track data records:

    RECNO()

To identify display locations:

    COL()
    PCOL()
    ROW()
    PROW()

To verify file marks, file existence, and data elements:

    BOF()
    DELETED()
    EOF()
    FILE()
    TYPE()

To use the macro function:

    &

II. Summary of Built-In Functions

&

Substitutes an alphanumeric string for the name of a database file or data field.

    STORE "ACCOUNTS.DBF" TO FILENAME
    STORE "ACCT_NO" TO FIELDNAME
    USE &FILENAME
    LOCATE FOR &FIELDNAME="10005"

ASC( )

Returns the ASCII code of the left character of an alphanumeric string.

    ?ASC("Smith")
    83

AT( )

Returns the starting position of the first alphanumeric string within a second alphanumeric string, such as

    ?AT("ABC","XYZABC")
    4

BOF( )

Tests for the beginning of the file and returns a .T. if the beginning is found.

CDOW( )

Returns the name of the day of the week from a date variable. For example, if today is 6/01/85, the function shows

    ?CDOW(DATE())
    Saturday

CHR( )

Returns the ASCII character from a numeric code, such as

```
?CHR(85)
S
```

CMONTH( )

Returns the name of the month from a date variable. For example, if today is 6/01/85, the function returns

```
?CMONTH(DATE())
June
```

COL( )

Returns the current column location of the cursor.

```
?COL()
5
```

CTOD( )

Converts the specified alphanumeric string to a date.

```
STORE CTOD("12/25/85") TO CHRISTMAS
```

DATE( )

Returns the system date. If the system date is 6/01/85, the function shows

```
?DATE()
06/01/85
```

DAY( )

Returns the numeric value of the day of the month from a date variable. For example, assume that CHRISTMAS is 12/25/85. The program shows

```
?DAY(CHRISTMAS)
25
```

DELETED( )

Tests for deletion mark at the current data record (assuming that the current data record has been marked for deletion).

    ?DELETED()
    .T.

DOW( )

Returns the numeric code for the day of week from a date variable. If the date is Saturday, June 6, the function returns

    ?DOW(DATE())
    6

DTOC( )

Converts a date to an alphanumeric string, such as

    ?"Today's date is "+DTOC(DATE())

EOF( )

Tests for the end of the file and returns a .T. if the end of file has been found.

EXP( )

Returns the exponential value of the numeric variable.

    ?EXP(1.00000000)
    2.71828183

FILE( )

Verifies the existence of a specified file name.

    ?FILE("EMPLOYEE.dbf")
    .T.

INT( )

Converts a numeric value to an integer, such as

    ?INT(3.568)
    3

LEN( )

Returns the length (in number of characters) of the specified alphanumeric string.

?LEN("James Smith")
11

LOG( )

Returns the natural logarithm of the specified value.

?LOG(2.71828183)
1.00000000

LOWER( )

Converts the specified alphanumeric string to lowercase characters.

?LOWER("James Smith")
james smith

MONTH( )

Returns the numeric code for the month from a date variable (assuming that CHRISTMAS is 12/25/85)

?MONTH(CHRISTMAS)
12

PCOL( )

Determines the current column position on the printer.

?PCOL()
10

PROW( )

Determines the current row position on the printer.

?PROW()
5

RECNO( )

Returns the record number of the active data record.

?RECNO()
5

ROUND( )

Rounds the specified value to a given number of decimal places.

?ROUND(3.71689,2)
3.72

ROW( )

Determines the current row location of the cursor.

?ROW()
5

SPACE( )

Creates an alphanumeric string of blanks.

?SPACE(10)+LAST_NAME+SPACE(5) +AREA_CODE
+PHONE_NO

SQRT( )

Returns the square root of the specified value.

?SQRT(9)
3

STR( )

Converts a numeric expression to an alphanumeric string.

ANNUALPAY=25950.50
?"Annual salary = "+STR(ANNUALPAY,8,2)

SUBSTR( )

Returns a specified substring of a given alphanumeric string.

```
?SUBSTR("ABCDEFG",4,3)
DEF
```

TIME( )

Returns the system time (assuming that the system time is 22:15:35).

```
?TIME()
22:15:35
```

TRIM( )

Removes trailing blanks from an alphanumeric string.

```
?TRIM(FIRST_NAME)+" "+TRIM(LAST_NAME)
```

TYPE( )

Returns a single character code for the type of the specified expression, such as

```
?TYPE(BIRTH_DATE)
D
?TYPE(ASTRING)
C
```

UPPER( )

Converts the specified alphanumeric string to uppercase letters.

```
?UPPER("James Smith")
JAMES SMITH
IF UPPER(ANSWER)="Y"
  . . .
ENDIF
```

VAL( )

Converts an alphanumeric string to an integer value.

?VAL("34.567")
34
?VAL("34.567")*1000
34567

YEAR( )

Returns the numeric code of the year from a date variable (assuming that the system date is 06/01/85).

?YEAR(DATE())
1985

Index

More Computer Knowledge from Que

Que Order Line: 1-800-428-5331

All prices subject to change without notice.

0215